Emergency Numbers

Emergency Heart Care Hospital ______________________

Paramedics ______________ Fire ______________

Police ______________ Ambulance ______________

The best place for fire, police, and paramedics numbers is on the cradle of your telephone. If you don't have a sticker supplied by a service organization, make one yourself on a Dymo® tape (those black tapes with the raised white letters) or print the numbers on sturdy paper and secure them to the telephone with transparent tape.

Doctors:

____

____

____

____

Hospitals:

____

____

Family:

____

____

____

Friends or neighbors:

Insurance Agents:

Repair Services:

Transportation:

Info Line

Other:

Be sure your family and friends or neighbors know these numbers are here.

Identification Numbers

In addition to your own identification numbers, you may wish to list those of other household members.

Bank Accounts:

________________ ________________

________________ ________________

________________ ________________

Car License Plate:

________________ ________________

Driver's License:

________________ ________________

Employee or Retirement Number:

________________ ________________

Insurance Policies:

Auto ________________ ________________

Homeowner's ________________ ________________

Life ________________ ________________

Others ________________ ________________

Social Security:

________________ ________________

Credit Cards:

Miscellaneous:

THE SENIOR CITIZEN HANDBOOK

A SELF-HELP AND RESOURCE GUIDE

Marjorie Stokell
Bonnie Kennedy

PRENTICE-HALL, INC., Englewood Cliffs, New Jersey

Printed in the United States of America.

This book is not intended to replace the services of a physician or an attorney. Any use of the recommendations in the following pages must be at the reader's discretion and sole risk.

Library of Congress Cataloging in Publication Data

Stokell, Marjorie, 1915–
The senior citizen handbook.

Includes index.
1. Aged—United States—Handbooks, manuals, etc.
I. Kennedy, Bonnie, 1916– . II. Title.
HQ1064.U5S7435 1985 646.7'9 84-22353

ISBN 0-13-806522-5

ISBN 0-13-806514-4 {PBK}

Prentice-Hall International, Inc. *London*
Prentice-Hall of Australia, Pty. Ltd., *Sydney*
Prentice-Hall Canada, Inc., *Toronto*
Prentice-Hall of India Private Ltd., *New Delhi*
Prentice-Hall of Japan, Inc., *Toyko*
Prentice-Hall of Southeast Asia Pte. Ltd., *Singapore*
Whitehall Books, Ltd., Wellington, *New Zealand*
Editora Prentice-Hall do Brasil Ltda., *Rio de Janeiro*
Prentice-Hall Hispanoamericana, S.A., *Mexico*

This book is dedicated with affection and gratitude to Robert D. Kennedy, who helped us in innumerable ways.

Author's Note: The names, addresses, phone numbers, and office descriptions given in this book have been thoroughly checked and were accurate as of early 1984. However, because of new legislation or reorganizations implemented after this printing, some information may no longer be current. We regret any inconvenience this may cause and urge you to keep delving until you find a new address or number. A letter (not a postcard) will be returned to tell you that the address is incorrect. Telephone Information can help you if the organization is still located in the same city.

Contents

R

S

T

U

V

W

X

Preface

Welcome to the *Senior Citizen Handbook,* a guide designed to help you meet the challenges and demands of your later years. Not all the topics will apply to you now, and perhaps some of them never will, but they are here at your fingertips. We expect that this comprehensive reference book will eliminate a lot of searching for information and interminable telephoning.

All of life is an adventure, no less at sixty than at sixteen. Choices must be made and actions taken. Wise decisions are based on the best information available, which is what we have tried to provide.

These last decades of the century (and the millenium) are an exciting time. New technologies and research are leading to longer and more productive lives, and many major diseases have been eliminated or controlled. More advances can be expected if our national resources are used wisely and humanely.

One thing we have learned is that an active and involved person often avoids many of the ills associated with advancing years. Another is that sensible diet and exercise release our energies for better living at any age. Practical pointers on these aspects of life are part of this volume.

If you are anticipating retirement, there are questions about pensions, retirement accounts, investments, social security, and medical coverage. If you are already retired and experiencing the exhilaration that comes with a new way of life, you have many options. Are there old ambitions you can now fulfill? Long-neglected talents you would like to develop? Do you want to continue your education where it was interrupted, or start a second career? Would you like to share your expertise? Do you have problems of housing, medical care, or loneliness? Topics in this book will help you.

We have had to be selective because of space limitations. We hope we have selected the topics of most concern to most of our readers. We also hope that you will often exclaim, as you read, "Oh, I'm glad to know that!" We said it often as we were compiling the information.

ACKNOWLEDGMENTS

A work of this kind requires the help and advice of many people and organizations; we are deeply grateful to all those who gave generously of their time and expertise.

Particular thanks go to the following marriage and family counselors for help in their specialties: Jane Haly in alcoholism, Diane Sanson in assertiveness training, and Dorothy Leichner in widowhood and in relaxation techniques.

Bonnie Liebman, staff nutritionist, and Dr. Bambi Batts Young, biochemist—both of the Center for Science in the Public Interest—aided with and reviewed the sections on nutrition and nutrition-related diseases.

Dr. Lucille Forer, psychologist, assisted with the material on depression and Beryl Barone with appearance; Victor Rose helped with the editing and selection of material to be included.

We are grateful also to the Pergamon Press and Drs. R. H. Holmes and R. H. Rahe for permission to reprint the Social Readjustment Rating Scale; to the National Cancer Institute for the use of the Breast Self-Examination Chart taken from the booklet "Breast Exams, What You Should Know," NIH Publication No. 82-2000; and to the government agencies, both state and federal, that allowed us to excerpt material from their publications, most particularly the *FDA Consumer* and the National Institute on Aging's *Age Page*.

Professor Harold Borko of the UCLA School of Library and Information Science gave valued advice on the preparation of the index. We, however, are responsible for any and all shortcomings in this or in any other sections of the book.

A

ABSENTMINDEDNESS

You go to another room to look for something; you forget what you came for. You lock yourself out of the house. You hide something and can't remember where. You're in despair, thinking that you're losing your mind. Your children say, "C'mon, it happens to me all the time too." But you don't for a minute believe them; you know that it didn't happen to you when you were younger—at least not so often.

Not to be confused with memory deterioration, absentmindedness is just that—the mind is absent, wandering. And although it *does* occur in the young, it often increases with age; let's not pretend that it doesn't. Your mind is much more cluttered than it used to be—stuffed up like Fibber McGee's closet.

Keep reminding yourself that absentmindedness is not forgetting; it's not attending. By forcing yourself to pay attention, you can reduce the number of lapses.

The best solution may be, after all, to learn to laugh about the problem; you have lots of company. (See also: ALZHEIMER'S DISEASE; MEMORY LOSS.)

ACCIDENT PREVENTION

At home—as a pedestrian—as a motorist—disabling accidents can ruin more than your whole day; they may change your whole life. The accident statistics for age groups above fifty-five are sobering, making awareness of our vulnerability a necessity. Accidents happen so unexpectedly; it's only afterward that the victim is likely to realize that with care and foresight the catastrophe might have been prevented.

Preventing accidents has three elements: recognizing hazards, avoiding or eliminating them, and adopting attitudes that minimize the risks.

How well do you score on the following true-false tests that measure your chances of beating accident odds?

Quiz

I. Avoiding Accidents at Home

A. Hazard Recognition — *Yes* / *No*

1. Are the traffic patterns of your home relatively stable, so that coffee tables and ottomans don't seem to pop up in unexpected places? ______ ______
2. Have you tossed out throw-rugs that don't stay put, so they won't have a chance to throw you? ______ ______
3. Have you eliminated long telephone cords? If not, do you make sure that the cord is systematically stored away after its use so that it can't ensnare you? ______ ______
4. If you still use wax on the kitchen linoleum, is it the nonskid variety? ______ ______
5. Does your bathtub or shower sport nonskid strips to keep you from taking a dive where there is no deep end? ______ ______
6. Is your middle-of-the-night trek to the bathroom lighted by adequate night lights? ______ ______
7. Have you removed or replaced worn carpets and stair runners that have dangerous threadbare areas? ______ ______
8. Do stairs, inside and out, have strong hand rails? ______ ______
9. Are thresholds, porches, and stairs in good repair and well lighted at night? ______ ______
10. Do you use a properly designed stepstool when reaching for stowaways on the top shelves? ______ ______

B. Attitude Changing — *Yes* / *No*

1. Do you recognize your limitations and hire someone to do the work that may be too risky for you now—roofing, painting, second-story window washing, heavy lifting, or garden tasks that may cause strain? ______ ______

I. Avoiding Accidents at Home (cont.)	*Yes*	*No*
2. Are you extra cautious when you have houseguests (or when you are one), and the normal routine is a little unsettled?	____	____
3. If you are emotionally upset or under stress, do you try to settle yourself down before rushing into action?	____	____
4. Do you pause for a moment to get your bearings when you get up in the middle of the night?	____	____
5. Do you remember the danger of careless smoking? Do you check that cigarettes or cigars are out before retiring—and never, never smoke in bed?	____	____
Home Safety Score Total	____	____
	Yes	*No*

II. Avoiding Accidents as a Pedestrian

A. Hazard Recognition	*Yes*	*No*
1. Do you keep aware of all moving vehicles—automobiles, bicycles, skateboards, and roller skates—and try to judge the best place to be out of their way?	____	____
2. Do you move quickly and promptly across the street when the light is GREEN and not attempt to scamper across on the YELLOW?	____	____
3. When crossing in front of several lanes of traffic, do you pause to check for oncoming vehicles at each lane before stepping into it?	____	____
4. When cutting across parking lots, do you keep a sharp lookout for the cement bumper strips that define the parking spaces?	____	____
5. In those parking lots, do you choose your way carefully, aware that cars may be behind you or backing out?	____	____

(Remember that the motorist has a ton of steel behind him. Your upraised

II. Avoiding Accidents as a Pedestrian (cont.) *Yes* *No*

hand, if seen, may alert the driver to your presence, but he or she may not be able to stop.) ______ ______

B. Attitude Changing

1. Recognizing that you are probably shorter and, hence, less visible than you used to be, do you give others enough time to see you before you step into the street, in and out of elevators, up and down stairs? ______ ______
2. If you are unsteady on your feet, do you forget your pride and use a cane or a walker? ______ ______
3. Do you allow for the carelessness and thoughtlessness sometimes demonstrated by children and young people? Do you stay out of their way? ______ ______
4. If your eyesight is dimming, do you try to go with someone for marketing and shopping expeditions? ______ ______
5. Do you wear walking shoes with sensible heels so that a misstep will not send you flying? ______ ______

Driving schools teach defensive driving.
Defensive walking is often necessary for safety.

Pedestrian Safety Score Total ______ ______

Yes *No*

III. Avoiding Accidents as a Motorist

A. Hazard Recognition *Yes* *No*

1. Do you plan your driving to avoid rush hours? ______ ______
2. Recognizing that your reaction time is now probably slower, have you increased the distance between you and the car ahead of you? ______ ______
3. Do you keep up with the flow of traffic so that others are not tempted to dart around you? ______ ______
4. Do you reduce the distractions

III. Avoiding Accidents as a Motorist (cont.) *Yes* *No*

when you drive under hazardous or nerve-wracking conditions by turning off the radio and discontinuing conversations? ______ ______

5. Remembering that most accidents take place less than twenty miles from home, are you doubly cautious on short runs? ______ ______

B. Attitude Changing

1. Do you fasten your seat belt, even for short trips? ______ ______
2. If your night vision is not so good as it used to be, are you willing to admit it and stay home or let someone else drive? ______ ______
3. On a long trip do you stop when you are tired, even if you haven't equaled your old record of 400 miles for the day? ______ ______
4. Have you abandoned quarrels about back-seat driving and made driving a team effort, accepting warnings from passengers about potential hazards? ______ ______
5. When conditions are unfavorable for driving, have you learned to leave the driving to someone else or take a taxi or bus? ______ ______

Motor vehicle accidents are the most common cause of accidental deaths among people between the ages of sixty-five and seventy-four and the second most common cause among older persons in general. Your driving ability may be impaired by reduction of peripheral vision, increased sensitivity to dark, slower reaction time, diminished hearing ability, and reduced coordination. Realizing that you may be subject to age-related changes and compensating for them increases your chance for a safe journey.

Motorist Safety Score Total ______ ______

Yes *No*

Total your "Yes" answers:

Home Safety Score	________
Pedestrian Safety Score	________
Motorist Safety Score	________
Total Safety Awareness Score	________

Your chances of beating the odds:

28–30 You are on the safe side.
25–27 Better check back to see how you can improve your chances.
24 or less You may be tempting fate.

ACTION

ACTION, the federal volunteer agency, enables Americans to volunteer their services where needed, at home or abroad. ACTION programs offer part-time or full-time service up to two years, some volunteers serving on a stipend or small wage, others on a nonpaid basis.

For further information on these programs, see the following entries: FOSTER GRANDPARENT PROGRAM; PEACE CORPS; RSVP (Retired Senior Volunteer Program); SENIOR COMPANION PROGRAM; VISTA (Volunteers in Service to America).

ADVOCACY

The Older Americans Act, passed in 1965 and revised in 1978, is largely responsible for whatever advances have been made in services and equal rights for older people.

The fight for equality, however, is never completely won; and advocacy—active support of any or all aspects of the cause—should be of concern to all of us. Seniors can fight most effectively through senior organizations, such as:

American Association of Retired Persons (AARP)
Gray Panthers
National Alliance for Senior Citizens (NASC)
National Association for the Visually Handicapped (NAVH)
National Association of Mature People (NAMP)
National Association of Retired Federal Employees (NARFE)

National Council of Senior Citizens (NCSC)
Older Women's League (OWL)

See the chart on page 158 for further information about these groups and join as many as you can. Their newsletters will alert you to important issues about which you can write to your congresspersons, and for which you may be able to agitate in other ways. It's better to be active, but even if you prefer to be passive, you can aid by adding one more name to the list of members behind the fight. (See also: GRAY PANTHERS; OWL.)

AGE DISCRIMINATION

Do you feel that you didn't get a job, are being paid less, or were let out early because of your age? Because older workers face such discrimination, the Federal Age Discrimination in Employment Act was passed in 1964. Under terms of the act, it is illegal to discriminate against workers from forty to seventy years old in hiring, discharge, pay, promotions, fringe benefits, or any other aspect of employment. The act applies to federal, state, and local governments, to all employers of twenty workers or more, and to most labor organizations with twenty-five or more members.

The Equal Opportunity Commission is responsible for enforcement. Some states have similar agencies. If you feel that your right to earn a living has been abused because of discrimination, you can file a protest with the EEOC.

You also have a right to file a private lawsuit. However, the act requires reasonable promptness in filing an action, so it's best to contact the Equal Employment Opportunity Commission first. The EEOC will guide you in the correct steps to take.

In larger cities the EEOC office is listed in your telephone directory under United States Government Offices. To write the EEOC:

Equal Employment Opportunity Commission
2401 E Street NW
Washington, DC 20506

AGE SPOTS

Forget Porcelana, Esoterica, and those other highly advertised fade creams if you want to lose those miserable brown age spots quickly. Find a good dermatologist and have them frozen off. The treatment is quick, easy, and relatively painless. Within three weeks the offending spots will be gone. One visit is usually all that is necessary, and your medical insurance may cover the cost.

If you prefer to have Mother Nature help you, try rubbing a slice of lemon over the spot daily. It sometimes works, especially with new spots.

Having removed the demons, keep them off by using sunscreen lotion. These lotions are numbered according to their screening power; the lower the number the weaker the protection. The highest number—fifteen—gives the maximum protection.

And remember that even on dull days the harmful rays may filter through, so make the use of the sunscreen a habit. (See also: SKIN CARE.)

ALCOHOLISM

Rutgers University's Center for Alcohol Studies defines an alcoholic as "one who is unable consistently to choose whether he shall stop drinking or not." Alcoholism is a specific disease, sometimes hereditary. For the true alcoholic, one drink is too many and one hundred are not enough. But a person who needs even one or two drinks daily, is unable to abstain for a week or more, becomes restless or combative when no alcohol is available, or must have a drink at a particular time may be an alcoholic.

A long list of diseases can be related to alcoholism: cirrhosis of the liver, alcoholic psychosis, neuroses, heart disease, high blood pressure, gastritis, duodenitis, pancreatitis, diabetes, respiratory diseases, vitamin deficiencies (partly due to the generally poor eating habits of alcoholics), traumas, and several types of cancer. Depression, mood changes, and memory loss can be caused by alcoholism. Not surprisingly, it reduces life expectancy by twelve years.

Alcoholism is especially dangerous to older people. Their bodies have slowed down, not eliminating alcohol as quickly as do young bodies; this slowdown can be aggravated by chronic illness. Tranquilizers and other prescription drugs also intensify the effects. Alcoholism is harder to diagnose in seniors; it is often mistaken for senility, and the situation is dismissed without any efforts to correct it.

Many older people start to drink after age sixty in reaction to the stresses that often accompany old age. Recently retired or widowed men over age sixty-five are at especially high risk. And most alcoholics remain hidden in society; fewer than 3 percent are on skid row.

Alcohol is connected with 80 percent of fire deaths, 22 percent of home accidents, 77 percent of injurious falls, 36 percent of pedestrian accidents, and from 35 to 64 percent of fatal automobile accidents.

If you live alone and you have recognized some of the symptoms in yourself, ask yourself whether you want to risk becoming one of these statistics; if not, seek help.

If you realize that your spouse or your parent has become a problem drinker, what can you do? Neither arguing nor ignoring the situation will avail. Only after an alcoholic has admitted that there is a problem can outside help be beneficial.

But it isn't enough to persuade the alcoholic to get treatment; the whole family needs it. Alcoholism must be considered a family disease. The spouse feels resentment and anger, and guilt at the gut level. ("Maybe if I had been different, kinder...") Adult children of long-time alcoholics share these feelings, even when intellectually they know them to be irrational. ("If I hadn't been naughty...")

Prolonged resentment because of the money squandered on liquor and unease about bringing friends home exacerbates the family malaise, so whatever treatment is chosen for the alcoholic should be supplemented with psychological treatment for the family.

Alcoholics Anonymous and its support group for the families of alcoholics, Al-Anon, (both free) are the most successful combatants of alcoholism. (See your telephone directory.) AA, a strictly volunteer organization, provides places for meetings where reformed alcoholics share their experiences with those who are still struggling and give, on a one-to-one basis, support and guidance at any time of day or night. They consider themselves spiritual but not religious.

Care units, located in many hospitals throughout the country, are medically supervised treatment centers offering medical and psychological help and educational programs for both the alcoholic and the family. Their information and crisis line (twenty-four hours a day) is 1–800–845–0318; in California, 1–800–422–4427.

Chains of commercial alcoholism treatment centers such as the Schick Centers and the Raleigh Hills Hospitals are listed in your classified telephone directory under *Alcoholism.* Some may use aversion therapy, which can be physically damaging, and/or Antabuse, which should be taken only under strictest supervision.

Recovery homes and halfway houses also exist, some on a free or sliding-scale basis. Ask your family doctor for recommendations, and remember that Medicare pays for thirty days of hospitalization.

For further information:

The National Council on Alcoholism
733 Third Avenue
New York, NY 10017

The National Clearinghouse for Alcohol Information
1776 East Jefferson
Rockville, MD 20852

(See also: MENTAL HEALTH.)

ALZHEIMER'S DISEASE

Absentmindedness, forgetfulness, failing memory or memory lapses, woolgathering—all these are common. But now that we're older, and now that Alzheimer's disease (pronounced Altz-hi-merz) is increasingly in the news, many of us have come to fear that any of the above are symptoms or precursors of that irreversible, incurable disorder. Also known as senile dementia of the Alzheimer's type (SDAT), it is the most common cause of severe intellectual impairment in older people.

But there are other symptoms, and also many reversible disorders, with which it may be confused. According to the U.S. Public Health Service, the victim at first experiences only minor symptoms and gradually becomes more and more forgetful, especially about recent events. As memory loss increases, however, there are other changes, such as confusion, irritability or high temper, agitation, and restlessness. Judgment and concentration are impaired, and speech may be affected. Though the symptoms are progressive, there is considerable variation in the rate of progress.

About one-half of all the seniors with severe intellectual impairment have Alzheimer's; one-fourth suffer from vascular disorders, especially small strokes; the remaining fourth may have other conditions that may be reversible: brain tumors, thyroid problems, infections, pernicious anemia, alcoholism, or adverse drug reactions.

We must not forget that some forgetfulness occurs during normal aging and that severe depression can also affect memory.

The victim suspected of having Alzheimer's, therefore, should be thoroughly examined for all other possibilities; only after these have been checked can a diagnosis be made.

Alzheimer's disease has no known cause, and no known cure. Elevated aluminum levels appear in the brain, but nobody is sure how or why that happens. However, a Washington, DC toxicologist, Armand Lione, has suggested (in *Food and Chemical Toxicology*, vol. 21, no. 1, 1983, p. 198) that minimizing the amount of aluminum in your diet may possibly prevent SDAT; although the evidence is far from conclusive, it would appear wise to take precautions.

Where does the aluminum you ingest come from? From certain nonprescription drugs: some antacids, buffered aspirins, and antidiarrhea and hemorrhoid medicines. Chief among the foods are some pancake mixes, baking powders, presliced process cheeses, and pickled cucumbers. Read the labels. And avoid aluminum cookware and cans if possible.

The SDAT patient must be under the care of a physician; your internist or family doctor will recommend the specialists he or she deems necessary, and these may change from time to time.

Health services feel that during the early stages of the disease, the victim should be kept at home if possible, and should be encouraged to continue the daily routine. The same calendar and lists of daily tasks that help all of us are particularly helpful now. Labeling some items may also help.

As the disease progresses, however, the family has increasingly greater difficulty in coping with the patient. Families should by all means turn to the Alzheimer's Disease and Related Disorders Association (ADRDA) for emotional support, encouragement, information, and advice. The association has a twenty-four-hour free telephone number to receive calls for information and referral. There is probably a local chapter near you; if not, national can advise you how to form one, to help yourself and others at the same time. For further information, write:

ADRDA
360 North Michigan Avenue, Suite 601
Chicago, IL 60601
(Tel. 800–621–0379. In Illinois 800–572–6037.)

(See also: ABSENTMINDEDNESS; MENTAL HEALTH; SENILITY AND PSEUDOSENILITY.)

APPEARANCE

Women

Image makers, those experts of makeup and fashion, admit that the older woman is neglected both on the fashion scene and in the beauty columns. Leaf through any high-fashion or glamour magazine and the upper age limit of the size-six models is about forty. Obviously, the older woman has to rely on her own good judgment and experience to be tastefully and appropriately dressed and well groomed.

But figures, hair color, and skin tones change. Alterations must be made in order to keep a chic, well-groomed appearance. Those same image-makers, when interviewed on the subject, *do* have some advice for older women.

- Number one priority—keep your weight down.
- Have a good haircut. Short is better, and keep the lines sweeping up.
- Experiment with styles and colors.

There is no charge for trying on clothes, so search the racks and keep trying. Be daring. Try colors, necklines, styles you haven't worn before. Keep searching until you find the garments that are perfect for you.

To get the most from your wardrobe dollar, stick to one basic color—which can be anything, as somber as grey or as dazzling as purple. Then find good solid colors you can mix with your choice. For blouses, summer suits, and dresses, try ivory instead of white. If pastels don't work for you, and they don't for all women, stick to more vibrant colors. And give full rein to separates, those superb and versatile budget stretchers—skirts, sweaters, blouses, pants, jackets—that can be mixed and matched and layered for versatility and warmth.

Acknowledge your bad points and work around them.

- Hippy? Try tunics, A-line or pleated skirts.
- Overweight? Opt for floats, envelope dresses, kaftans, overblouses, tunics.
- Double chin? Be selective about necklines. Relegate turtle necks to the rummage sale.
- Skinny or crepey arms? Conceal them with long or three-quarter length sleeves. (Full, flowing sleeves call attention away from less-than-beautiful hands.)
- If you like pants, select the style that is best for your figure and your age. Try pants pleated at the waist, or with an elasticized waist. Jeans are serviceable, but are not for everyone, nor are shorts. Shorts, like sleeves, need to be long—Jamaicas.

Cultivate a look, an ageless look, that gets compliments. Feed these positive comments into your memory bank and work in that direction as you select wardrobe additions.

Experiment with makeup. Try coral and pink lipstick and rouge or blusher, avoiding the harsher reds. Heighten eye drama with eyeshadow, eyeliner and mascara. Experiment with different colors and combinations of color in eyeshadow. Fair-skinned women should steer clear of black mascara and black eyeliner.

Black women, conversely, need stronger, brighter lipstick and blushers and can use dark brown or black eyeliner, mascara and eyebrow pencil.

Face saver: To hide circles under the eyes and laugh wrinkles beside the mouth, cover with liquid Erase or a similar concealer product, several shades lighter than your skin. Blend it in and cover with your regular makeup.

Makeup is an art well worth mastering. Cosmetic manufacturers such as Merle Norman, and department store cosmetic sections at times of special promotions, give instructions in its application.

Men

Men writing for men have noticed what women have noticed, often enviously—that many men are frequently better looking at sixty than they were at thirty. If a man has kept fit and has retained his self-esteem and interest in life, he may well be more attractive than younger men.

Advice to men parallels that given to women.

1. Keep your weight down.
2. Have your hair cut or styled regularly.
3. Buy good shoes and keep them in good repair. Women can get away with trendy shoes, but for some reason they diminish a man's appearance.
4. Dress in clothes appropriate for a forty-year-old, neither too young nor too old. Choose classic styles, simply cut, in the best fabrics you can afford. A really good suit in a becoming color, and a navy blazer, coupled with well-cut slacks, will carry a man through most occasions. Add to these the casual clothes that fit your daily lifestyle. Try some new colors in shirts. Striped, ivory, or colored shirts are usually more flattering than white for older men.

Now you are all set. Almost any man looks dashing in a light-blue shirt, the shade selected on the basis of his skin tone, a red tie (or one with red in it) and his blue blazer.

Quick Tricks for Both Sexes

Ten-pound weight loss! Good posture makes anyone appear slimmer. Walk, stand, and sit erect with spine straight, head up with chin parallel to the floor, chest up and buttocks tucked under. Voilà!

Instant face lift! Brush eyebrows up at the arch. (Check Sophia Loren's.) If they stubbornly won't stay, use a toothbrush moistened with hairspray.

Thicker hair! Bend forward, brush your hair toward the floor. Straighten up and arrange it.

Relaxation and a glowing face! Spend fifteen minutes on a slant board, or on your back across your bed with your head over the side. You will feel and look rested and radiant.

Be your own magician. Make your bad points disappear and your good ones appear through intelligent wardrobe choices, mirrors, and a few tricks. (See also: AGE SPOTS; COSMETIC SURGERY; HAIR; SKIN CARE.)

AREA AGENCIES ON AGING (AAA)

Services for senior citizens, established in 1965 under the Older Americans Act (OAA), have increased in number until recently. The total program, funded largely by the federal government with some aid from state and local governments and nonprofit organizations, has been known since 1976 as AAA—Area Agencies on Aging—the umbrella agency for government efforts to help older citizens.

The money comes from your tax dollars and is no more a form of charity than are farm subsidies and supports for many kinds of business.

Among the many programs are senior multipurpose centers, transportation discounts and aids, information and referral, legal aid, Meals on Wheels, homemaking and personal care for the housebound, and case management (sticking to a complicated problem and following it through to a resolution).

If, after reading about AAA programs described in this book, you want community addresses and further information, call your city hall or county administrative offices. If the operator doesn't recognize the name, explain that you want information about local services for the elderly. In the unlikely event that you still have difficulties, call your local library and ask for help from the reference librarian.

ARTERIOSCLEROSIS AND ATHEROSCLEROSIS

*Arterio*sclerosis is the condition of thickening and rigidity of the arteries that is thought to occur as a normal change during aging, but it can occur earlier. A hereditary tendency or an association with diabetes, gout, or high blood pressure may be the cause.

*Athero*sclerosis is the clogging of the arteries with cholesterol and other lipids: fat → cholesterol → plaque in the arteries → narrowing of the arterial passages → blockage → heart attack or stroke, depending on whether the blockage occurs in the coronary arteries (heart attack) or in the brain (stroke). High blood pressure will aggravate the condition.

Both high blood pressure and the tendency to high cholesterol levels may, if not hereditary, be caused or controlled by diet. A low-fat, low-salt, high-fiber diet is recommended.

Recommended Reading

Stress, Diet, and Your Heart, by Dean Ornish, M.D. New York: Holt, Rinehart, and Winston, 1982.

(See also: CHOLESTEROL; EXERCISE; HEART DISEASE; HIGH BLOOD PRESSURE; NUTRITION; STROKE.)

ARTHRITIS

Bones of the Java Ape Man, Neanderthal Man, and Egyptian mummies show the crippling effects of arthritis—there is nothing new about this disease. Today some 11 million Americans suffer from it and related diseases. The incidence of arthritis increases with age, so it is a serious concern of older people.

The most common forms in older people are rheumatoid arthritis, osteoarthritis, and gout.

Rheumatoid arthritis is the most serious and often the most crippling; it can cause bone destruction, deformity, and disability, but it may also be mild and intermittent. Some think it is caused by a virus, others that it is a disruption of the immune system.

Osteoarthritis (or degenerative bone disease), called the "wear-and-tear disease," often comes with age. It may be mild and show no symptoms, but it can be painful and disabling. It occurs most often in hips, knees, fingers, or spine. Overweight can aggravate it because of the added load on the joints.

Gout usually affects the joints of the foot, especially the big toe. Once attributed to high living and heavy drinking, we now know it is caused by an excess of uric acid in the blood. Curiously, an unusually large percentage of exceptionally bright people have such an excess.

Symptoms

Though no cure has been found for arthritis, there are ways of alleviating it. Early detection and care can help avoid severe crippling. With rheumatoid arthritis, the warning signs are tenderness, pain, and stiffness or swelling in one or more joints (especially in the morning). Osteoarthritis is indicated by a single stiff, creaky joint and pain of varying degree. Gout usually appears suddenly, with excruciating pain in the affected joint.

Treatment

Four kinds of treatment are used for rheumatoid arthritis: rest (during the active stage), exercise, moist heat, and drugs. Aspirin is often used, but if large doses are needed they can have bad side effects. Newer drugs are available by prescription, but some may also have severe side effects. Check with your physician or druggist, or the *Physician's Desk Reference* in your library.

Osteoarthritis is progressive, but can be slowed down by weight loss, physical therapy, or braces, canes, and crutches. Heat and drugs can reduce the pain. Total joint replacements are becoming common for hips and knees and are often highly successful.

Acute attacks of gout are treated by rest and medication. Your physician may also prescribe a drug to be taken daily in order to prevent further attacks.

Claimed Cures

Cures for arthritis have been touted from earliest times, but with no consistent results. They range from copper bracelets to high colonic enemas, magic boxes, uranium, diet, vibrators, and more. DMSO has been in the news but has not been approved by the FDA for arthritis and can, if impure, be dangerous. Although the FDA does not believe that diet helps arthritis, some people claim to have been helped by eliminating caffeine or red meat, or eating a cupful of canned sour (Queen Anne) cherries daily. Since these diets are not harmful, you might want to try one for a month or two.

Managing with Crippling Arthritis

See the entries under DISABLED for advice and information on how to manage if arthritis makes normal activities impossible. Note that if you can't hold a book easily, you're eligible for the same free talking books and magazines that are offered to the blind (see EYES and BLIND).

For further information:

Arthritis Foundation
1314 Spring Street NW
Atlanta, GA
Tel (404) 872-7100

You can obtain useful pamphlets and booklets as well as local referrals either from the Foundation or from its local chapter, which you will find in your phone book.

Recommended Reading

Arthritis: Relief Beyond Drugs by Rachel Carr. New York: Harper & Row, Pub., 1981.

Overcoming Arthritis by Frank D. Hart. New York: Arco, 1981.

Living with Your Arthritis by Alan L. Rosenberg, ed. New York: Arco, 1979.

ASSERTIVENESS TRAINING

If you have been in a position of authority for many years, your habit of command may no longer be appropriate. If you have always taken orders, or feel dependent because of your age and situation, letting other people tell you what to do may not be appropriate either.

If you're used to giving orders, you may be astonished at the irritation or anger you arouse in others when you say something that seems to you justified. Or if others are always telling you what to do, you may be resentful when you find yourself doing things you don't want to, putting up with things you shouldn't, or not getting what you're entitled to.

A comparatively new discipline, assertiveness training, can help you. Courses, seminars, and workshops are given in many adult education programs, community colleges, university extension programs, and YMCAs and YWCAs. Some are inexpensive or free. If money isn't a problem, look for a private counseling center, where groups are smaller (perhaps six to eight rather than twenty to thirty) and you get more individual attention.

After an introductory session, you will learn the elements of successful assertiveness. These include nonverbal elements such as posture, gestures, facial expression, and eye contact. Verbal elements include not only *what* you say but your delivery: tone, volume, emphasis, pitch, speed, and timing.

Working in a group with a trained leader is probably most effective, but if you can't find a group, don't despair. You can buy (or get from the library) books that will help you learn assertiveness.

Remember that you're attempting to change the habits of a lifetime; cure is not instant. Be content with one small (or large) step at a time. It's helpful to keep a diary to record the situations where you asserted yourself successfully and those where you failed by being too aggressive or too timid. You'll be astonished at the change in the reactions of those around you.

Recommended Reading

Your Perfect Right, by R. E. Alberti and M. L. Emmons. San Luis Obispo, California: Impact Publications, Inc., 1982.

The New Assertive Woman, by L.Z. Bloom, et al. New York: Dell Pub. Co., Inc., 1976.

When I Say No, I Feel Guilty, by Manuel J. Smith. New York: Bantam, 1975.

For additional books, see *Assertiveness Training* in your library catalog.

B

BACKACHE

One out of every two Americans either is or will be troubled by backache, 80 percent of which is caused by accumulated muscle stress or joint strain, common in older people.

Overweight is a leading cause of strain, for it increases the mechanical load on the back. Weak stomach muscles are another cause, strong abdominal muscles being essential to the support of the back. More than half of all lower back pain is due to poor tone and flexibility of the back and abdominal muscles. Structural inadequacy (chronic back pain) because of poor posture, long hours at a desk, and the like is another factor to be considered. Even psychological factors like anxiety or stress can create muscular tensions that result in backache.

The second most common cause of backache is arthritis. Spinal osteoarthritis, a normal development of aging, usually responds to bed rest and heat and massage treatments; these should be prescribed by an orthopedist.

The third cause is invertebral disc abnormality or disc herniation—more simply, a ruptured, herniated, or slipped disc. Symptoms may include low back pain radiating down to the back of the thigh or calf and aggravated by coughing, sneezing, or defecation; or numbness in the back, buttocks, legs, or feet. These can be very serious symptoms indeed; consult a physician immediately. Injection of chymopapain, which can dissolve the core of herniated discs, is a comparatively new alternative to surgery, the last resort. Bed rest, local heat and massage, or traction should relieve acute symptoms.

Disc abnormalities occur more rarely in the upper back. Other causes of pain—a pinched nerve, kidney or gallbladder problems, spinal curvature or scoliosis, and injury—may need to be ruled out before you embark on a program to reduce discomfort.

Prevention and Alleviation of Pain

1. Sit firmly against the back of a chair low enough so that both feet are on the floor, and the knees are slightly higher than the hips. Resting the arms on the chair also helps.

2. Bend at the knees, not from the waist, when you lift something heavy. Get as close to the object as you can before lifting, and never lift higher than the level of the elbows.
3. When you stand for an extended period, try to stand with one foot on a stool, a step, or something else higher than the floor, in order to relieve swayback.
4. Never sleep on your abdomen. The best way to sleep is on your side, with hips and knees bent, almost in the fetal position.
5. If you must sleep on your back, place pillows eight to ten inches thick under your legs so that your knees are flexed; or see to it that in some other way both knees and feet are raised.
6. Keep shifting positions during the night to keep muscles from stiffening. (If you're a sound sleeper, this is hard to do.)
7. Use down, feather, or fiber pillows rather than foam rubber.
8. Avoid possible "back-pocket sciatica" by keeping your wallet out of your back pocket. If you use a shoulder-strap purse, alternate shoulders frequently.
9. Wear sensible shoes.

Devices to alleviate pain may be found in a catalog from The Back Store (address follows), which sells chairs that transfer pressure from the lower back to the legs, special pillows and car-seat cushions, automatic massage tables, and much, much more.

But passive aid alone is unlikely to cure you completely. Do abdominal and back-strengthening exercises on your own, or enroll in your local YMCA's back program. Try biofeedback and physical or psychotherapy. Along with exercise, learn to relax, for tension causes more muscle stress and back pain than any other single cause.

To obtain the Back Store catalog, send to:

The Back Store
33 Highland Avenue
Needham, MA 02101

Recommended Reading

The New Approach to Low Back Pain, by Dr. Bernard E. Finneson. Send $3.80 to:

Materia Medica
1775 Broadway
New York, NY 10019

The Y's Way to a Healthy Back, by Dr. Hans Kraus. (Send $12.25 for the hard-cover or $8.00 for the paperback to:

The YMCA Healthy Back Program
236 East 47th Street
New York, NY 10017

Backache, Stress, & Tension, by Dr. Hans Kraus. New York: Simon & Schuster, 1978.
(See also: EXERCISE; STRESS; YOGA.)

BANKING

If you haven't investigated services for senior citizens at your bank or savings institution, you may be missing out on some money-saving opportunities and conveniences. (Some services start at age sixty). You may be entitled to free checks, a checking account, travelers' checks, a safe deposit box, document photocopying, and who knows what else. Compare them with the freebies at other banks and S & Ls.

While you are deciding where you will get the most for your account, don't forget the interest on your money. Where will you get the highest possible return? Compare both the interest rate and the way it is paid. Not all banks or S & Ls pay the maximum rate, and even if they do, the way it is paid makes a difference. One good way to find out is to ask, "What is the exact amount of interest $1,000, for example, will earn in six months?"

In her *Complete Consumer Book,* Bess Myerson describes a *Consumer Reports* experiment involving four banks. All paid 6 percent interest but computed it by different methods. On the same amount at the end of six months, Bank A paid $44.93 interest; Bank B, $52.44; Bank C, $58.44; and Bank D, $73.30! The difference is more than the price of an ice cream cone. Bank D gave interest from the day of deposit to the actual day of withdrawal; it's as fair and simple as that.

This is a good time to examine the type of account you now have. Ownership can be arranged in many ways to suit individual circumstances. You may want to change the way your account or accounts are held.

Note: Legal aspects of any of these accounts may vary from state to state. Before changing any account consult your banker, accountant, or attorney so you are aware of the impact the change may have on your taxes and estate.

Individual Account. An individual account is held in one person's name only. In the event of death, the funds become part of the individual's estate.

Joint Tenants Account. Two or more persons share a joint tenants account, which may require one, all, or any combination of signatures. In the event of death, the account goes to the survivors—subject to inheritance clearance.

Tenants-in-Common. A tenants-in-common account is owned by two or more persons, each owning a share, not necessarily equal. Upon the death of one of the participants, his share becomes part of his estate (rarely used except by advice of attorney).

Community Property Account. A community property account is established by a husband and wife. Withdrawals require one or both signatures. Upon the death of one spouse, the survivor has access to one-half of the account.

Trust Accounts. Trust accounts consist of funds set aside for individual beneficiaries or institutions and are controlled by one or more trustees. Trust accounts may be set up in many ways. Since they involve income tax liability and inheritance tax questions as well as problems of ownership, consult your attorney and tax advisor before setting up such an account.

Some Words of Caution. Don't assume the bank is always right. Many a deposit has gone astray and many a check charged to the wrong account. Keep all deposit slips until the amount appears on your statement, and balance your checkbook when your monthly statement arrives.

Read all the notices the bank sends. With the present state of flux in the industry, charges and policies are changed as often as bed linen, and, unless you keep on top of everything that is going on, you may find charges are eating up your savings account or you are paying out more in fees than you are earning in interest. If you are, change banks.

BARGAIN HUNTING

"You can save time or money, but you can't save both."

If you've always had to economize, you may not need any hints; but if the necessity for your economizing is new, you can get help from government agencies, consumer protection agencies, consumer magazines, advocacy organizations like the Nader groups, and consumer programs on TV and radio.

Following are a few tips to begin with.

Supermarkets

Learn the prices of the foods you use most so that you can recognize a true bargain. Most supermarkets have weekly loss leaders; if you have storage space for the staples, buy in quantity. Check the prices of the three nearest markets for the best buys in the Thursday (perhaps another day in your area?) ads, and choose the market with the most best buys.

Don't assume that a large package is cheaper than a smaller one. That used to be true but often isn't now. Likewise, a "30¢ off regular price" marked on an item doesn't necessarily mean that it's a bargain. Another brand may be cheaper. A calculator comes in handy for figuring cost per ounce.

Frozen vegetables with sauces are more expensive than the plain ones. Add your own herbs and spices or sauces, and you'll come out ahead. Even plain, frozen vegetables taste much better than canned vegetables, contain less salt, and are often cheaper; you're paying a lot for the liquid in the can, so compare drained weight.

Frozen entrees and TV dinners are no bargains. If you have freezer space, it's much cheaper to prepare a roast, a chicken, or a turkey, divide it into meal-sized portions, and freeze it. (And speaking of frozen turkeys, they're the best of bargains before Thanksgiving and Christmas.)

Do you know whether that boneless roast at $3.99 a pound is much more expensive than the bone-in roast at half the price? Are chicken breasts at $1.49 a pound dearer than a cut-up whole chicken at 49¢? Note how many meals you get out of the purchases and compare the price per meal.

Department Stores

Watch for clothing sales in quality shops; discounts at the end of a season are often enormous. But DON'T buy a great bargain unless you know you'll use it; in the end you lose more than you save.

The two best bargain months are January and February, with July and August next, particularly for out-of-season items. The biggest sales of the year come immediately after Christmas, New Year's Day (inventory), Easter, and July 4th. You'll have to fight the mobs to get near a sale table or find a vacant dressing room, and you may conclude that you no longer have the stamina for that sort of thing. Try late in the afternoon before the big sale day; merchandise may be already marked down, and you won't have to hassle with crowds.

Discount Stores

General merchandise discount stores are usually best for brand-name items, but some may make up for it on items you can't comparison-check. Other good places to shop are clearance rooms or shops, close-out stores, factory outlets, and sample shops.

Secondhand Items

It's now chic to buy your clothes in consignment shops. Often the clothes are new or almost new; the price may be one-fourth of the original or less; and the fabric and workmanship will be of highest quality.

Recommended Reading

Consumer Reports. Published monthly by Consumers Union, 256 Washington Street, Mt. Vernon, N.Y. 10550.

The annual buying guide may be purchased separately. Analyzes foods, appliances, household equipment—almost anything you can think of. Gives you best buys as well as quality comparisons and prices. If you don't want to buy it, you can usually get it at the library reference desk, where it's often sequestered to prevent rip-offs.

Sylvia Porter's New Money Book for the 80's, by Sylvia Porter. New York: Avon, 1980.

This encyclopedic book contains not just shopping tips, but practical information on how to save money, invest it, borrow it, and use it to better your life. Betty Furness says that the book "should be on every family's bookshelf along with the Bible and the dictionary."

Local or regional factory-outlet or bargain-hunters' guides. These paperbacks can be found in your local bookstores and libraries.

BEREAVEMENT, PREPARATION FOR

We all know that every life comes to an end, but with loved ones we prefer to ignore the inevitable. References to death are likely to be turned aside with, "Oh, don't talk like that."

Actually, the spouse who brings up the subject with a view to preparing for it is doing both partners a loving service.

There is no way to lessen grief, but steps can be taken to assist the one who is left to pick up the remnants and continue.

Sitting down together to discuss the options open to the survivor or survivors serves three purposes: the acceptance of one's mortality, a recognition of the fragile hold we have on life, and a review of the practical matters that must be faced.

If the roles have been the traditional ones, much information needs to be shared. A wife needs to know the family assets, the status of the mortgage, what to expect from social security, what part of the pension and health insurance will continue for her. Does she know how to drive, to handle a checkbook? Acquiring a knowledge of her husband's business may enable her to keep it afloat, even manage it. If, recognizing the possibility of being alone, a wife develops a set of friends and activities not dependent on couple relationships, she will have a part of her life that requires little adjustment, and one that will help her through that difficult first year of widowhood.

Where will the husband go? He may want to stay in the family home. Does he have a rudimentary knowledge of how to keep it clean, of how to operate the washer and dryer and the microwave oven? Does he know how to prepare a roast, create a salad, pop a frozen pie into the oven? A man, too, needs to have interests and connections not solely couple-oriented. Clubs and service organizations provide a source of support if he is left alone.

More delicate but equally important questions should be settled also. In *The Good Age,* Alex Comfort suggests preparing for the period of bereavement by a rehearsal, just as families hold fire drills. In other words, map out a plan of action that should be taken when the unthinkable becomes a reality.

Who should be called first?
Who will help?
Is there a problem of whom to trust?
Where are the insurance policies, important papers?
What arrangements have already been made?
What arrangements will have to be made?
What kind of funeral service is desired?
Are there any special requests for the disposal of personal belongings not mentioned in a will?

All of the questions that should be raised between a husband and wife are equally pertinent between parents and children, or sisters or brothers, or any relatives and those who are likely to survive them.

A record of these discussions kept in a looseleaf notebook, or another readily accessible file, will make the practical considerations of bereavement easier when it comes.

Reviewing in advance the many details that accompany bereavement will help in settling them when the time comes. In addition, the survivor will be able to say, "This is the way he/she wanted it." And it will be true.

Few of us would embark upon a voyage without plans, and bereavement is another phase of life's journey. (See also: LIVING TRUSTS; LIVING WILLS; RECORD KEEPING; WIDOW AND WIDOWER; WILLS.)

BLIND, SERVICES FOR THE

There is no frigate like a book
To take us lands away....
EMILY DICKINSON

National Library Services (NLS)

The world of literature, whodunits, sci-fi, and current magazines is not closed to you because you can't read in the ordinary way. Through a nationwide network of cooperating libraries, the Library of Congress distributes recorded and Braille materials to anyone eligible.

You're eligible if you have certifiably lost 70 percent of your vision or if you can't hold a book because of arthritis or other disability—eligible no matter where you live, even abroad.

Special phonographs or cassette players; records, tapes, or Braille books; catalogs of materials; mailing costs both ways—all are *free.* The holdings are enormous, with books and magazines for every taste. Some magazines, like the books, must be returned, but others are mailed directly from the publisher and may be kept.

To return the materials, replace them in the container and reverse the mailing label so that the library address shows—it's that easy. Enrich your life by taking advantage! Ask your local librarian or get an address list of libraries from NLS.

Recording for the Blind, Inc. (RFB)

W. H. Prescott, eminent nineteenth-century dramatic historian, became visually handicapped early in life. Not allowing his disability to keep him from his chosen career, he formulated the chapters of his books in his mind after listening to hired readers repeat again and again the source materials on the Spanish conquests.

Today his task would be much simpler because although NLS doesn't produce or distribute textbooks or professional books, Recording for the Blind does. Any professional worker or student may request RFB to record books needed for work or study.

Send two copies of the book to RFB headquarters; it will be recorded and taped within a few months. If it has already been recorded, taped copies are available sooner.

National Federation of the Blind (NFB)

The National Federation of the Blind publicizes job opportunities for the blind through twenty-six job bulletins a year, recorded on cassette tapes and available through the NLS network.

For further information write to:

Library of Congress
Division of the Blind & Physically Handicapped
1291 Taylor Street NW
Washington, DC 20542

Recording for the Blind, Inc.
725 Park Avenue
New York, NY 10021

Guide Dogs

Would you like to get around more freely? You can: Seven nonprofit groups supply free seeing-eye dogs and many supplementary services to qualified persons. The facility in San Rafael, California, for example, asks only that you pay for your transportation—if you can. Their twenty-eight-day training period is free, as are board and room. Annual follow-up visitors check on the welfare of dog and owner, and, should the latter become sick or go on vacation, the group provides kennel care.

Each group differs in the services offered; check with the ones closest to you. If you have any problems, contact your state rehabilitation department.

Guide Dog Foundation for the Blind, Inc.
109–19 72nd Avenue
Forest Hills, NY 11375

Guiding Eyes for the Blind
Yorktown Heights, NY 10599

The Seeing Eye, Inc.
P.O. Box 375
Washington Valley Road
Morristown, NJ 07960

Pilot Dogs, Inc.
625 West Town
Columbus, OH 43215

Leader Dogs for the Blind
1039 Rochester Road
Rochester, MI 48063

International Guiding Eyes
13445 Glen Oaks
Sylmar, CA 91342

Guide Dogs for the Blind, Inc.
Box 1200
San Rafael, CA 94902

Eye of the Pacific Guide Dogs and Mobility Services, Inc.
2723 Woodlawn Drive
Honolulu, HI 96822

BLOOD PRESSURE

Blood pressure is like alcohol and avoirdupois—it's not a good idea to have too much of it—at any age. Even a little high blood pressure (hypertension) can become dangerous. Because it often has no symptoms, it may go undetected. It is the commonest of the diseases affecting the heart and blood vessels. An estimated 60 million adults in the United States are afflicted, and every year many Americans die prematurely from related conditions: stroke, heart disease, congestive heart failure, and kidney disease. Untreated hypertension can affect other vital areas of the body also, including the brain.

High blood pressure can make your heart pump harder or enlarge it. It can also accelerate *atherosclerosis,* a thickening of the artery walls, and contribute to coronary attacks, which are three to five times more common in those with high blood pressure. Wear and tear on the blood vessels in back of the eyes may cause hemorrhaging and blindness. The vessels of the kidneys are often hardest hit, and these vital organs may no longer be able to clear wastes from the bloodstream.

Although a stroke is not inevitable, it is one further complication that may result from high blood pressure.

Hypertension is a serious threat. The outlook is not so grim, however, if the condition is detected early and treatment is instituted. With medical assistance, most people are able to live with high blood pressure and continue their regular activities. Having your blood pressure checked several times a year insures that treatment may begin promptly, if needed.

Normal blood pressure is considered to be 120/80. A reading under this seldom causes trouble. An occasional high reading may be nothing to worry about, but when the pressure goes to 140/90 or over and remains at this level (forget the old adage about 100 plus your age), medical treatment may be in order. However, many doctors put the treatment point at 150/90 or even 160/90.

Cutting back on salt or losing weight may be enough to lower your blood pressure. If not, there is an arsenal of medications for high blood pressure. Since people respond to medicine in individual ways, your doctor may have to try out a variety of drugs—and check you regularly—to see what is right for you.

So far this has been gloom-and-doom news, designed to get you to your doctor or to your fire department or a local bank—any place that provides a blood-pressure reading service.

Now the good news: The important thing to remember is that 85 percent of all hypertensive persons, regardless of the severity of their disease, can keep their blood pressure under control. Keep tabs on yours.

Recommended Reading

The Relaxation Response, by Herbert Benson, M.D. New York: William Morrow, 1975; New York: Arco, 1976.

The Mind-Body Effect, by Herbert Benson, M.D. New York: Simon & Schuster, 1979; New York: Berkley, 1980.

The following pamphlets are available free:

Watch Your Blood Pressure, Public Affairs Pamphlet No. 483B. Write to:

The High Blood Pressure Information Center
120/80 National Institutes of Health
Bethesda, MD 20205

Blood Pressure. Write to:

The American Kidney Fund
7315 Wisconsin Avenue
Bethesda, MD 20205

(See also: EXERCISE; NUTRITION; STRESS.)

BREAST MALADIES

Shirley M. discovered two lumps in her breast, panicked, and rushed to her internist, who sent her to a surgeon, who scheduled her for surgery. Luckily, a friend persuaded her to see an oncologist (cancer specialist) first. After palpating her breasts, he told her that lumps like hers are not cancerous and can often be expressed (suctioned out by needle) in the office or will disappear shortly without treatment.

About 45 percent of all women develop mastitis or fibrocystic disease—Shirley's problem. Benign lumps, sometimes painful, come and go each month. Many physicians, unable to distinguish benign cysts from cancerous tumors, recommend frequent surgery in order to be safe. It's best, then, to get as many as three independent opinions before surgery.

Because 7 percent of American women will develop breast cancer, it behooves them to learn and practice regularly the technique of breast self-examination (BSE). Lumps are discovered more quickly and more often by women themselves than by physicians during routine physicals. (See chart for method.)

If self-examination reveals any changes or abnormalities, seek medical attention, preferably from a breast specialist and an oncologist. They may recommend mammograms. Should they conclude that surgery is necessary, act quickly; a tumor can double in size every two months. The sooner it is removed, the less chance of metastases (spreading).

Until recently, the patient was prepared for major surgery, and the breast was removed at once, if cancerous cells were discovered. Nowadays more and more women are insisting on a simple biopsy at first, so that they may decide afterward what they want done. You may decide on a lumpectomy and radiotherapy, as Shirley Temple Black did. You may decide on a simple or modified radical mastectomy if the doctor recommends either. You may even decide to have both breasts removed, particularly if yours is the type of tumor that is likely to spread laterally. Get several opinions.

Remember that speed is essential, but remember also that it's YOUR body and you must be a party to any decision. And

Breast Self-Examination Chart

BREAST SELF-EXAMINATION (BSE)

Here is how to do BSE:

Breast self-examination should be done once a month so you become familiar with the usual appearance and feel of your breasts. Familiarity makes it easier to notice any changes in the breast from one month to another. Early discovery of a change from what is "normal" is the main idea behind BSE.

If you menstruate, the best time to do BSE is 2 or 3 days after your period ends, when your breasts are least likely to be tender or swollen. If you no longer menstruate, pick a day, such as the first day of the month, to remind yourself it is time to do BSE.

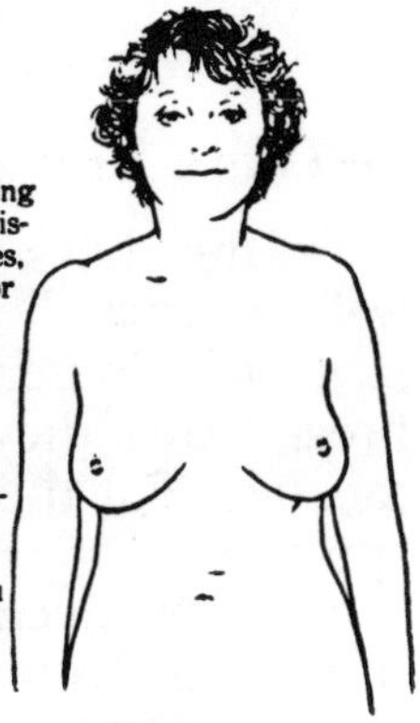

1. Stand before a mirror. Inspect both breasts for anything unusual, such as any discharge from the nipples, puckering, dimpling, or scaling of the skin.

The next two steps are designed to emphasize any change in the shape or contour of your breasts. As you do them you should be able to feel your chest muscles tighten.

2. Watching closely in the mirror, clasp hands behind your head and press hands forward.

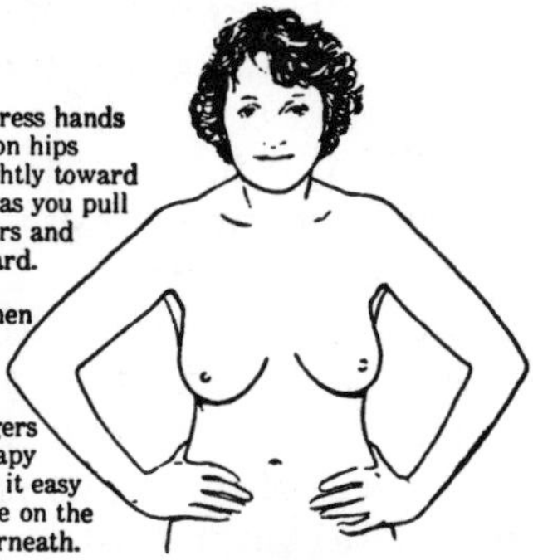

3. Next, press hands firmly on hips and bow slightly toward your mirror as you pull your shoulders and elbows forward.

Some women do the next part of the exam in the shower. Fingers glide over soapy skin, making it easy to concentrate on the texture underneath.

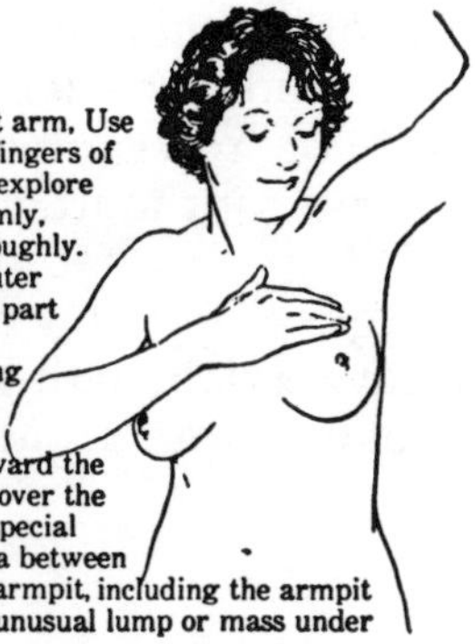

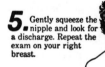

4. Raise your left arm. Use three or four fingers of your right hand to explore your left breast firmly, carefully, and thoroughly. Beginning at the outer edge, press the flat part of your fingers in small circles, moving the circles slowly around the breast. Gradually work toward the nipple. Be sure to cover the entire breast. Pay special attention to the area between the breast and the armpit, including the armpit itself. Feel for any unusual lump or mass under the skin.

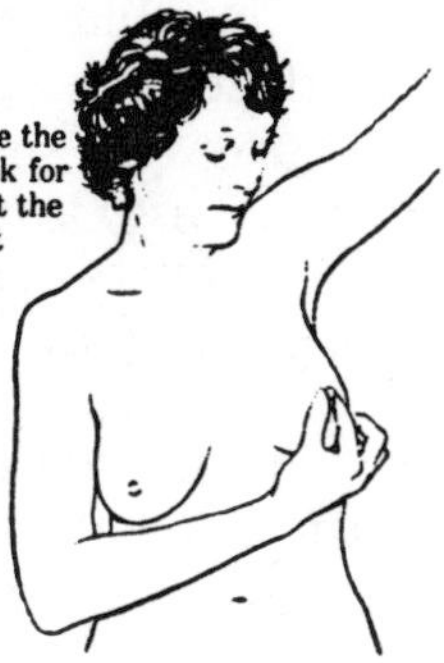

5. Gently squeeze the nipple and look for a discharge. Repeat the exam on your right breast.

6. Other women do steps 4 and 5 lying down. If you wish to, lie flat on your back, left arm over your head and a pillow or folded towel under your left shoulder. This position flattens the breast and makes it easier to examine. Use the same circular motion described earlier. Repeat on your right breast.

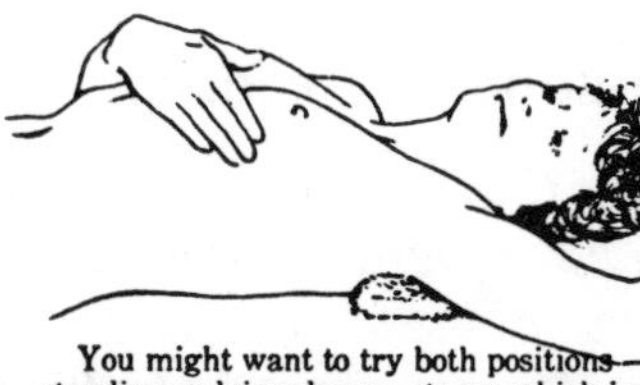

You might want to try both positions—standing or lying down — to see which is more comfortable for you. However, the most important choice is the decision to do breast self-examination each month.

Author's note regarding item 6: ALWAYS try both positions; you may miss some lumps while standing.

remember that the older you are, the less virulent and swift a cancer is likely to be; age does have some advantages.

Is There Life After Breast Surgery?

After the shock wears off, you'll be grateful that you're alive and well, and you'll adjust. You may want to consider breast reconstruction. Some women have had such difficulties with these false breasts that they regretted getting them; others are completely satisfied. For this plastic surgery also, search out the best possible specialist.

If you decide against breast reconstruction, you will want a prosthesis. In many hospitals a Reach-to-Recovery volunteer will visit to offer encouragement and to supply you with a dacron-filled form to be worn until you heal. She will also give you a list of shops where prostheses and special bras may be bought.

Within four to six weeks, you can probably begin wearing a permanent prosthesis. Heavier forms, filled with silicone gel or thick liquid, are more expensive than the lighter foam-rubber or polyester-filled types. Many women feel that the heavier ones give better balance and look and feel more natural, but some find the weight uncomfortable and damaging to the posture. Others find that the lighter types cause balance problems, back or shoulder pain, and poor posture.

If possible, go for your fitting with a woman who has been through it. Wear a form-fitting dress or sweater so that you can judge size and shape. Take your time, and don't let yourself be pressured into anything you're not sure of. You can buy bras with special pockets for the prostheses or you can, more cheaply, sew pockets into your own bras.

Yes, there is life after breast surgery, and you can make it pleasant and rewarding. You don't have a debilitating handicap; just think what it would have been like to lose an arm or a leg instead, or even a hand.

Recommended Reading

The Breast Cancer Digest: A Guide to Medical Care, Emotional Support, Educational Programs, and Resources. NIH Publication No. 80–1691.

U.S. Department of Health & Human Services
National Cancer Institute
Bethesda, MD 20205

Breast Cancer: A Personal History and an Investigative Report, by Rose Kushner. New York: Harcourt Brace Jovanovich, 1975.

First You Cry, by Betty Rollin. Philadephia: Lippincott, 1976.

(See also: NUTRITION; STRESS; SURGERY, SECOND OPINION.)

C

CALL-A-DAY

Operating under such names as House-Calls, Care-Line, and Call-a-Day, this program, usually manned by volunteer seniors, arranges daily calls for the isolated elderly. Criteria for being part of the program vary from one group to another, but the purpose remains the same—to serve those who are elderly and alone. The calls, made at the same time each morning, check on the person's welfare, bringing reassurance. If the person doesn't answer or needs help, the volunteer will call family or friends or the appropriate emergency number.

To determine if the program is operating in your area call your senior center.

CANCER

Cancer is, surprisingly, one of the most curable of the major diseases in this country, according to the American Cancer Society. More than 1½ million Americans alive today have defeated this most dreaded disease. A diagnosis of cancer is not a death sentence; it increases the odds of defeating it.

An increasing number of reputable scientists and health agencies feel that you may be able to prevent certain cancers through a diet low in fat, high in fiber, strong in crucifers (members of the cabbage family), and rich in vitamin A (from vegetables like carrots, not from pills).

Abstention from smoking will greatly reduce your chances of getting four different kinds of cancer: lung, larynx, esophagus, and mouth.

Be aware of your body's warning signals for all cancers:

C Change in bowel or bladder habits
A A sore that doesn't heal
U Unusual bleeding or discharge
T Thickening or lump in the breast or elsewhere
I Indigestion or difficulty in swallowing
O Obvious change in a wart or a mole
N Nagging cough or hoarseness

Diagnosis and Treatment

Before undergoing surgery for any kind of cancer (except perhaps melanoma, which requires utmost haste), get at least three *independent* opinions. Many unnecessary operations are performed in this country. On the other hand, some physicians have on occasion ignored certain symptoms until too late; if you feel uneasy about continuing symptoms, consult a reputable oncologist (cancer specialist). Nowadays most insurance covers payment for more than one diagnosis.

Before you undergo *any* kind of treatment for cancer—surgery, radiotherapy, or chemotherapy—put yourself in the hands of an oncologist. Even better, go to one of the 21 cancer centers in the country, where you will be examined by a board of specialists who will confer about your case. You may elect to remain and be treated there or to take the information given you back to your own physician.

And please, please, don't rely on strange diets, high colonic enemas, megavitamin therapy, or unproven drugs to cure you; they may or may not harm, but they will waste precious time.

Resources

The National Cancer Institute (call 1–800–4–CANCER) gives referrals to a variety of community resources for social, psychological, and financial aid to cancer patients and their families. Its volunteer workers will also answer questions about many aspects of cancer, or will recommend another source. Another of their numbers, the Hotline (1–800–638–6694), is open to calls from 8 A.M. till midnight, seven days a week.

Write to the Institute for its list of free pamphlets and booklets. If you're undergoing chemo- or radiotherapy, be sure to ask for "Eating Hints: Recipes and Tips for Better Nutrition." Write to:

The National Cancer Institute
9000 Rockville Pike, Building 31, Room 10A18
Bethesda, MD 20205

Your local American Cancer Society branch answers questions and offers useful free booklets. The number is in your telephone directory. ACS may also offer counseling, sickroom equipment, aid in buying medication, and nursing and homemaker services on a sliding-scale fee basis.

Try also the American Cancer Research Center (1–800–321–1557) for free information, psychological counseling, and financial advice. They invite family and friends to call for advice about how to handle tense emotional situations.

Many hospitals offer cancer patients and their families workshops where they can learn about resources that will help them live with their disabilities and cope with daily problems.

More groups exist to give support and advice for this disease than for any other. Make your life easier by taking advantage of the help they offer. (See also: BREAST MALADIES; NUTRITION; PROSTATE PROBLEMS; SKIN CARE; STRESS.)

CARDIOPULMONARY RESUSCITATION (CPR)

CPR is a life-saving technique that everyone should master, even children, but especially those who live with older people. One learns how, with pressure and mouth-to-mouth breathing, to try to revive anyone who has stopped breathing because of heart attack or some other trauma.

The American Heart Association, the Red Cross, local hospitals, and fire-department paramedics give free (usually three-hour) courses in CPR. The course trains one to recognize the "sudden death" crisis and to handle it expeditiously.

You will learn the ABCs of the the technique: A is forAirways, which must be kept open by tilting the victim's head back. B is for Breathing, which you will learn to do by mouth-to-mouth or mouth-to-nose resuscitation. C is for Circulation, which must be brought back by timed chest compression. You will get a chance to practice these techniques on a delightful mannikin named Resusci-Anne or Annie.

Since approximately 1.5 million Americans suffer heart attacks annually, and almost 25 percent of these die before reaching a hospital, you feel a lot safer if the people in your home can apply the technique to you in case of need, and you to them.

Also used for victims of drowning and electrocution, the technique is a MUST for those who live with a heart patient. The course should be repeated every year or, better still, every six months—memory being fleeting. (See also: PARAMEDICS.)

CAREERS, SECOND

For the person who has been productive in a stimulating career, retirement may soon lose its charm. The drive and motivation of the working years seldom grind voluntarily and abruptly to a halt because you have reached a chronological cut-off point.

You might want to try something new and different, like selling. According to a recent *Wall Street Journal* article, manufacturers and distributors are finding that older people often do better than younger. A study shows that some 13 percent of salespeople are over sixty-five; in some firms the percentage is even higher. Many of these seniors had never before been in sales.

Selling real estate is a popular second career. Generally, you have to take an examination and be licensed.

The Department of Defense helps retired servicemen embark on second careers—even third. Displaced Homemaker Centers counsel, sometimes train, and help find jobs for women who have too long been out of the work force. And civil service examinations and positions are open to anyone under age seventy.

If you're reluctant to work for someone else, consider a small business. If it can be run from your home and the capital investment is low, it's worth trying; you have little to lose but your time, and you may even enjoy the attempt, win or lose. The best chances for a post-retirement venture seem to evolve around a special talent or skill that a person can put to work with only a small investment in equipment, rent, materials, advertising, and other expenses.

According to the Small Business Administration (SBA), 50 percent of small businesses fail by the third year. What are the usual causes? Poor location, poor management, inadequate advertising, lack of sufficient capital, too narrow a market for the product, too much competition, and/or inadequate business sense. But again—if it costs you little, it's a gamble that could pay off.

Having chosen your product, you have several ways to market it:

- by direct sales, from your home
- by mail order
- through a wholesaler or agent
- through stores, on consignment
- at flea markets

SBA-sponsored Service Corps of Retired Executives (better known as SCORE) and Active Corps of Executives (ACE), and SBA itself, offer invaluable advice either personally or through seminars; check your telephone directory or write for information.

If you'd like some of the same freedom without any investment, consider a job as a Motel 6 manager. This budget chain is interested in mature couples without live-in dependents. It requires a short training course and an apprenticeship before assignment to a resident manager position with "a good salary and excellent benefits."

For further information:

Small Business Administration
1441 L Street NW
Washington, DC 20416

Motel 6, Inc.
51 Hitchcock Way
Santa Barbara, CA 93105
Attention: Training Department

(See also: DISPLACED HOMEMAKERS; EMPLOYMENT; SCORE/ACE.)

CARRIER ALERT

Even if you feel isolated, someone passes your home nearly every day who is aware of and concerned about you. That person is your friendly mail carrier, loaded to the hilt with junk mail but faithfully completing an appointed round and willing to check on your welfare.

Because of their unique role, the nation's mail carriers have become pivotal figures in an operation called Carrier Alert.

Carrier Alert is a system of monitoring senior citizens who are infirm or live alone and fear that they may be unable to summon help should they fall or have a stroke or some other incapacitating misfortune. As the carriers make their deliveries, they check to see if the mail has been picked up from mailboxes that display a simple, unobtrusive sticker. (This sticker varies from one location to another, so it is not a signal to others.) If the mail is still in the box, the carrier contacts the cooperating Carrier Alert agency, usually the senior center. The agency summons help (a relative or physician) from names and numbers supplied by the participating senior.

If such a check would add to your peace of mind, call your post office to see if it is operating in your neighborhood. Don't get angry at the postal employees if it isn't; they are willing, but someone out there has to keep the records and make the telephone calls.

If Carrier Alert has not been implemented in your area, you might be able to get one started. Could you or a friend work as the liaison between the carriers and the people on the emergency lists? Call your senior center or Area Agency on the Aging to tell of your interest and suggest someone or some group that may be willing to accept the responsibility for this important task. You may be the moving force that gives Carrier Alert service to those who need it in your neighborhood.

CATARACTS

A cataract is a clouding of the crystalline lens of the eye that gradually obscures the vision; the most common form, senile cataract, often begins at age fifty. The first symptom, usually, is the appearance of spots in the vision—not the floating kind, but stationary. Then vision becomes increasingly clouded and blurred, and bright objects appear to be multiple. Although the waiting period before the ophthalmologist is ready to correct the problem is burdensome, the success rate for all forms of correction is high, unless the eye is in some other way diseased.

During the time when your vision has severely deteriorated, many aids available to the blind are also available to you, even though your vision loss is temporary and not total.

Treatment

Surgery is the ONLY treatment; the old lens with the cataract is removed. But the operation has become so simple that most patients now have the job done as outpatients in the hospital or in the physician's office. You may move around freely afterward, so long as you don't stoop, lift anything heavy, strain in any other way (such as a difficult bowel movement), or make abrupt head movements.

Vision is restored in one of three ways: eyeglasses, contact lenses, or intraocular lenses (lens implants). Your doctor will determine which is best for you, but the intraocular lens is often the best solution for elderly patients. The lenses are implanted in front of the iris and sewn in directly after the cataract is removed. You no longer have the nuisance of eyeglasses or contact lenses unless there's another vision problem, and the success rate has been high. If you're lucky, you can see well the next day, but sometimes it takes months or even a year for the vision to stabilize. For further information and booklets write:

The National Society for the Prevention of Blindness
79 Madison Avenue
New York, NY 10016

Public Citizen Health Research Group, Dept. 501
2000 P Street NW
Washington, DC 20036

(See also: BLIND, SERVICES FOR THE.)

CERTIFICATES

Are you having trouble locating a birth, death, or marriage certificate? Apply in the county where the event took place, to:

Vital Records Division
County Registrar-Recorder's Office

For divorce papers apply to:

County Courthouse
Small fees are usually charged, but are sometimes waived if the certificates are for social security applications.

CHARITY DONATIONS

Older Americans are noted for giving generously to causes they consider worthwhile. Many have experienced the deprivation others are experiencing; many are champions of the underdog. The empathy is commendable, but does the money go to the proper place and is it used wisely?

Frequently, an appeal is made at your door. If you know the solicitor and the cause is well known, you can be reasonably sure the money will reach the right hands. You sign the collection information sheet and receive a receipt.

Suppose you know the drive is being made, but the person at your door is a stranger. Does your community require that those making collections carry a copy of a permit given by the Department of Social Services or some similar agency? Do you recognize the form? Is the person required to wear a badge? Ask to see both, before you even open the door.

If you know little or nothing about the charity, should you give?

Not all groups are equally worthy of support. The name may be misleading. The money may go to a group you violently oppose. In some cases a high percentage of the donations is used for "administrative costs," with only a trickle reaching the person or group whose name is used.

More and more appeals come in the mail. These well-worded, professionally crafted letters are designed to bring in a shower of checks. The money may go to the starving orphans of Upper Altafirma. Again, it may not. That address in a respectable neighborhood may be a mail drop or a mail-collection service.

Radio appeals are equally suspect. More than one self-made millionaire has traveled the road to riches over the air waves, asking for a dollar now, a dollar later.

This is not to imply that most solicitations for funds are dishonest. The reverse is true. But if you don't know, investigate before you give.

If you could use assistance in deciding which charities have legitimate fund-raising practices, request a copy of the *Wise Giving Guide* from:

National Information Bureau
419 Park Avenue South
New York, NY 10016

The Philanthropic Advisory Service
1515 Wilson Blvd.,
Arlington, VA 22209
(also has up-to-date lists of legitimate charities)

Recommended Reading

Charity USA, by Carl Bakal. New York: Times Books, 1979.

CHILDREN, RELATIONS WITH

> *All happy families resemble one another; every unhappy family is unhappy in its own fashion.*
>
> TOLSTOI, *Anna Karenina,* part I, chap. 1

If your relations with your children are totally satisfactory, read no further. But why not try to change and improve the relationship if you're dissatisfied for any of the following reasons?

- They don't give you the time and attention you'd like, and you suspect that they would prefer to see you less often than you consider reasonable.
- They seem to find your conversation boring.

- They are bossy and officious; they have started parenting you and treating you like a child.
- They make too many demands on your time and perhaps even your purse. They expect you to drop whatever you're doing and baby-sit or cook or take care of little emergencies.
- They remain dependent.

If you have the first two problems, just don't count solely on your children for friendship and entertainment. Work up your *own* social life and friendship network so that you don't have to sit around waiting for them to call. Refuse their invitations sometimes, on the grounds that you're busy. Free them of a sense of guilt for not calling so regularly or so often as you'd like.

The most admired parents and grandparents we know are those who have such an absorbing interest or occupation that they have to squeeze family occasions in. YOU be the one who's hard to get, and you'll be astonished at the rise in your popularity rating.

For your long-term peace of mind, and to be free of lingering resentment, it's best not to give anything you can't give freely. This may mean money, unless you have more than you'll ever need or want, even with galloping inflation. It may mean hospitality, if you can no longer cope with visiting children or grandchildren who want to come for extended stays. It may mean substituting potluck dinners or take-out foods for the huge gourmet meals you used to spend days preparing. It's important to live life as generously and fully as possible, but it's more important to honor your own needs.

If you must take your adult child back into your home—with or without grandchildren—because of divorce or job loss, decisions should be made and clearly stated in advance about how finances and household responsibilities will be shared. Drawing up a contract is an excellent idea, because people tend to forget what they'd rather not remember.

Of course, if you love baby-sitting, cooking, serving big family dinners, and having children and grandchildren come for overnight or extended visits, don't cheat yourself out of such pleasures. But don't for a moment think that you're an unnatural parent or grandparent if you'd rather be doing something else. You waited a long time for leisure, and you have a right to enjoy it in your own fashion. You don't do children a favor by keeping them dependent.

Remember: Now that your children are adults, you have the right to be a person first and a parent or grandparent second. Troubled relationships continue because the comfortable limits for each member are unclear. If they can be clarified without hurt or anger, you and your children might join those happy families that all resemble one another. (See also: STEPFAMILY ASSOCIATION OF AMERICA.)

CHOLESTEROL

Most of us didn't even know the word *cholesterol* when we were younger; but when it becomes a *Time* cover story (March 26, 1984) and even General Foods runs a full-page ad recommending avoidance of excess saturated fats and cholesterol in the diet, it's time to take notice... time to question our consumption of bacon and eggs, steak, ice cream, and other targeted foods.

Even before extensive tests proved the connection between diet and high cholesterol readings in the blood, it was known that Americans and Finns, whose fat consumption is the highest in the world, have the highest cardiovascular disease rate; the Japanese, who consume very little fat, have the lowest.

Cholesterol travels through the bloodstream packaged in high-density lipoproteins (HDLs), which help prevent heart disease; and also in low- or very low-density lipoproteins (LDLs and VLDLs), which clog the arteries. A nonfasting cholesterol blood test doesn't tell the whole story. A blood test taken after a fourteen-hour fast reveals all these components; so if your blood cholesterol level is high (some say over 200, some over 250), request these tests from your physician. Call your local American Heart Association about your level; some doctors don't know.

The connection between fats in our diet and cholesterol in our blood and arteries is now clear. Although some people can eat anything—well, almost anything—without ill effects, others seem to have a hereditary propensity to high levels of cholesterol. But most of us can, with care, maintain low levels or reduce the levels in our bodies; although it's still uncertain whether the build-up of plaque in the arteries can be reversed.

It would obviously be wise to put yourself on as strict a regimen of diet as you can manage if you want to extend your life span. And alert your children and grandchildren, if they aren't already alerted. Age two is a great time to start. (See also: ARTERIO- AND ATHEROSCLEROSIS; EXERCISE; NUTRITION.)

CONSERVATORSHIP

A conservatorship is a legal procedure by which one person, the conservator, is given power over the living arrangements, property, and/or finances of another person, the conservatee. Conservatorships are established to help persons who cannot handle their own lives. Granting of such power to another is a very serious matter, restricted by legal safeguards for the person who needs the help. Courts try to make the help as unrestrictive as possible. However, a person may lose numerous civil rights under conservatorship, such as: 1) the right to manage property or personal or financial affairs; 2) the right to enter into contracts; 3) the right to vote; 4) the right to drive; 5) the right to choose a residence; and 6) the right to refuse or to consent to medical treatment.

When persons are senile or gravely ill, a conservatorship may be necessary. When such a condition exists, a person (usually the spouse, a relative, or a friend) petitions the court requesting the conservatorship, stating why it is necessary and who is to be the proposed conservator.

To protect the rights of the conservatee, a court investigator:

- interviews the intended conservatee
- explains the serious nature of the proceedings
- tells the conservatee his rights
- determines if the conservatee wants to contest the proceedings and/or desires legal counsel
- defines what measures the court should take to protect the interests of the conservatee

The report of the investigation, in writing, is submitted before the court proceedings start. What rights are taken away will be determined by the court, which will also evaluate the qualifications of the conservator.

There is more than one type of conservatorship, depending on the nature of the conservatee's disorder and condition.

If such proceedings seem necessary, seek legal advice. (See also: POWER OF ATTORNEY.)

CONSUMER COMPLAINTS

Get any two persons together and the horror stories start: This doesn't work; that was broken when it was delivered.

Most businesses do their best to supply good products and services, but sometimes they fall short of what may reasonably be expected: A part is left out of a package, or the product doesn't do what the manufacturer advertises it will do. When these or similar problems arise, it's time to complain.

Steps to Take

- Identify the problem in your mind. Why is the product or service unsatisfactory? What do you believe would be a fair settlement: getting your money back or receiving an exchange or free repair?

- Get your documents together to substantiate your claim: sales receipt, warranty, repair order, contract, cancelled check.
- Call or see the person who sold you the item or performed the service and calmly state both the problem and the action you would like taken. If this person is not helpful, ask for the supervisor or manager. Repeat the complaint.

  (Usually "the buck stops here" and the problem is resolved. If it is not, don't give up.)
- If the company has a local office (not where you complained), call there. Ask for their customer service department. Repeat your complaint.
- Does the company operate nationally or is the product a national brand? Write a letter to that customer relations department or to the company president. (Labels will help you find the address.)

Your letter

- Make it *brief* and to the point.
- Include all the pertinent facts: date and place of purchase, clear identification of the item involved, and your idea of a fair and just settlement.
- Attach COPIES of your documentation. DO NOT SEND ORIGINALS.
- Be courteous. The person you are writing to is not responsible for the problem.
- Include your name, address, and telephone number.
- Keep a copy of your letter.

If you have only the name of the product and need to know the name of the manufacturer, ask your librarian to look in the *Thomas Register.* Other good sources of help are state, county, and city consumer offices. Look in your phone directory under "Consumer Complaints," or ask information. Your Better Business Bureau is sometimes helpful.

Media programs—newspapers, radio, and TV stations sometimes have "Action" programs that you can phone or write to. A listing of "Call for Action" services may be obtained from the Call for Action National Center. Their address is:

Call for Action National Center
575 Lexington Avenue
New York, NY 10022

(See also: CONSUMER PROTECTION.)

CONSUMER PROTECTION

Motto of the marketplace: *caveat emptor* (let the buyer beware). You are not out there alone, though; the cavalry is coming in the form of government help—if you summon it.

Product Safety

For the latest word on the safety of toys, recreational vehicles, and/or other products or to report defects, call or write:

Consumer Product Safety Commission
1111 18th Street NW
Washington, DC 20207

Dial 800 Information for the toll-free number for your state. All numbers serve deaf persons with TDDs.

Other Consumer Products

An invaluable reference for consumers is the *Consumer's Resource Handbook,* a ninety-one page publication of the U.S. Office of Consumer Affairs. The book lists offices, private and corporate, which you may contact to help solve your consumer problems. Names, addresses, phone numbers are given for consumer-protection offices, banking authorities, insurance regulators, utility commissions, Better Business Bureaus, offices on aging, and a host of companies doing business nationwide.

To get your free copy send your request to:

Handbook
Consumer Information Center
Pueblo, CO 81009

(See also: CONSUMER COMPLAINTS.)

COSMETIC SURGERY

One of the wonderful things about today's world is that we don't have to be stuck with the face that we were born with, or even the one that we have grown for ourselves over the years. People change noses, ears, chin lines; they shape their eyes, even their bodies—all through the magic of plastic, or cosmetic, surgery. So if you are depressed by the reflection you find in your mirror every morning, and you have the tariff, you can step right up and make a change—if you want to. Even if it means stretching pennies, you may decide that a new you is worth it. It's being done every day by some of the people you see most often. You didn't think those Hollywood glamour gals and guys arrived at sixty without a little wear and tear like the rest of us, did you?

Some caution and planning are required. As in all fields, search for the best professional you can find. Your local medical association will help you by providing names of plastic surgeons. Once you evince interest you may discover that friends have recommendations. (You may not want anyone to know, and that's all right, too. Many people have the job done in another city, state, or even country.) Back up any recommendations by checking with your own physician and the medical association. One of the best sources of information is a former patient. But again, do the back-up checks.

Many plastic surgeons specialize, so before you are given an appointment you will be asked what you want done. Be as specific as you can.

Before you go in for the initial consultation write down any questions you want answered so you won't forget to ask them. In addition to the cost, you will want to know:

- *Where will the operation be done?* Some surgeons have an office operating room, which saves the cost of hospitalization. Others require at least an overnight stay in a hospital. Is this an extra charge?
- *What improvements does he or she recommend?* If you want just minor modifications be sure to say so. Perhaps all you want is your eyelids tightened, or your double chin eliminated.
- *How long must you allow for recovery?*

If you live in a rural area or a small town you will probably have to go to a larger city, but most of your recovery will take place at home, usually a minimum of about three weeks.

Many surgeons are real artists. You may be better looking than you have ever been.

COUNSELING

Aging can open a Pandora's box of problems: Roles alter, earning powers dwindle or cease, health may fail, housing needs change. Stresses like unfulfilled life expectations, alcoholism, loss of friends, new patterns of unstructured living, depression, and various long-hidden problems may now surface. Inability to cope with these fast-changing times may also give concern.

Difficulty in adjusting to any or all of these is understandable, and one should not be embarrassed to take advantage of whatever help exists. Both group help and individual counseling are available on a no-fee or sliding-scale basis.

Counseling skills may include those of peer counselors, social service workers, marriage and family therapists, psychologists, and psychiatrists. Circumstances and fees will dictate your choice. Don't hesitate to switch if you're not satisfied.

For emotional disturbances arising from recent widowhood, much group help is available through senior multipurpose centers, Family Service, and churches or synagogues.

Day-care centers for the frail and elderly, supported by grants from government and industry, often provide (in addition to food, medication, and care), art, dance, journal workshop, and other therapies, as well as group, family, and individual counseling.

For health-care needs and referrals, screening centers exist, free or low-fee. These may also be found through the services previously listed and city or county health agencies.

If specialized medical or emotional counseling is needed, many of the health organizations—Diabetes, Cancer, Alzheimer's Disease, and others—encourage and foster support groups for both victim and family, and often provide professional personnel to lecture and counsel.

If your mental and physical health is OK, but you need advice on either long-term or immediate economic problems, start with Family Service or a multipurpose center; if they can't help you, they're great for referrals, and they care.

In contrast to former years, there is a growing body of counseling resources functioning in ever-widening problem areas. Take advantage! (See also: DAY-CARE CENTERS; HOUSING; LEGAL AID; MENTAL HEALTH; WIDOW AND WIDOWER.)

CREDIT DISCRIMINATION

Do you find it more difficult to get credit now than when you were younger, even though you're as creditworthy as you were then, or at least solvent enough to be a good risk even though you're retired? The Federal Trade Commission (FTC) may be able to help you under the Equal Opportunity Credit Act (EOCA). They can and do file suits against companies that deny loans to otherwise qualified seniors because of age. The companies can also be prosecuted for excluding income from pensions and public assistance from these standards.

A company may also be charged with violating the Fair Credit Reporting Act (FCRA) if it won't disclose to you the name of the agency that gave your unfavorable credit report and the reason for denial.

The Federal Trade Commission has regional offices in Atlanta, Boston, Chicago, Cleveland, Dallas, Denver, Honolulu, New York, San Francisco, Seattle, and Washington, D.C.

CREDIT UNIONS

Many people assume that when they retire they can no longer use their credit union. Not only is this not true, but there is even a National Association for Retired Credit Union People (NARCUP). At no cost to you NARCUP can help you rejoin your original credit union or locate one near your home that will serve you.

For information, write to:

NARCUP
P.O. Box 391
Madison, WI 57701

CRIME, PROTECTION FROM

The rates of the most serious crimes—murder, rape, and assault—are low among older Americans. Street crimes and burglary are our biggest threats. We resourceful older Americans can do something about that—outwit the rascals. It's partially a question of tactics.

Foiling the Street Bandit

Know your neighborhood or the place you are going.

Know when it is safest to be out.

Avoid potentially dangerous areas. Parking lots, alleys, dark doorways, corridors, and streets are good hunting grounds for muggers.

Be alert at all times. Be aware of those around you and their actions. Walk purposefully, stride. Studies show would-be-attackers look for easy marks—strollers, dawdlers.

Leave your valuables at home—gold chains, diamonds, furs.

If you must carry money or credit cards:

Women

If possible, do not carry a purse. Carry your money and credit cards in an inside pocket or a soft cloth container attached to your bra or slip. Some department-store notion counters stock these, but you can make your own.

Men

Wear a money belt. NEVER carry your wallet in your hip pocket unless it's a decoy holding a few dollars and outdated cards and you have another, the functional one, in an inner or secret pocket.

But should you be accosted, give up your valuables. No heroics!

If You Drive

Put your purse and valuables on the floor or under the seat.

Keep your car windows closed if you can.

If you think you are being followed, drive to a police station, the fire station, an open business.

Always lock your car doors—while you are driving and when you park.

Thwarting the Burglar

Ask your police department for a burglary audit—a check on how secure your home is.

Have sturdy locks, a strong night chain.

Install and use a peephole.

Lock up when you are at home and when you step out, even for "just a minute."

Leave lights on, preferably on timers, if you are out for the evening or go on vacation.

Add noise—a dog, a radio playing.

Double-protecting Your Valuables

Mark valuable property by engraving it with your social security number.

Keep photographs of hard-to-engrave items.

Inventory your valuables; keep the list in your safe deposit box.

Install a camouflaged safe (at least 250 pounds).

Never open the door to a stranger.

Security Apartment Houses

Don't open the security door to strangers or graciously allow them to walk in with you.

Know *absolutely* who is there before you push the buzzer to let anyone in.

Joining an anticrime crusade

Neighborhood Watch is an organization that spies with a purpose—to sight criminals in the neighborhood. Volunteer Security Patrols get into action—traffic duty, bike registration, security checks, patrolling. Ask your police department about the above programs.

Report all crimes so the police know where the problems are.

Get license numbers and descriptions if you see suspicious actions or a crime committed, or if you are a victim.

If, heaven forbid, you should be a victim, inquire about state or private assistance programs for victims of crime.

For information write:

National Organization for Victim Assistance
1757 Park Road NW
Washington, DC 20010

D

DAY-CARE CENTERS

A day-care center is a place elderly patients come to during the day; they return to their homes at night. It may be a day club, a workshop, a rehabilitative center, or a day hospital.

In a day club or workshop the elderly members engage in activities planned to suit their energy levels, abilities, and interests.

In a rehabilitation center, usually connected with a hospital, the day patient, commonly a stroke victim or an amputee, strives for mobility and self-sufficiency, learning to use a walker or a wheelchair, or to adjust to a prosthesis. Here too, in a home-style kitchen and bathroom, the patient practices the skills he or she will need at home.

Day hospitals provide medical supervision. This may include administering drugs, checking blood pressure, and giving physical therapy.

Lunch is served at the centers. Games and exercise may be part of the daily program. Sometimes there are beds for napping. Ideally, transportation is provided both ways.

The benefits to the elderly patients and their families are obvious. Family members can feel secure knowing that their spouses, parents, or other charges are well cared for during the day. The home situation is less likely to become stressful because of the daily respite.

For the patients, the pluses are many: continued contact with other people, a sense of getting out into the world, and regular medical attention as needed, coupled with the emotional support of remaining with their families.

Unfortunately, day-care centers are not available in all communities, their development having been hampered by the reluctance of government as well as private health insurance suppliers to cover such care. The picture may be changing, however.

If a day-care center might help you, contact your local area Agency on Aging, local hospitals and medical associations, or your senior center.

For a list of such day-care centers order the Directory of Adult Day-Care Centers by writing to:

Public Information Specialists
HCFA/DHHS
330 Independence Ave., SW
Washington, DC 20201

DEPRESSION

Elderly patients are frequently classified as senile when they are actually suffering from depression. Loss of a loved one, even fear of losing a loved one, a change of surroundings, and feelings of abandonment, guilt, or inadequacy are but a few of the causes of depression. Retiring into a world of one's own, lying in bed all day, sitting immobile for hours watching television, spending abnormally long hours buried in books, or a pronounced reluctance to communicate may indicate depression.

Any four of the following symptoms persisting for more than a week indicate a person is suffering from clinical depression and should seek help from a psychiatrist and/or a physician.

A severe change in appetite or weight, either increase or decrease
Insomnia or over-long sleep sessions
Loss of energy, feelings of fatigue
Loss of pleasure in usual activities, including sex, social contacts, work, etc.
Complaints of diminished ability to think or of indecisiveness
Recurrent thoughts of death or suicide
Feelings of self-reproach or excessive or inappropriate guilt

Antidepressant drugs, a better diet, and the addition of vitamins will often help the patient out of his unhappiness and back to his or her normal self. Some doctors suggest a dexamethasone suppression test (DST), a test for depression. Sometimes counseling is indicated.

The treatment for depression, whether by drugs or counseling or both, must be accompanied by an analysis of the factors helping contribute to the depression. Is the person ill, alone, feeling neglected? Struggling with alcoholism, poverty, fear, guilt?

Anyone besieged by depression needs all the help possible: drugs, counseling, great doses of hope, TLC (tender loving care), perhaps a change of environment, and certainly—once the immobility induced by the depression starts to lift—being drawn into action, encouraged to take responsibility, and given a sense of being needed. (See also: LONELINESS; MENTAL HEALTH; PETS; SENILITY AND PSEUDOSENILITY.)

DIABETES

Are you overweight? Does diabetes run in your family? Do you have any of the following symptoms: blurred vision, unusual drowsiness or fatigue, tingling or numbness in hands and feet, skin infections, slow healing of cuts (especially on the feet), itching, or excessive thirst and urination?

If you answered yes to any of the above, it would be wise to have yourself checked regularly for diabetes, even though any of the listed symptoms might be indications of some other problem.

Non-insulin-dependent diabetes (formerly called maturity-onset) usually occurs in adults over forty. The onset is usually gradual, according to the American Diabetes Association; in this type of diabetes, the insulin produced by the pancreas can't be used effectively because of a cell receptor defect.

This type can often by controlled by diet and exercise, but sometimes requires oral medication. Problems relating to the heart and circulation are common. Because onset is gradual, the disease may go undetected for years.

Eighty percent of all victims are overweight at the time of diagnosis. Many cases could probably be prevented if individuals maintained desirable weight and kept physically fit throughout life.

Diabetes is a serious disease. Diabetics are twenty-five times more prone to blindness than others, seventeen times more prone to kidney disease, twice as prone to heart disease and strokes, and five times more prone to gangrene, which often leads to amputation. Diabetes with its complications is the third leading cause of death in the United States; approximately twenty-three percent of these deaths are caused by the disease itself, and the rest by complications.

Are you now frightened enough to have yourself tested? The simplest test is a urinalysis. (You can even get a kit from your pharmacy that enables you to do it yourself, but the test may be unreliable and shouldn't be used for final diagnosis.) Blood tests are more accurate. The most sensitive and unpleasant of these is the glucose tolerance test (GTT). This usually isn't necessary unless one of the other two tests indicates abnormality.

Should you be diagnosed as diabetic, see your physician regularly and follow his or her directions. Join the local branch of the American Diabetes Association, or contact national headquarters if you can't find an address in your phone book. The association has a wealth of material and advice for you: pamphlets on foot care, recipes for party and snack foods, suggestions for eating out, principles of diet and alcohol consumption, and much more.

It offers help also through a one-to-one program, which provides contact with diabetics who have successfully adapted to the disease and who offer emotional support during times of stress through encouragement and a sharing of experiences. This contact may be made, however, only with the consent of your physician.

Since the physical and psychological problems that arise after diagnosis of diabetes can be great, the association sponsors monthly educational sessions at various locations and also teaching programs at many hospitals. You'll learn that if you lose your excess weight, adhere to your diet, and get plenty of exercise, you can still expect to live happily ever after.

For Further Information

American Diabetes Association (ADA)
2 Park Avenue
New York, NY 10016

Recommended Reading

The ADA Family Cookbook, by The American Diabetes Association and the American Dietetic Association. Englewood Cliffs, N.J.: Prentice-Hall, 1980.

Diabetes in the Family, by the American Diabetes Association and the American Dietetic Association. Englewood Cliffs, NJ: Prentice-Hall, 1982. To help the whole family adapt to your diabetes and the changes necessary because of it.

The Diabetic's Sports and Exercise Book, by Jane Biermann and Barbara Toohey. Philadelphia: Lippincott, 1977. To help you work out a program of healthful exercise.

The Diabetic's Total Health Book, by Jane Biermann and Barbara Toohey. Los Angeles: J.P. Tarcher, 1980.

(See also: EXERCISE; FOOT CARE; MEDICAL ID CARDS; NUTRITION; PARAMEDICS; SECURITY SYSTEMS: INDIVIDUAL.)

DIETING

In an attempt to lose weight, people often try remedies that don't work and can do much harm. For example, body wraps or custom garments claim to melt away the fat. They merely reduce body dimensions temporarily by removing fluids through perspiration. Creams in combination with the wraps are a variation on that theme.

There is no evidence that *any* diet pill, prescription or nonprescription, is effective in achieving long-term weight loss. In addition, there is substantial risk associated with many or most of them:

- Danger of addiction and fairly serious mental disturbances with amphetamines (benzedrine)
- Danger of harmful increase in blood pressure with others

Drugs are a crutch, useful for only a limited time. The FDA is reconsidering the legal status even of prescription pills, because of the danger of abuse.

Almost all diet pills belong to the same class and can cause wakefulness, agitation, insomnia, and even hallucination. The loss of weight that occurs may easily be from the agitation and restlessness induced. Many cases of drug dependence and psychosis have been reported.

- Starch blockers, which caused nausea, vomiting, diarrhea, and stomach pains in some dieters, have been pulled from the market.
- Liquid diets are still being marketed, but several deaths have been associated with them.
- Spirulina, a type of algae sold in health food stores, is, according to the FDA, useless in small quantities and in large quantities may cause heart problems; it may also be impure.

Crash diets rarely work; when weight is lost too quickly, it is soon regained. Repeated gains and losses are more harmful even than obesity, according to many authorities. Fad diets rarely work permanently either and can damage your health with too much or too little of certain nutrients.

What, then, is left? Regular exercise and increased activity will help. Unwanted weight gain in the middle and later years often comes because no reduction in calories accompanies the reduction in activity.

Some people find hypnotism or psychotherapy helpful, but support groups are probably most helpful in the long run. Try Weight Watchers or Overeaters Anonymous.

Jane Brody (see below) suggests an eating diary—a record of the time, place, and circumstances of every morsel eaten and the amount. Learn to eat only when you're hungry, and nibble on nonfattening snacks (carrot or celery sticks, lettuce, etc.) when hunger pangs strike too often. And remember that to be permanent, weight loss must be gradual—not more than a pound or two a week.

For further information and encouragement, read: *Jane Brody's Nutrition Book.* (W.W. Norton & Co., Inc. 1982.) The whole book will help you change your eating habits, but see especially pages 288–296. An inexpensive paperback edition is available.

For a support group, check your telephone directory or write:

Weight Watchers International
800 Community Drive
Manhasset, NY 11030

Overeaters Anonymous
World Service Office
2190 190th Street
Torrance, CA 90504

(See also: EXERCISE; NUTRITION.)

DIGESTIVE PROBLEMS

Children have bellyaches, and even young people can get ulcers, but aging can bring on or intensify certain digestive diseases that the young are mercifully spared.

Hiatal Hernia

A hernia is a protrusion of an organ through a wall of a cavity in which it is enclosed; in hiatal hernia, a portion of the stomach protrudes through a teardrop-shaped hole in the diaphragm where the esophagus and the stomach join. Anybody can get a hiatal hernia, but it is considered a condition of middle age. Many people over fifty have at least small ones, usually harmless.

The most frequent known cause is an increased pressure on the abdominal cavity produced by coughing, vomiting, straining with bowel movements, obesity, or some sudden physical exertion.

Heartburn is not caused by hiatal hernia, but symptoms may be similar; these include difficulty in swallowing and distress under the breastbone.

Suggestions: Avoid lifting, bending over, or straining at bowel movements. If you're overweight, reduce. Elevate the head of the bed about eight inches. Physicians sometimes prescribe antacids, but do not take them over a prolonged period and avoid those containing aluminum.

Heartburn

The causes of heartburn are complex; the only important consideration is how to cope with it. First, be sure you're not having a heart attack. Then try an antacid that doesn't contain aluminum. Sometimes the removal of certain foods from your diet will alleviate or eliminate the problem. Giving up smoking often helps. And elevating the head of the bed about eight inches (as for hiatal hernia) may give you relief at night. Avoid lying down for a while after eating. And again—if problems persist, see your doctor.

Diverticulosis and Diverticulitis

Diverticulosis is a condition of the digestive tract characterized by small protrusions of intestinal lining (diverticula) through the large intestine's muscular wall. Often there are no symptoms. If the sacs become inflamed, the condition is called diverticulitis.

For unknown reasons, this condition is found more often in women than in men. Causes are unknown, but it's thought that chronic constipation and the use of strong cathartics may contribute.

Symptoms. Diverticulosis usually produces pain in the lower left side of the abdomen, but the pain can occur also on the right side, where it may be confused with appendicitis. Nausea, vomiting, bloating, and alternating diarrhea and constipation may occur, as well as abdominal tenderness or contraction of the abdominal muscles. Acute diverticulitis includes all these symptoms plus fever and a high white blood count.

Suggestions. For diverticulosis, a supervised diet is indicated; laxatives and enemas may be harmful. Diverticulitis treatment includes bed rest, antibiotics, and pain killers, prescribed by your physician.

Constipation

Constipation is not a disease, and there is no accepted rule for the correct number of weekly bowel movements. "Regularity" may be a twice-daily bowel movement for some, or two or three bowel movements a week for others. Many older people become overly concerned with having a daily bowel movement and take harmful measures to assure it.

If your bowel movements are neither so regular nor so easy as you'd like them to be, what can you do? Exercise; eat more high-fiber foods (including dried fruits and small amounts of unprocessed bran); try to develop a regular time for your bowel movement (after breakfast is good); limit your intake of antacids; drink plenty of liquids (unless a heart, circulatory, or kidney problem forbids); avoid enemas and laxatives; and DON'T worry about missing a movement for a day or two.

For further information:

Digestive Diseases Clearinghouse
1555 Wilson Boulevard, Suite 600
Rosslyn, VA 22209

A service of the Arthritis, Diabetes, and Digestive and Kidney Diseases section of NIH (National Institute of Health), this agency provides inquiry response and referral; and distribution of easy-to-understand, scientifically accurate materials (from which this section was excerpted) about these and other digestive diseases.

You can also write to:

American Digestive Disease Society (ADDS)
7720 Wisconsin Avenue
Bethesda, MD 20854

This group distributes materials about specific disorders, diagnosis, treatment, and more. It also sponsors GUTLINE (301–652–9293), a telephone service that provides counseling by gastroenterologists and other health professionals. (See also: NUTRITION.)

DIRECT DEPOSIT

Behind the scenes of the nation's banking system is electronic wizardry designed to transfer your government pension or compensation check from Uncle Sam's coffers to your savings or checking account—effortlessly—for you. There need be no more anxious waiting for the postperson on check-delivery day, no trip to the bank or savings and loan, no more lock-stepping your way along the zigzagged velvet-roped path to the teller's window, no worry that you may be mugged as you leave the bank.

Government reminders have begged you to start this *direct deposit* by electronic funds transfer (EFT). Individual transactions are more costly to both the bank and the government. The cost savings to the government, if everyone did it, is estimated at $30 million a year—not enough to balance the budget but a sizable little chunk, nevertheless.

To start direct deposit take the necessary data with you to your financial institution.

You'll need:

- your claim number shown on each government check
- the suffix under the claim number
- the type of payment
- names of beneficiaries (payees on checks)
- your checking or savings account number

Your bank will supply you with the application for EFT transfer.

You will be doing yourself a favor. In addition to the convenience, government statistics reveal that although one in 700 home-delivered checks is stolen or lost, only one in 450,000 direct deposits goes astray. That's quite an improvement in any odds.

Word of Caution

Although EFT functions well most of the time, as indicated in the odds, occasionally a foul-up occurs and your money may not be deposited. Keep a close watch. The bank is responsible for sending you a deposit slip. If you don't get it and are worried, or if you need to know the status of your account, call the bank—usually the bookkeeping department.

THE DISABLED

Alathena Miller, stricken with polio at age 25, lost the use of both legs and lower torso, and has been confined to a wheelchair for 38 years. She lives alone, cooks for herself, and entertains elegantly, with little or no help. She goes to the theater, concerts, art exhibits. A travel agent, she has gone completely around the world four times, twice alone, and makes several trips a year, mostly to exotic places.

Jim Taylor, an amputee from the age of nine, clambered with his one leg and crutches in and out of tenders and across rugged volcanic terrain on a Galapagos trip. Stan Levy, a muscular dystrophy victim and nature lover, still goes to national parks and wilderness areas with his family, which slows down gladly to keep pace with him.

These people became disabled in their early years. Older people who have enjoyed good health for more than half their lives frequently adapt less well to disabilities. They may sequester themselves at home and grieve. They may avoid admitting disability by refusing to use available aids that would make life easier. They may refuse to associate with others who have similar problems, or they may go to the opposite extreme and stay solely with them.

Depression, even despair, almost always follows disablement. If it has occured in you, allow time for grieving, mourning, readjustment.

But then ask yourself: Where do I go from here? If certain avenues are now closed to me, what new ones can I explore? What can I do to make life as easy as possible? What pleasures can I substitute for the accustomed ones now denied me? How can I remain as independent as possible?

Learn to accept proffered help graciously when you need it, to refuse it as gracefully when you don't. Be as independent as you can, but don't alienate those who would gladly help you.

The visually handicapped have an enormous and wonderful support system waiting for them; unfortunately, there is much less help for those who are otherwise disabled, and the help varies throughout the country in both quality and quantity.

To get help, start with the closest senior multipurpose center. It can help with referrals, as can Family Service. Medicare pays for a limited amount of physical and occupational therapy.

The number and variety of physical aids are astonishing: gadgets to make eating, drinking, bathing, brushing teeth, shaving, and applying cosmetics easier; walking and wheelchair accessories to aid mobility; appliances for kitchen, bath, bedroom, and laundry.

There are even aids for leisure and recreation, from writing to riding, chess to crafts, Scrabble® to gardening. Life tends to narrow as we age, especially if we become disabled; try to broaden yours in unexpected ways.

Recommended Reading

Directory of National Information Sources on Handicapping Conditions and Related Services. U.S. Department of Education Publication #E-82-22007.

Office of Special Education
and Rehabilitative Services
Washington, DC 20202

This directory is probably available at your library reference desk.

International Directory of Access Guides, by Rehabilitation International USA.

RIUSA is the American affiliate of a worldwide network that brings information on new treatments, programs, and technological innovations to our country, publishes this free annual guide for the disabled, and works intensively with audiovisual materials and for "greater ease and dignity in air travel for the disabled and elderly."

The Source Book for the Disabled, edited by Glorya Hale. New York: Holt Rinehart & Winston, 1982.

Covers psychology, sexuality, education, transportation, employment, physical aids to be made or bought, and much more. A resource list includes national organizations and agencies, reference books, suppliers of equipment, and access to sports and leisure activities. Invaluable.

A Handbook for the Disabled: Ideas & Inventions for Easier Living, by Suzanne Lunt. New York: Scribner, 1982.

Describes aids for easier living, to be made or bought. Excellent bibliography, and appendix listing sources of equipment and information.

Free Commercial Catalogs

Aids for Daily Living

Cleo, Inc.
3957 Mayfield Road
Cleveland, OH 44121

Sears Home Health Catalog

Sears, Roebuck & Company, Department 141
5555 South Archer Avenue
Chicago, IL 60638

Self-Help Items for Independent Living

Fashion Able
Box S
Rocky Hill, NJ 08533

Medicare may be willing to pay for up to 80 percent of the price of durable medical equipment prescribed by a doctor—items able to withstand repeated use and not generally useful in the absence of illness or injury. (See also: ACCESS; TRAVEL.)

DISABILITY BENEFITS

Severely disabled persons under sixty-five are entitled to certain benefits under social security. These disability benefits are based upon your qualifications and work credits.

You are considered disabled if you have a severe physical or mental condition that:

- prevents you from working, and
- is expected to last (or has lasted) for at least twelve months, or is expected to result in death.

Disabling conditions eligible for benefits are spelled out in the social security regulations, but conditions not included are sometimes covered. Each case is considered individually. Impairments on the social security list do not automatically qualify you, just as having a condition that is not on the list does not automatically disqualify you.

It's important to remember the following:

- You don't have to be completely unable to work or to function in order to qualify.
- Since benefits don't begin until six months after you file an application, it's a good idea to apply as soon as your disability begins.
- If you are legally blind, you can receive disability payments even though you are working. (However, the allowable amount of earnings was limited to $550 a month in 1983.)
- Widows or widowers (or those divorced after ten years of marriage) may qualify on the work credits of a deceased spouse. (Limitations: You must be at least fifty years old and your disability must have begun before his or her death or within seven years after.)

Persons receiving disability payments may test their ability to work while getting benefits. Under a 1980 law, disabled widows or widowers, as well as persons disabled before age twenty-two, can work for a trial period up to nine months before losing benefits.

- If you return to work but your condition forces you to stop within a year after your benefits end, notify social security. In most cases your checks can be started again without a new application.

If you work while disabled, the amount you earn will be the major factor in determining whether your disability checks can continue. (Remember: expenses related to your disability can be deducted from your earnings. This may make the difference in your continued eligibility for financial help.)

Generally deductible

- medical devices and equipment
- wheelchairs
- attendant care
- drugs and services required because of your impairment

Medicare Coverage

Disabled persons qualify for Medicare. Contact any social security office for information on disability benefits.

Remember that rules and laws change and that the answer you get from the first person you talk to may be different if you reach someone else. If you think you are qualified, or your benefits should be resumed, try, try again.

DISCOUNTS

Do you know that:

- At least five of the big motel chains give a 10 percent discount to senior citizens?
- Amtrak gives a 25 percent discount on round-trip fares to senior citizens?
- By law, transit systems that use federal funds (and that's most of them) must give senior citizens reduced rates?
- Some state, county, and city parks and all national parks have lower fees for seniors? (See GOLDEN AGE PASSPORT).
- Many restaurants, including fast-food establishments, post lower prices for older citizens, list a discount on their menus, or have "senior days"? ("Early Bird" dinners are aimed at the senior market.)
- Some counties or states license and neuter pets free for seniors?
- Sports attractions frequently reduce or waive entrance fees on "Senior Days"?

In many communities, merchants and service businesses join a program to lower prices for seniors. Discount cards (sometimes called gold cards) are issued, with directories of the participants, at senior centers or nutrition sites.

The businesses are usually small—beauty shops, small clothing stores, pharmacies, gas stations, and repair operations. Big chains seldom participate.

The penny saved may be the penny earned if you take advantage of the discounts available to older Americans, sometimes to those as young as fifty-five.

It's almost a soup-to-nuts banquet. All that is required is proof of age, variously interpreted as a Medicare or Medicaid card, a driver's license, or an AARP (American Association of Retired Persons) membership card. Depending on how often you ride the bus, eat out, go to the theater, travel, or patronize discounted services or businesses, you can save a little or a lot.

It's good economics to watch the senior citizen publications and local papers to increase your awareness of discount opportunities and to ask *always,* "Is there a discount for seniors?" (See also: BANKING; BARGAIN HUNTING; TRANSPORTATION; TRAVEL.)

DISPLACED HOMEMAKERS (FOR WOMEN ONLY)

You married young and raised a family, working happily at home, unaware of your dependence and its dangers. Unexpectedly, you lost your husband and your financial support through death, divorce, or separation. Lack of job history and your age make you a poor prospect for employment. Your home-making and child-rearing skills are not likely to be of much help to you. Not having had a remunerative job, you are not eligible for unemployment insurance. In addition, you probably lost your health insurance with the loss of your husband. You're not eligible for social security until you're sixty-two, nor for Medicare till age sixty-five.

Approximately 5 million displaced homemakers are in the same boat with you. If you haven't been able to improve your financial lot through the courts, you need to search out groups that will help you get back into the paid work force.

The Displaced Homemaker's Network, 1531 Pennsylvania Avenue SE, Washington, D.C., 20003, through its national office and regional affiliates, serves as an information clearinghouse, providing technical assistance to displaced-homemaker programs. It is your advocate throughout the country. It will send you a list of centers in your area that will encourage and counsel you about continuing education, help you with job reentry, and function as a support group.

If you need to earn money immediately, search out employment agencies that specialize in finding jobs for older people. (Emergency? Contact the local social service department.)

Explore also assistance that may be given by:

- women's centers
- YWCA's
- trade-technical schools
- community colleges and their counseling services
- Family Service
- senior multipurpose centers

You need a lot of support from other women in similar circumstances; you'll find it also in OWL, Gray Panthers, and women's centers. You'll need all the strength you can get, for you're going to have to become a new person—strong and independent. Who knows—you might end up liking the new you better than the old one. (See also: ADVOCACY; EDUCATION; EMPLOYMENT; GRAY PANTHERS; OWL.)

DIVORCE AFTER 60

Founded in Ann Arbor in 1982 with thirty women and one man who were either contemplating a divorce, in the process of getting one, or had recently undergone this traumatic experience, Divorce After 60 seeks to help group members to:

- share experiences and provide emotional support for one another
- educate themselves on the legal, financial, and other practical aspects of their new situation
- work through legislation for more equitable divorce settlements
- encourage research in this new and growing problem

Unlike the younger divorced or the widowed, older newly divorced persons often don't know anyone else in their situation. They need help in recovering from the emotional impact of this often unsought alteration in their lives and in facing the new realities forced upon them. Although the members are mostly women because they usually face a greater number of problems after divorce, the organization welcomes men also.

To find out whether a similar group exists in your community, call your local Information Line, which should be able to refer you if they don't know.

For advice in starting such a group, write to:

Nell Stern, Counselor and Resource Person
Divorce After 60
University of Michigan Hospitals Turner Geriatric Clinic
Ann Arbor, MI 48105

or telephone (313) 764–2556 for the name of the current chairperson.

Recommended Reading

The Disillusionment of Divorce for Older Women, Gray Paper No. 6, by Frances Leonard et al.

Older Women's League
3800 Harrison Street
Oakland, CA 94611

DONATING THE BODY OR ITS ORGANS

Suppose you could wave a magic wand and make a child doomed to dwarfhood grow, or restore a young mother to health and family, no longer dependent upon daily dialysis to live another day. Would you? Of course you would.

The magic wand is the Uniform Donor Card or its equivalent. By filling out this card, you make the anatomical gifts that can make others well or contribute to medical research.

Around the world thousands of people are benefiting from donated organs. The list of body parts that are transplanted now, or may be in the future, is long. Thousands of corneal transplants have been made with a high (90 to 95 percent) success rate. Material from a donor's bones can be used to spare an accident victim a crippling handicap. The human growth hormone (HGH) can be taken from a donor's pituitary gland and used to promote growth in children who would otherwise be dwarfs. Useful now or for broadening the scope of research are the middle-ear bones and ear drums, the parathyroid gland, the membrane covering the brain, the lungs, the heart, the chest cartilage, sections of the intestines, the blood vessels.

Donating your body or organs is not for everyone. You may have very strong reservations about such a decision. You may want to talk it over with your family, your doctor, or your spiritual advisor.

If you do want to give this added chance to others, don't hold back because you are elderly and can't see or hear or you suffer from arthritis or some other affliction. Some parts of your body can still be used, and scientists need to examine afflicted parts to get information about the disease and the effect of drugs or surgery.

If you want to donate your body or only specified parts of your body, the process is simple. In some states you may indicate on your driver's license that you wish to be a donor. Find out the next time you renew your license. The National Institute of Health suggests using a Uniform Donor Card. The card is signed by the donor and two witnesses in the presence of each other. On the card the donor lets his or her wishes be known about the gifts, including any special limitations.

If you donate your body to a nearby medical school, call the school to get complete instructions before entering your name on your donor card. Embalming may be prohibited or done in a special way.

If you sign the Uniform Donor Card or some similar instrument, inform your family, attorney, and doctor. Give them complete instructions: Who is to be called, how soon after death the body must be delivered, where. (For some donations, a few hours delay is too much. Kidneys, for example, must be removed immediately after death.) Readily available answers to these questions will make it easier for the grief-stricken family. Record the location of your card on page 195.

The Uniform Donor Card can be ordered free from:

National Society for Medical Research
1000 Vermont Ave.
Washington, DC 20005

National Institute of Health
9000 Rockville Pike
Bethesda, MD 20014
(Ask for the pamphlet "How to Donate the Body or Its Organs".)

DOOR-TO-DOOR SALES

The handsome young man had an engaging smile, a convincing sales talk, and here you are with an agreement for siding for your house or a new driveway. You can't really afford it and now that he has gone are not sure you need it. What can you do?

Seniors are often rooked by door-to-door salesmen, but did you know that a Federal Trade Commission regulation now requires a "cooling off period" for door-to-door sales?

The FTC ruling requires that the salesperson (1) inform consumers of their right to cancel the contract, (2) give consumers two copies of the cancellation form, and (3) give consumers a dated receipt or contract that shows the name and address of the seller.

The ruling includes not only sales made at home, but also those made anywhere that is not a normal place of business, such as "parties" in homes, and sales in rented hotel rooms. Exceptions are: sales made totally by mail or phone, sales under $25.00, real estate, insurance or securities sales, or sales of emergency home repairs.

So if you have decided you don't want the siding or the driveway after all, call the number on the sales agreement now and sign and date one copy of the cancellation form and mail it to the address given. It must be sent before midnight of the third business day after the contract date. For safety's sake imagine that you have only forty-eight hours to change your mind. That will get you moving and get your cancellation form in the mail on time.

DRUGS, LOWER COST

The price of prescription drugs can be a crushing expense, but buying drugs under their generic names (that is—the name of the compound instead of its brand name) does lower the cost. Tetracycline, for instance, is the generic name for a widely used antibiotic; chlordiazepoxide hydrochloride is the generic name of the tranquilizer Librium. Physicians may write prescriptions under either the brand name or the generic name, but the generic name may save you as much as $10 on an average prescription.

When a new drug is developed it is usually patented under a single brand name. The patents run for seventeen years, during which time the company recovers the cost of the research and development that went into the product and usually makes a healthy profit as well. After that, the drug may be put on the market by the same company or others under the generic name. Indeed, 90 percent of all generic drugs are made by the major companies, so a popular misconception that most generics are made by small, unknown companies that are pirating the drugs is unfounded.

To get the savings that are yours by buying generic drugs, ask your doctor to specify the generic name or write the words "or generic equivalent" on your prescriptions. If you are fearful that generic drugs might not be safe, be reassured. Walter Reed Hospital in Washington, D.C., and Bethesda Naval Hospital use generic drugs exclusively. These are the medical facilities that treat our congressmen and presidents.

Comparison-shopping for drugs, generic or otherwise, can result in dramatic savings. Use the listing "Pharmacies" in your classified telephone directory and comparison-shop by phone.

The Prescription Bargain Counter: Commonly Prescribed Drugs and Their Generic Equivalents

GENERIC NAME	*COMMONLY PRESCRIBED BRAND NAMES*	*PURPOSE OF DRUG*
Ampicillin	Amcill Omnipen Polycillin Principen	To fight infection (antibiotic)
Tetracycline	Achromycin V Panmycin Sumycin Tetracyn	To fight infection (antibiotic)
Acetaminophen/codeine	Tylenol with Codeine	To relieve pain, fever, and cough
Hydrochlorothiazide	Esidrix HydroDIURIL Oretic	For hypertension and edema (diuretic)
Penicillin V-K	Pen-Vee K V-Cillin K Veetids	To fight infection (antibiotic)
Chlordiazepoxide hydrochloride	Librium	To relieve anxiety and tension
Propoxyphene hydrochloride, aspirin, phenacetin, and caffeine	Darvon Compound-65	To relieve pain (analgesic)
Erythromycin stearate	Erythocin Stearate	To fight infection (antibiotic)
Amitriptyline hydrochloride	Elavil Endep	To relieve symptoms of depression
Diphenhydramine hydrochloride	Benadryl	Antihistamine (also for motion sickness and parkinsonism
Diphenoxylate hydrochloride with atropine sulfate	Lomotil	To help control diarrhea
Meclizine hydrochloride	Antivert	To control nausea and vomiting, and dizziness from motion sickness
Chlorothiazide	Diuril	For hypertension and edema (diuretic)
Erythromycin ethyl succinate	E.E.S.	To fight infection (antibiotic)

Reproduced from HHS Publication NO. (FDA) 80-3068

Another source of lower-cost drugs is mail-order pharmacies. One is Pharmacy Service of the AARP. Service is reasonably prompt. Prescriptions are sent by return mail and usually reach you within six days. If you have difficulty getting to a pharmacy, mail-order is a boon.

At your request Pharmacy Service will fill your prescriptions with generic rather than brand-name medicines. Send only original prescriptions. Copies cannot be filled. Send no money; the Service will bill you.

Among other mail-order discount pharmacies are Federal Prescription & Vitamin Company and Pharmaceutical Services. With catalogs from all these, you can truly comparison-shop.

For catalogs and price lists write to:

AARP Pharmacy Service
National Headquarters
510 King Street, Suite 420
Alexandria, VA 22314
(They will send you the address of your regional AARP outlet.)

Federal Prescription & Vitamin Company
200 Main Street
Madrid, IA 50516

Pharmaceutical Services
Belton, MO 64012

DRUGS—USE AND MISUSE

Are seniors drug addicts?

- According to the *New England Journal of Medicine,* elderly persons (about 11 percent of the population) receive about 30 percent of all prescriptions written. Additionally, almost 70 percent of the elderly use over-the-counter medication regularly, as compared with approximately 10 percent of the general population.
- According to the National Institute on Aging, about 25 percent of the elderly take four to six drugs concurrently, often prescribed by different doctors.
- And according to Dr. Jonathan Lieff, chief of geriatrics at a Boston hospital, *one out of every four older persons hospitalized is suffering from an adverse drug reaction.*

Do you take medications for hypertension, arthritis, gout, high cholesterol, heart disease, diabetes, and/or some other ailment? If you now have additional problems, these may be caused by the mixture of medications.

Furthermore, medications may act differently on older people from the way they do on the younger. The length of time the drug remains in the body, the amount absorbed by body tissues, and the body reaction have changed. Because older kidneys and liver probably function less efficiently, drugs leave the body more slowly.

For your own welfare, tell each physician you see, and your druggist, what other drugs you're taking. Ask about possible side-effects and interactions. Doctors sometimes hesitate to tell patients that there could be a problem with any prescribed medication, not wanting to alarm them unduly or stir up their imaginations.

To find out for yourself about side-effects and drug interactions with foods as well as other drugs, refer to one or more of the following:

Pills That Don't Work, by Sidney M. Wolfe with C.M. Coley and Ralph Nader's Health Research Group. Washington, DC: A Health Research Group Publication, 1981.

Over-The-Counter Pills That Don't Work, by Joel Kaufman. New York: Pantheon, 1983.

The People's Pharmacy, and *The People's Pharmacy—Two,* by Joe Graedon. New York: Avon, 1977 and 1980.

The Essential Guide to Prescription Drugs, by James W. Long, M.D. New York: Harper & Row, 1982.

The Essential Guide to Non-Prescription Drugs, by David R. Zimmerman. New York: Harper & Row, 1983.

Prescription Drugs, by the editors of *Consumer Guide* with Thomas A. Gossel and Donald W. Stansloski. New York: Crown, 1978.

The Physician's Desk Reference (PDR) and *The Physician's Desk Reference for Non-prescription Drugs.* These annuals are published by the Medical Economics Company.

Both books consist of purely voluntary information from drug manufacturers, and indicate, for each drug, dosage, administration, interactions, contra-indications, precautions to be taken, and possible adverse reactions. They are difficult to use, but your reference librarian will have them and help you with them.

E

EDUCATION

If you feel that your world has narrowed, you can broaden it with education. Whether you want to sharpen your mind, learn new skills, investigate new subjects, or get a diploma or a degree, ample opportunities exist, usually close to home.

The doors are open to free or inexpensive courses at your local high school (evening classes), your nearby college or university, in senior citizen and community centers, YMCAs-YWCAs, churches, clubs, and retirement communities. Classes run the gamut from auto repair to zoology.

AARP's Institute of Lifetime Learning will send materials for a variety of minicourses to any group requesting them. See NATIONAL MEMBERSHIP ORGANIZATIONS for the address.

The Senior Center Humanities Program offers to senior organizations and centers a variety of study units with guides, books, cassette tapes for the visually disabled, and other resources. Write to:

The National Council on Aging, Inc.
600 Maryland Avenue SW
Washington, DC 20024

If you want to get that high school diploma you couldn't manage before, take the General Educational Development (GED) examinations given locally in every state; without even going back to school, you can earn part or all of a high school equivalency certificate. Write to:

GED Testing Service
One Dupont Circle NW
Washington, DC 20036

If it's college you want, there are programs where the nontraditional older student can earn a degree through a combination of on- and off-campus study, often with credit for life experience and knowledge gained over the years. Some schools, called Universities without Walls, work on a tutorial basis. The student meets weekly with a tutor to get assignments and review lessons. No formal class attendance is required.

Outreach programs such as those offered by Antioch, Goddard, and other colleges have local classrooms in various cities. They too give credit for life and work experience and knowledge gained outside the classroom. They encourage class attendance, but you can work on your own under the supervision of a tutor. If you plan to get a graduate degree, make sure that the undergraduate college you attend is accredited.

Another approach to obtaining credit for knowledge acquired outside of school is the College-Level Examination Program (CLEP). Multiple-choice tests measure knowledge in five broad areas and a wide variety of special subjects. Each college or university makes its own decision about acceptable scores on these exams and the amount of credit it will accept. Write to:

CLEP College Board, Department C
888 Seventh Avenue
New York, NY 10019

Educational pursuits are still open to you even if you are housebound, live in a remote corner of the world, or just prefer to skip class. The postman can be your tie to the academic world. Two catalogs of university correspondence courses are published by:

The National University Extension Association
One Dupont Circle NW, Suite 360
Washington, DC 20036

The Directory of Home Study Schools is published by the national correspondence school accrediting agency:

The National Home Study Council
1601 18th Street NW
Washington, DC 20009

Gerontologists maintain that a well-exercised mind keeps its elasticity, just like a well-exercised body. More than 2000 years ago Aristotle said, "Learning is an ornament in prosperity, a refuge in adversity, and a provision in old age." It's still true. (See also: ELDERHOSTEL.)

ELDER ABUSE

Until recently the abuse of elders has been hidden even more effectively than wife or child abuse. All are equally abhorrent, and known or even suspected cases should be reported to the proper authorities (your district or city attorney) at once. (If immediate help is needed call the police.)

Cases of elder abuse reported in hearings before the U.S. Congress and in several states reveal physical, psychological, and even sexual abuse. Exploitation is not uncommon. Relatives or caretakers—self-appointed or otherwise—deprive the older person of his income, possessions, or even his home.

Because of the fear of retaliation, many elders, no matter what the extent of their suffering, are loath to come forward. Often they are ashamed of having been victimized or believe, mistakenly, that they have caused the mistreatment.

The abused are both men and women from sixty up, but those most often mistreated are women seventy-five years or older who suffer from some physical or mental disability and who live with a relative. Patients in poorly run nursing homes who have no friends or relatives to keep close watch on them are sometimes abused, as are those who are so disoriented that they can't make their complaints known or believed.

Families who have members in nursing homes will help assure better care for them if they visit regularly, and *vary the time of the visit.* Arriving at different times of the day and on different days of the week, not just during visiting hours, will give a better picture of what goes on.

Most nursing homes are profit-making institutions. Often the help is employed at minimum wage and is unskilled in handling the infirm and the elderly. There are good nursing homes, but if you think the care is inadequate or practices are questionable, tell the nursing home director. If conditions do not improve, consult:

Long Term Care Ombudsman Program
[Your state division on aging]
Titles vary from state to state. The division on aging is under your state government listing in your telephone directory.

(See also: NURSING HOMES.)

ELDERHOSTEL

A change of scene, a broadening of intellectual horizons—all with a minimum for tuition, room, and board! Elderhostel is waiting for seniors sixty or over and accompanying spouses of any age. It is a network of more than 400 colleges and universities in fifty states and Canada offering low-cost, one-week residential summer programs. A wide range of courses explores all aspects of the human experience from Tracing Your Roots to The American Experience, from Music from the Movies to the Scope of the Universe. Three courses may be taken in one session.

There are no exams, no grades, no required homework, and no requirements for previous formal education.

Elderhostelers live in the college dormitory and eat most meals in the college cafeteria. Charges for tuition and room and board in 1984 were $190 per week.

All that is needed is an adventurous spirit. This summer you could be attending college at Amherst, Yale, the University of Colorado, or the University of Southern California.

To determine the price of the catalog and how to get an application write:

Elderhostel
100 Boylston Street, Suite 200
Boston, MA 02116

A similar program for study in Europe, sponsored by the University of New Hampshire, is Interhostel, offering two-week programs in eight European countries—Denmark, France, Greece, Ireland, Spain, Switzerland, and West Germany. For information write:

University of New Hampshire
Interhostel Program
Durham, NH 03824

(See also: EDUCATION.)

EMPLOYMENT

Self-Employment

You no longer have to retire at sixty or sixty-five, but you did. Now you're bored or restless, you miss that glow of achievement, you feel cut off from the world, or *you need more money*. You want to get back to work, full or part time—but does anyone want a senior citizen for other than volunteer work?

If you were self-employed, can you go back to whatever you gave up? If you sold a business, can you use your expertise in some related way?

Professionals frequently become consultants, offering services in their previous line of work or a related one. Often the consultant's fees are greater than the previous salary (but with no fringe benefits), and he or she still has a pension.

Teachers can tutor, or even open a tutoring school at home. Accountants can be as busy as they want at tax time, or can keep accounts all year for small businesses or for individuals. Writers can continue writing as before or do small jobs, such as résumés or speeches. Psychologists and social workers can start private practices.

An expert in almost anything can give seminars or teach an extension course at an adult school or a university; it's essential only to round up enough students so that the course is self-supporting.

Look around, use your imagination, build bridges between your skill and ways to reach those who need it.

Employment Agencies

If being an employee sounds more comfortable to you than being self-employed, a good place to start is your state employment office. It charges no fees, and some offices have special sections for older workers. All provide free job counseling and, sometimes, referrals to training programs.

Private employment agencies that offer full-time jobs are not a good bet for the older worker. They often require fees and rarely do more than file your résumé. Temporary employment agencies (check Employment—Temporary in your classified telephone directory) are another story. You have a much better chance of getting work and they charge no fee, since you become their employee.

Among the nation-wide agencies are Mature Temps, Kelly Services, Manpower Temporary Services, and Accountemps. Local temporary agencies sometimes specialize in older people also.

The Senior Community Service Employment Program (SCSEP) is a federally funded job program specifically for older people, providing retraining and job placement. The twenty-hour-a-week jobs, in day-care centers, schools, hospitals, senior centers, and the like, are open to those over fifty-five with subpoverty income levels and pay at least federal minimum wage. Following the training, supervisors try also to find nonsubsidized jobs for trainees, in private industry or public agencies.

SCSEP projects are sponsored by AARP, the National Farmers' Union, and the National Council of Senior Citizens. Get the SCSEP number in your telephone directory, or write or call any of the sponsoring agencies.

Some YMCAs and YWCAs offer job counseling and help in finding jobs.

Your Area Agency on Aging often has arrangements with groups that provide day care for children and adults, workers for nutrition centers, and similar services. Volunteers do much of the work, but some jobs are paid, and people over sixty get preference.

Keep in mind that volunteer work can lead to paid work, especially where funds for senior citizens are being used. (See also: ACTION; CAREERS, SECOND; DISPLACED HOMEMAKERS; INTERNATIONAL EXECUTIVE SERVICE CORPS [IESC].)

ESTATE PLANNING

Once a problem for only the wealthy, estate planning now is recognized as a need by many middle-class Americans.

A quick survey of a few estate-planning books will convince you that it is not an easy task. Your reasons and intent in planning the disposition of your estate may not change, but inheritance and tax laws do—frequently, so the advice you glean may be out of date or simply not apply in the state in which you live. Your best insurance that your estate planning is handled properly is to seek expert advice, your own attorney and accountant if you have them, or others who are specialists in the field. (The Bar Association or a faculty member at a local law school may be able to recommend an attorney for you. Accountants have a similar organization, frequently called the Society of Certified Public Accountants (CPAs) that will also make recommendations.)

Your estate is the total of everything that you own and is owed to you, minus anything you owe—your net worth. This is what you want to pass on to specified individuals and not to others. In doing this you want a minimum of probate and administrative cost and of estate and death taxes. And you want this accomplished with dispatch and the least amount of dissension among your heirs.

Responsibility for drawing up a good estate plan starts with you. Before you see your advisors, make a list of your wishes about the distribution of your estate, general division of property, and specific bequests that may or may not be in your will. Assemble all of the documents and facts that will enable your attorney and accountant to make sound judgments in analyzing your assets and liabilities and carrying out your wishes.

Necessary Documents and Facts

Your will and that of your spouse
Real estate deeds and/or leases
Insurance policies
List of bank accounts—checking, savings, and certificates of deposit
Lists of safe deposit boxes and their contents

Copies of all contracts

Any property agreements you are involved in

Records of all lifetime gifts and gift-tax returns

Income tax returns for the last five years

Lists of any stocks or bonds or government securities

Title to major chattels: cars, jewelry, boats, artworks, etc.

Your family tree, to give a picture of family members who are involved or may have a claim on your estate

Records of any previous marriages or divorces and terms of settlements

The name of your executor, ideally someone who has had business experience and is concerned with the welfare of your heirs. This person must be willing as well as able to accept the responsibility.

You will probably also be asked to grant a power-of-attorney to someone who will act in your behalf should you be ill (death cancels a power-of-attorney).

Your advisor will draw up an estate plan for you. Check it over carefully, making sure it expresses your wishes and instructions. Review the administrative provisions, making sure your executor has power to act without having to get the consent of a probate court for each step, entailing delays that drag out settlement.

One more word of advice: Review your plan regularly. If you move, marry, divorce, gain or lose property, acquire or lose children, grandchildren, relatives, or any of a dozen other events that may occur, your whole plan may require alteration. It will be time to see your advisors again.

EUTHANASIA

If you feel that suicide under any circumstances is a sin, euthanasia will be abhorrent to you. If, however, you feel that taking one's own life is justifiable when pain makes it unbearable, when each day is only a new agony, and when there is no real hope for recovery—a group exists to help you even in this extremity.

The Hemlock Society, founded in 1980 by Derek and Ann Humphry with the help of Gerald Larue, professor of Biblical History at the University of Southern California, supports active voluntary euthanasia for the terminally ill.

By September 1983 membership had grown to over 9,000. Mr. Humphry says: "The rapid expansion of membership reflects a growing concern with securing the right of the terminally ill to die in a planned and dignified way....

"Who joins Hemlock and for what reasons?...The membership is an interesting cross-section of people from all walks of life. They are individuals who rationally face the complex issues that the technological revolution in medicine has confounded society with...."

The society has published five books on euthanasia; the most important, helpful, and explicit of these is *Let Me Die before I Wake,* which has already sold 13,000 copies by mail order and may now be distributed to bookstores by the Grove Press. (An alternative is to send $10 to Hemlock. Add $1 for shipping.)

Passive euthanasia, the right to refuse life-sustaining treatment, is somewhat less controversial. California passed a law in January 1984 that gives a person the right to sign a Durable Power of Attorney, giving power to make life-or-death decisions to some trusted person in the event of the patient's incapacity.

If you feel that you would not want a terminal illness lengthened, check to find out whether your state is considering a similar law.

For further information write to:

Hemlock
P.O. Box 66218
Los Angeles, CA 90066

(See also: HOSPICE; LIVING WILLS.)

EXERCISE

No one can prove that exercise will make you live longer, but there is ample proof that it can improve the quality of life. Exercise has been shown to do lots of good things. It can:

- Aid digestion and elimination, improve circulation
- Strengthen and tone muscles of the abdomen, back, legs, and feet
- Repair and improve the aging body, increase flexibility
- Reduce the risk of cardiovascular disease
- Reverse the slowing of reflexes
- Lower blood fats and blood pressure
- Burn calories to help control your weight
- Strengthen your heart and lungs and increase oxygen intake
- Invigorate, and increase energy and resistance to fatigue
- Increase your ability to dissolve blood clots
- Help you cope with anxiety, depression, and stress
- Help you relax and feel less tense, improve the quality of sleep
- Arrest osteoporosis (thinning of the bones with age)

Aerobic Exercise

Aerobics, according to Kenneth H. Cooper, M.D., "refers to a variety of exercises that stimulate heart and lung activity for a time period sufficiently long to produce beneficial changes in the body." (See Recommended Reading at the end of this section.) Most sports are not sustained enough to qualify. As the American Heart Association puts it, "Only those exercises which significantly increase the blood flow to the working muscles for an extended period of time promote cardiovascular fitness and endurance."

In other words, muscle-building exercises such as weightlifting and isometrics won't do the job, nor will most sports. Only regular, brisk, sustained exercise such as fast walking, swimming, and stationary cycling can give you the benefits listed. Jogging is excellent also but not recommended for people over sixty. Outdoor bicycling is good only if you can sustain the pace without having to stop or slow down. The idea of aerobic exercise is to increase the maximum amount of oxygen your body can process within a given time.

If you're not used to this kind of exercise, take it easy. See your doctor before you start any serious exercise program, especially if you have a heart condition, high blood pressure, insulin-controlled diabetes, or fairly severe arthritis or if you have a family history of premature heart disease. In these cases he or she may advise modified exercise. Just to make sure, you might ask about a treadmill test (an electrocardiogram taken while you are exercising).

Recommended schedules for aerobic sessions range from twenty to thirty minutes at least three times a week to half an hour twice daily. If limited to three times a week, space your sessions throughout the week, rather than exercising on successive days. A five-minute warm-up period should precede each session, and an equal cool-down period end it; don't stop vigorous exercise abruptly.

Tips for Aerobics

- Wear appropriate, comfortable clothing; easily removable layers are sensible. Avoid rubberized or plastic garments except maybe in the rain. For walking, be sure to wear good shoes and cotton or woolen socks. For swimming, you're on your own.
- Take it easy in hot or humid weather. Dr. Cooper suggests not exercising on any day that is over ninety-five degrees (or ninety degrees with 80 percent humidity) or very cold.
- Build up gradually to your maximum. If you have to miss a few

sessions, start again at half or two-thirds of the normal level. If you feel any tightness or pain in chest, arm, or shoulder, or any difficulty in breathing, stop at once.

The objective of aerobic exercise is to reach your optimum degree of exertion. How can you know when you've reached it? You need to determine your target zone (TZ). First subtract your age from 220; that should be your maximum heart rate. Now take 60 to 80 percent of that number (authorities differ) to get your TZ. For age sixty, 220 minus 60 equals 160; 70 percent of that is 112, your TZ. The National Institute of Health has a simpler formula:

Age	*TZ*
60	96–120
65	93–116
70	90–113

Your TZ is the heart (pulse) rate you want to reach and sustain for the duration of your exercise; if your rate is lower, you're not exercising hard enough; if it's higher, you're overdoing. Check your pulse at the wrist or, more easily, at the throat. Count the beats for five seconds and multiply by twelve. Five minutes after the end of the exercise period your rate should be lower than the TZ, and by ten minutes it should be under 100. If it's not, slow down for a week and try again.

Other Kinds of Exercise

Flexibility Exercises. Suppleness is important to seniors because our range of motion tends to decrease with age, and a sudden movement can cause injury, such as strains or even broken bones. Yoga (see entry) is a good way to stretch every part of the body and at the same time learn relaxation and deep breathing, but there are other flexibility programs.

Body Movement to Music. This kind of exercise may be sustained and vigorous enough to take care of your aerobics, or it may be more like stretching exercises.

Breathing Exercises. These are described in *Total Breathing* by Philip Smith. New York: McGraw Hill, 1980.

Sedentary Exercises for the Disabled. Some of these you can think of by yourself, such as stretching often and comfortably like a cat. Isometric exercises pit one set of muscles against another, as when you clasp your hands together and try to pull them apart. It's important to move as much and as often as you can; sitting or lying without movement is bad for you.

Exercise Through Imagery. Interestingly enough, some scientific tests have indicated that going through certain exercises in your mind can actually improve muscle tone.

Even being on your feet at least one hour every day will strengthen your long bones. Remember that the amount of work you do in any kind of exercise should depend on your own capacity, which exercising will improve. Also remember that exercise can't be banked; last year's exercise won't help you this year. Whatever your situation, some kind of exercise will make you feel better and improve your health.

Recommended Reading for Everyone

The Aerobics Way, by Kenneth H. Cooper. New York: Bantam, 1978.
(See also: SENIOR OLYMPICS; YOGA.)

Recommended Reading for the Disabled

The SAS In-the-Chair Exercise Book, Issued by Scandinavian Airlines. Call your local SAS office or ask Information for an 800 number. Designed for airline passengers, this is useful to anyone confined to a chair.

Exercise for the Prone Patient, by Etter, Mildred F. Detroit: Wayne State University Press, 1968.

EYEGLASSES

Are your glasses usually misplaced? Then you are probably wearing glasses only for reading, and, if you are comfortable with the inexpensive magnifying eyeglasses sold at Woolworth's or the department stores, you can buy a couple of pairs, station them strategically around the house, and solve the problem. That's for convenience.

Now for saving money. It's possible to reduce the cost of prescription lenses. Some optical companies have cut prices dramatically. Obtain a prescription and then order your glasses there. If you already have your prescription glasses, go to one of these companies for the second pair you need at home or to take along on trips.

Most authorities now say it is not necessary, as it was once considered, to check your prescription annually. Go back when you feel it needs changing. You will know.

Incidentally, don't let an optometrist charge you for or refuse to give you a copy of your prescription. A Federal Trade Commission ruling makes it illegal.

The place to send those discarded glasses—frames, lenses, or both—is New Eyes for the Needy, Short Hills, NJ 07708; you can take a tax deduction, and you'll be doing a good deed.

Recommended Reading

Know Your Eyes, by Ira A. Abrahamson. Melbourne, Florida: Krieger, 1977. Write to:

> **Robert E. Krieger Publishing Co., Inc.**
> P.O. Box 9542
> Melbourne, FL 32902

The Eye Book, by John Eden, M.D. New York: Penguin, 1978.

EYES, PROBLEMS WITH

Diseases of the Macula

The macula is that part of the retina responsible for central or "straight-ahead" vision. Some macular disease comes with aging and diminished blood supply to the macula. Diabetes, high blood pressure, and kidney disease may also cause impairment, as may certain drugs taken over a long period—certain tranquilizers and antimalarial or antirheumatic drugs. Check with your physician or the *Physicians' Desk Reference.*

The most common condition is macular degeneration, which occurs mostly in people over the age of sixty-five. Freckle-like spots on the macula may, if not in a critical area, never cause any difficulty; but they can in time cause a slight blurring or even loss of clear central vision. They never cause complete blindness, for peripheral or side vision remains.

You may be unable to read or to recognize people at a distance, but you can get around and take care of your personal needs. You can learn to use your residual vision for many activities if you put your mind to it. Many aids are available nowadays to make seeing easier: special magnifying glasses, special lighting, large-print books, and more.

Treatment of macular disease is not usually possible, but your case may be an exception, so have a complete ophthalmological evaluation if you start having problems. Early symptoms are blurred vision, blank spots in the central vision, and distortion.

Remember that using the impaired eyes will not harm them, and that total blindness will not occur.

Floaters or Spots

The sensation of seeing spots occurs most often in older people, particularly the near-sighted (myopic); it is caused by vitreous floaters that occur erratically and is usually insignificant. The spots appear to be moving beady or thready strands or dust particles, and are best seen when you look up at the sky or at a white or light background. If, however, they are red or brown, or occur in a sort of shower, see your physician at once.

Presbyopia

Presbyopia is the difficulty in focusing on close objects that accompanies the normal aging process. It may cause you to need bifocals or trifocals, but sometimes simple magnifying eyeglasses will do. (See also: BLIND, SERVICES FOR; CATARACTS; GLAUCOMA.)

F

FAMILY HISTORY

When Alex Haley's *Roots* took the country by storm, it generated a red-hot interest in genealogy. Mr. Haley's study was more the history of a people than a family, but most genealogical research is the record of families: their dates, relationships, migrations, occupations, and circumstances.

Tracing your roots can give you a greater sense of identity, understanding of your predecessors' trials and perseverence, and pride in their achievements. The history of a family, and records of family events and family folklore, and stories of occurrences are a priceless heritage. Now that retirement and reduced responsibilities give you more time, you may want to research the family history and preserve this private record for others.

The place to begin is with yourself. Test your own information.

What do you know of the origins of the family?

What events caused settling in a particular place or places?

What is the origin of the family name? Has it ever been changed?

Is there a recorded family tree?

Have any members distinguished themselves?

What did your grandparents tell you about their early lives?

Have any members taken part in any historical events? (Don't forget such things as military service, meetings with famous people, protest activities.)

Are there family heirlooms that have a story?

Are there skeletons in the family closet?

Next assemble all of the memorabilia (legal documents, school records, photo albums, letters—whatever) that are related to the family. What do they tell you? Don't forget diaries and the family Bible—favorite places for recording information.

When you have exhausted your own resources you are ready to interview others, especially the oldest members of the family. A family dinner may yield spectacular results. Plan ahead which direction you want the conversation to go, the stories you want to delve into, the pictures you hope to identify. Tape record the conversation. Put the recorder where it is inconspicuous so your guests, although you have alerted them, may be able to ignore it.

Once you have delved as far as you can with what is readily available to you, you may want to pursue a serious study. If you want to get into true genealogical research, the Library of Congress has every genealogical book written in English. The National Archives, also in Washington, contains all the immigration, naturalization, and military records.

The New York Public Library, on 42nd Street, has a superb collection, especially good for the Eastern states, but also including information for the rest of the U.S. and Europe.

For tracing turn-of-the-century immigrants, the collection of the Mormon Church in Salt Lake City is great. The main Los Angeles Public Library is outstanding for records of the West.

Many local or regional libraries also have genealogical departments, usually limited to the particular area.

For free assistance from the Genealogical Society of the Mormon Church write:

Church of the Latter Day Saints
General Correspondence Division
50 E North Temple
Salt Lake City, UT 84150

To assist you in assembling your family history you may order *Family Folklore,* an interviewing guide and questionnaire Stock Number 047-000-0352-1 from:

Superintendent of Documents
U.S. Government Printing Office
Washington, DC 20402

or *Family Folklore,* a 100-page book discussing family stories, expressions, traditions, memorabilia from:

Smithsonian Institution, Folklife Programs
L'Enfant 2100
Washington, D.C. 20560

(Enclose a $3 check payable to
The Smithsonian Institution.)

FLU, FLU SHOTS, AND COLDS

Two major kinds of germs can get you down: bacteria and viruses. Most colds and flus are caused by one or more of 100 different viruses, none of which responds to antibiotics. Since antibiotics should never be taken unnecessarily, don't ask for or take one when a virus gets you.

Sometimes it's difficult to tell the difference between a cold or upper-respiratory infection and flu or influenza. If you have a runny nose, weepy or itchy eyes, sore throat, and maybe a low fever, you probably have a cold. If the symptoms are more sudden and severe, your temperature is high, and you feel awful all over, you probably have the flu.

Cold or flu, resign yourself to having the malady for one to two weeks. (If you suspect bronchitis or pneumonia—*see your doctor immediately!)*

The many over-the-counter medications for colds and flu may be cough suppressants, expectorants (to get the mucus up), antihistamines, anti-fever, or anti-pain drugs—often in combination. Most of these can create problems as well as alleviate symptoms, and you're safer if you can manage with just aspirin or acetaminophens like Tylenol. Chicken soup is now known to be medically helpful, something Jewish mothers have believed for years.

Influenza can have devastating results, particularly in people over sixty-five or with chronic illnesses. Many experts recommend flu shots for those at high risk, even though the vaccine is only about 65 percent effective, effective for only one year, and can cause fever or sore arms.

If you do get the flu, either because you didn't get the shot or it didn't work, ask your physician about the drug amantadine, which can shorten the illness if you take it in the first day or two.

For further information:

"The Common Cold: Relief but no Cure." HHS Publication No. (FDA) 77-3029, reprinted from the September 1976 *FDA Consumer.* Available from:

FDA Consumer,
Office of Public Affairs
5600 Fishers Lane
Rockville, MD 20057

FOOD STAMPS AND FOOD ASSISTANCE PROGRAMS

Having trouble stretching your budget to provide adequate food? The Food and Nutrition Service of the U.S. Department of Agriculture has food assistance programs for those who need help, the largest of which is the food stamp program. Those who are eligible buy food coupons for a fraction of their value and then present them at the market in payment for their food purchases.

This government program, paid for by taxes, has been specifically designed to help you if you need it, so don't be reluctant to ask about it and accept the assistance. Contact your local or state welfare office or local health department, or write:

Administrator
Food and Nutrition Service
Department of Agriculture
Washington, DC 20250

Recently, surplus cheese and butter have been distributed to the needy. Don't be reluctant to accept the food—you're doing the government a favor, for it has cost a mint to keep it in storage.

Ask for details at your senior center. (See also: MEALS ON WHEELS; NUTRITION PROGRAM FOR THE ELDERLY.)

FOOT CARE

Feet often begin to hurt in later life (particularly if abused in earlier years) and need pampering. "The older your feet get, the more you have to baby them," says a Dr. Scholl's ad. Losing the desire or the ability to walk any distance narrows your world by restricting your activities prematurely.

Proper shoes are now even more important than they were; wear sensible heels and allow sufficient length and width for your toes. Shop for shoes in the afternoon, when your feet are larger from walking and standing all day.

Common Foot Ailments and What to Do about Them

Corns and Calluses. Don't cut or shave them off. Do rub gently with a pumice stone after bathing, and apply cold cream or other lubricants. Try over-the-counter medications only under supervision; used carefully, they may eliminate the need for surgery. Change shoes daily in order to change pressure points.

Bunions. Wear soft, wide, roomy shoes and a protective pad to provide relief. Whirlpool baths and certain antiinflammatory drugs may help. As a last resort, if the pain is unbearable, ask an orthopedist about a bunionectomy.

Falling Arches. Massage feet and soak them in warm water. Try arch supports.

Hard, Dry, Burning or Itching Feet. Use only cold-cream soaps, and sparingly. Apply lanolin or other lubricants twice a day. This may make your hose messy, but it will do wonders for your feet. If feasible, apply liberally at bedtime and wear cotton socks to bed.

Blisters. Dr. Subotnick of the American Podiatry Association says to apply tincture of Benzoine, cover with moleskin, and leave on till the area is healed—maybe as long as a week.

Ingrown Toenails. To prevent these, cut toenails straight across; then file till smooth with an emery board. If the condition occurs (but without infection) force a small piece of absorbent cotton under the nail to allow it to grow out properly. Replace cotton, containing a small amount of an antibiotic like Neosporin, morning and night.

Fungal and Bacterial Conditions (Including Athlete's Foot). After bathing, dry feet thoroughly, especially between the toes, and dust with a fungicidal or ordinary talcum powder. Dust powder into shoes and socks also. Wear cotton or woolen socks when possible; don't wear nylon hose at home. Wear shoes with leather (not "man-made") uppers, so that your feet can breathe. Dr. Subotnick says that soaking your feet two or three times a week in a pan of water with a half cup of white vinegar added will change the pH of the feet and kill the fungi. Expose feet to sun and air when possible. If all else fails, see a podiatrist or a dermatologist.

Poor Circulation. Try warm foot baths and gentle massage. Wiggle toes and flex feet frequently. Stretch feet and legs; walk, walk, walk. Don't wear garters. Sit with legs elevated whenever possible; lying on a recliner with feet higher than the heart is excellent. Avoid exposure to cold temperatures or water, long periods of sitting or resting, crossed legs, smoking. If feet are always cold, wear socks to bed. And check with your physician for causes of the condition.

Remember that jogging, running, and aerobic dancing may be too strenuous for the aging foot and may cause orthopedic problems. Remember also that if you suffer from diabetes or circulatory problems, you must assiduously avoid temperature extremes, pressure from poorly fitted shoes, cuts, bruises, and infections. See a physician *immediately* at the first sign of trouble.

For further information, write:

The American Podiatry Association
20 Chevy Chase Circle NW
Washington, DC 20015

Recommended Reading

Foot Notes, by Michelle Arnot. New York: Doubleday/Dolphin, 1980.

The Foot Book: Advice for Athletes, by Harry Hlavek. New York: World, 1977.

The Diabetic Foot, by Marvin E. Levin and Lawrence W. O'Neal. New York: Mosby, 1977.

FOSTER GRANDPARENTS

Sociologists, psychiatrists, and other professionals have observed that there is a special bond between youngsters and seniors. It is this special relationship that gave rise to the Foster Grandparents program under the sponsorship of the Office of Economic Opportunity in 1965. The venture, today administered by ACTION, has been phenomenally successful.

Foster Grandparents are low-income men and women sixty years and older who volunteer four hours a day, five days a week, through local public or nonprofit organizations. They serve children who suffer sight or hearing impairments, a language disorder, or specific learning disability or who are mentally or physically handicapped.

In return, they receive an annual physical examination, a hot meal each day they serve, transportation to and from their assignment sites, and a small nontaxable stipend.

Rewards go both ways in the program. Children benefit from the love and direction, often improving in dramatic ways. Foster Grandparents find themselves needed, loved, and involved in the world. There is a child out there who needs you.

To get information on the program call or write your regional ACTION office or call toll free 1–800–424–8580, ext. 239. (See also: ACTION; VOLUNTEERING.)

G

GLAUCOMA

A relatively common eye disease that, if unchecked, causes blindness, glaucoma is often age related or hereditary. It should not be one of the leading causes of blindness in this country, for it can be contained if diagnosed and treated quickly.

Signs of glaucoma may be loss of peripheral, or side, vision and delayed ability to adjust to semidarkness or low light levels.

Eyes should be tested regularly for aqueous humor pressure, even though no symptoms are discernible. The pressure is measured through tonometry, in which the force necessary to indent the eye is measured. The eyes are anesthetized by drops; the test takes but a moment, is painless, and is often done free in clinics.

High pressure isn't a sure sign of glaucoma, but it is an indication, so a high reading should be followed by a visit to an ophthalmologist. Glaucoma presents a danger when the reading is in the low twenties, but the victim may not notice pain from the pressure till it reaches the forties and has already done some damage.

Most patients are put on maintenance drugs (usually eyedrops) for the rest of their lives. The most popular of these is Timoptic, whose generic name is timolol maleate. It works better than pilocarpine and epinephrine. There are possible side effects from these eyedrops, as well as from tablets, which some older persons prefer.

Marijuana also reduces intraocular pressure and is now used legally in clinical investigations approved by the FDA.

Because of its furtive nature and because it affects so many older people, the possibility of glaucoma should be a major concern; so be sure to take the test once a year, and more often if it runs in the family.

For further information send for HHS Publication #80-3015, a reprint of the June 1980 *FDA Consumer,* from which this was excerpted. Write to:

FDA
Department of Health and Human Services
5600 Fishers Lane
Rockville, MD 20857

GOLDEN AGE PASSPORT

Off to visit the national parks this summer? The national government has a bargain for you. If you are over sixty-two, stop at a Forest Service office or the first national park, monument, or federally owned recreation center you come to and get your free Golden Age Passport, good from here to eternity.

The Golden Age Passport will admit you and any family or friends in your vehicle to any or all national parks, monuments, and recreation areas *and* give you a 50 percent discount on fees charged for federal facilities and services such as camping, boat launching, and parking. (Don't expect it at privately owned concessions, however.)

Golden Age Passports must be obtained in person. Proof of age is required: Medicare card, driver's license showing birth date, or a birth certificate.

Golden Age Passports may also be obtained at National Park Service regional offices (Department of the Interior) or from the Forest Service (Department of Agriculture), both listed in the telephone directory under United States Government.

For the disabled, the Golden Access Passport has the same privileges as the Golden Age Passport and is also free.

GOVERNMENT AGENCIES

The spectrum of programs, services, and assistance furnished by government agencies is as broad as our society is complex. To best serve the people, the government's offices are widely distributed around the country.

If you have questions about any program or agency in the federal (U.S.) government, call the Federal Information Center (FIC) nearest you. FIC staff members are prepared to help you find information or locate the right agency—usually federal but sometimes state or local—for help with problems. The offices are located in populous centers in each state.

To get the telephone number for the FIC nearest you, ask information for the Federal Information Center. (Ask for the toll-free number.)

In Florida, Iowa, Kansas, Missouri, and Nebraska toll-free 800 numbers serve locations outside the area code of the cities where the FIC is located.

Government offices and services in your area are listed in your telephone directory under United States Government, the name of your state (e.g., Florida, State of), the name of your county or parish (Fairfield, County of) or the name of your town or city (Glendale, City of).

Each state has consumer protection agencies that help resolve complaints and furnish information or helpful publications. Many states (and cities and counties) have separate departments of consumer affairs. In others, they are part of the State Attorney General's office—a consumer protection or consumer fraud unit.

State commissions and offices on aging are responsible for coordinating services for older Americans. They can provide information on programs, services, and opportunities for the aging. All have "aging" or "elderly" in their titles. To locate yours, contact your elected state representative.

If you are dissatisfied with the service you receive from any governmental agency, contact your elected representative on the appropriate level—national, state, city, or county. (See also: INFORMATION AND REFERRAL [INFO LINE].)

GRANDPARENTS' RIGHTS

If you have been barred from contact with your grandchildren because of divorce or family upheaval, legal avenues may be open to you to reestablish the relationship. Check with your representative in state government and your congressperson as to the present status of your rights. (Legislation has been pending.) If you have such rights, you may be able to tactfully change the attitude of the person or persons who are preventing you from seeing your grandchildren. If not, you can resort to legal action.

GRANNY FLATS

To help fill the need for senior housing, "granny flats" may be the wave of the future. The granny flat, started in Victoria, Australia, is a separate, self-contained unit installed as temporary living quarters in the yard of a single-family dwelling. By 1982, over 1000 granny flats, varying in size from a modest 280 square feet to 708 square feet—about the size of a single mobile home, had been installed in the Australian state.

Despite its economic advantages, the concept has gotten off to a slow start in the United States, where it has been dubbed "echo housing." (Cost compare: A federally subsidized housing unit in 1981 carried a price tag of $48,000, as compared to $18,000 for a granny flat!)

In general, zoning laws here prohibit extra living units on

single family lots. However, some communities, realizing that the granny flat is a viable alternative to rent subsidies or institutionalization of the elderly, have amended their codes to permit these second units.

An alternative to the detached flat, especially where questions of winter heating make a separate unit less feasible, is to remodel free space in the home for an accessory apartment. The advantages of both arrangements are obvious.

Advantages for the older person or couple

- continued independence
- more economical living
- emotional support of being near family
- help in case of emergency

Advantages for the family

- intergenerational relationships
- sense of fulfilling obligation to the elderly
- no long journey for monitoring the situation in a retirement or nursing home
- ease in giving support (meals, housekeeping, medication, etc.)

Local ordinances are not carved in stone. Changing codes to permit granny flats may be made palatable by a restriction that the housing must be removed once the need has passed and that the accessory apartment's continued use be for family members only.

This may be a step in restoring the unity of the American family—an idea whose time has come. (See also: HOUSING.)

GRAY PANTHERS

Not all of the Panthers are gray. Members of this enterprising, persistent organization come in all ages, from teens to nonagenarians. Young and old, they work together to improve the lot of the elderly.

Founded in 1970 by Maggie Kuhn and five friends after her mandatory retirement, the Gray Panthers have campaigned unceasingly for fairer treatment for older people. They fight against retirement forced because of age, for a just and reliable pension system, for a medical care system that really cares, for reform of the nursing home industry, and for measures that will promote independent living for seniors as long as possible.

Dozens of grassroots chapters across the country support these efforts. To find the chapter nearest you check your local telephone directory or write:

Gray Panthers
3635 Chestnut Street
Philadelphia, PA 19104

H

HAIR

Hair comes in two basic varieties—wanted and unwanted. It doesn't always stay where it is wanted and often appears where it isn't, especially on older people. It comes in a profusion of shades and colors that shift or fade as time goes by.

Baldness

For men it doesn't matter where it appears, but it often departs from the pate, and can inflict a staggering blow to self-esteem. The failure of hair follicles to continue to produce hair on male heads has given rise to a rash of products claiming to prevent hair loss or to stimulate hair growth—so many that the Federal Food and Drug Administration (FDA), exercising its power to regulate over-the-counter (OTC) drugs, has studied hair growth and the safety and effectiveness of these products.

According to the experts, if a man has inherited the gene for the classical M-shaped male-pattern baldness (alopecia), no cream, salve, or lotion is going to prevent his losing his hair or restore it once it is gone. Baldness is forever—not a comforting thought but, once it is accepted, it is a springboard for action to other remedies if remaining bald is unthinkable.

First, some of the most attractive men are bald—witness Yul Brynner and Telly Savalas—and it is possible to cultivate a sense of pride in the condition. This is the premise of the Bald-Headed League, a 4000-member club based in Dunn, North Carolina, to which former President Ford and actor Phil Silvers belong.

Second, there are alternatives. You can be fitted for a hairpiece that can be worn even swimming or in the shower. Or you can have a hair transplant.

In a hair transplant (a technique dating from 1954), 30 to 700 hair plugs are transferred under local anesthesia from parts of the head where they can be spared to the section where they are needed. The price is by the plug and varies, so it pays to comparison shop for price as well as expertise. The process is lengthy, sometimes painful, and in some cases unsuccessful. While the implants are taking hold, most men wear hats or caps to hide the unsightliness of the scalp. Nevertheless, many who have submitted to the process say it was worth every penny, every-minute, and any embarrassment that was involved. To date the most well-known beneficiary of the technique is Wisconsin's Senator William Proxmire.

(Don't go away, men. If you have thin or thinning hair you will find valuable tips in the following section directed toward women.)

Thin or Thinning Hair

Few women ever become bald, but many are troubled with thinning hair, a problem that may be alleviated by:

- A change of hair style. A clever cut can cover a thin spot or give the appearance of abundant hair.
- A permanent—body or otherwise. It's comforting to note that the FDA report on balding states that permanent waving, bleaching, and other trauma to the hair shaft itself does not harm the hair as long as the root is not involved.
- The use of one of the "texturizers" on the market. Texturizers cling to the hair shaft and make it seem thicker. Some are miracle workers.
- Use of hair spray to add body.
- A well-designed wiglet or a wig. Many actresses have whole wardrobes of them.
- That old trick (see also APPEARANCE) of bending over, head down, and brushing your hair toward the floor before arranging it.

Hair Color

Many people look stunning with gray hair, especially those with dark eyes or whose eyebrows and lashes have remained dark. For others gray hair is less than flattering. Tinting is now commonplace and widely accepted, and the tints on the market are excellent.

If you color your gray hair, according to hair stylist Don King, choose a shade lighter than your original color. Blond tones are youthful; dark colors looked more "dyed." Select a blond that has some depth, so that it contrasts with your face.

Hair coloring can be tricky; pinks or brassy tones creep in. Don't settle for them. If you go to a beauty shop, gently persuade your operator to keep trying, so you can both be satisfied. If you do your hair tinting yourself, start with lighter shades first.

If you prefer to keep your gray hair but don't like the shade, tints can change that for you. Perhaps grandmother's remedy, rinsing your hair with a bit of bluing in the water to keep down the yellow, may be all you need.

Facial Hair

Facial hair offers men an opportunity for expression: sideburns this month, a moustache next, or a beard. But for a woman, facial hair has no desirable qualities. Whether it's profuse or just coarse lip, neck, or chin whiskers, it is intolerable.

If the unwanted hair is limited to a few whiskers, tweezing can keep them under control. Eliminating them permanently can be accomplished by electrolysis, a process whereby a tiny wire is inserted in the hair shaft to destroy the growth-promoting follicle. (Repetition is sometimes necessary to make this effective.)

If facial hair is profuse, OTC depilatories (hair removers) or waxes, used periodically, will keep the hair under control. Be sure to read all of the directions carefully and follow them to the letter, including cautions that suggest testing. All these products are not the same, so try another if one is unsatisfactory.

It's worth time and effort to keep your hair attractive with whatever commercial, chemical, or surgical help is available. (See also: APPEARANCE.)

HEALTH FAIRS

Looking for a bargain? The biggest one around is, of all places, in the medical field. It's called Health Fair and there may be one coming to your neighborhood shopping mall, church, clubhouse, or retiree organization.

Older-American Health Fair programs have been an annual event since 1979. A grant from the Administration on Aging to the NHSCVO (National Health Screening Council for Volunteer Organizations—no wonder they shortened it!) set the program in motion. The Prudential Foundation took over the funding in 1981.

The fair offers a minimum of four screenings: measures of height, weight, blood pressure, and visual acuity. Some fairs test for glaucoma, hearing problems, and certain types of cancer.

Volunteer dentists, ophthalmologists, nurses, and other medical personnel do the more complicated tests. Lay volunteers assist with the easier tasks and the clerical work.

For a modest $8 fee, the 1983 Los Angeles Health Fairs also included a blood test. The twenty-three-item test result printout mailed to the participants informed them of their glucose, sodium, potassium, and cholesterol levels, as well as any evidence or lack of evidence of certain other problems. The purpose of each test was clearly stated and the normal range defined, making the printout easy to understand. If the tests revealed that a participant was in any danger, he was warned to see a doctor.

Where else can you get such a bargain? For further information watch your local newspapers or write:

NHCSVO
5161 River Road, Bldg. 2
Bethesda, MD 20816
Tel 1–800–638–8087
(in Maryland [301] 942–6601)

HEALTH MAINTENANCE ORGANIZATIONS (HMOs)

Under an HMO plan, you pay a single monthly or annual fee in order to receive, at little or no additional cost, any and all the medical care that you and your spouse need, including annual physical exams. And once you're a member, they can't throw you out.

But unless you enrolled as part of a group when you were working, you have to pass a physical exam; and any preexisting condition, like high blood pressure, diabetes, a mastectomy, and the like, can disqualify you. It's a good idea to apply while you're still healthy.

Many firms offer their workers a variety of health insurance options, including HMOs; you may switch while you're employed, but before retiring you must choose the one you want to remain with. Consider whether you'd prefer an HMO to Blue Cross or similar insurance.

HMOs aren't cheap unless your ex-employer is paying part or all of the bill, but as with medical insurance, you'll get a lot more than your money's worth in times of major or prolonged illness, and less than your money's worth if you remain healthy.

A great advantage is that all your doctors are in one building or complex, and you can get emergency care at any time of any day or night. Another plus is that the organization usually does *all* the paperwork you have to struggle with when your coverage is split between Medicare and a private insurance group.

The disadvantage is that you must choose doctors within the group, and when the one you've chosen isn't there, you have to make do with whoever is on duty.

Most HMOs reimburse you for emergency medical care in case of accident or hospitalization when you're traveling but not for ordinary visits to a doctor's office.

If you're eligible, an HMO may be the safest way to ensure your not going broke because of major medical expenses. For the name of an HMO near you, write to the Group Health Association of America. Ask also for booklets about HMOs, which they provide free. And ascertain, before you enroll in one, whether there are any exclusions whatsoever.

For further information, write:

Group Health Association of America
2121 Pennsylvania Avenue NW
Washington, DC 20037

HEARING AIDS

Picture Beethoven bent over his piano with a short stick of wood clenched in his teeth, keeping it in contact with the instrument so he could "hear" his new composition. What a tragedy and waste!

We have no way of knowing if a hearing aid would have helped Beethoven, but we do know that such aids help most people with a hearing loss.

The system consists of a tiny microphone to pick up sound waves from the air, an amplifier to strengthen the electrical signals from the microphone, a battery to provide energy, and a receiver that converts the amplified signals back into sound waves. These waves are then directed through an ear mold or bone conduction device, bringing hearing to the wearer.

Most people choose a monaural (one-ear) aid, but for some, a biaural (two-ear) aid is better. Your hearing specialist will select the best system for you, but you must select the model.

A good ear mold is essential to a successful hearing-aid system. Properly designed, it provides support for the aid and sends the amplified sound into the ear canal efficiently. If it doesn't fit properly, it may irritate the ear or distort sounds, setting up a horrible racket. Ready-made ear molds are available, but a custom-made mold, exactly fitting your ear, is worth the investment.

Getting a properly prescribed and fitted hearing aid is only the first step in being a successful aid user. You will need a month or two to adjust. (Many manufacturers and dispensers allow a thirty-day trial; try to obtain this advantage.)

You may have no trouble in rediscovering the world of sound, but you may be in for a shock. If sound has been blocked out for a long time, the confusion of sounds may be like a Tower of Babel peopled by fishwives and camel drivers. Background noises may drown out what you want to hear. People with normal hearing do "selective listening." You may be able to relearn this skill.

To get accustomed to your new electronic helper:

- Begin with a comfortable volume level.
- Break in gradually; turn it off or remove it if you're uncomfortable
- Try to concentrate on the person you want to hear despite background noises.
- In public places, sit near the front of the room.
- Try different settings of tone and volume control as you listen to people, TV, or music. Change your position in relation to the sound.
- Ask family and friends to help by attracting your attention with a gesture and by speaking slowly and distinctly.
- If you're having continued difficulty, ask your dispenser to check the fit and control setting with you.

When you buy an aid, you are also buying a set of services: mechanical and electrical adjustments, instruction in use, maintenance during the warranty period, and later repairs. Be sure that your supplier will continue to give satisfactory service. (See also: PETS; TDD AND OTHER TELEPHONE AIDS.)

HEART DISEASE

Good news! For the first time in our nation's history, heart attacks are decreasing in number, and cardiovascular death rates are going down. They have a long way to go to relinguish their place as the nation's number-one killer, but at least they are headed in the right direction. Americans are changing their life style, and the change is paying off.

Except where there is a family history of heart disease, a person's potential for a heart attack is determined by his habits and traits: smoking cigarettes; being overweight; developing high blood cholesterol, high blood pressure, or diabetes; engaging in little physical activity; or having what is known as a Type A personality.

The Type A personality, characterized as the "hurry and hostility sickness" by Drs. Meyer Friedman and Ray Rosenman, authors of *The Type A Personality and Your Heart,* is one who is highly competitive, impatient, intolerant, and goal-driven.

Both physical and behavioral elements are risk factors that increase the chances of having a heart attack by two or three times. A person with two risk factors has three to four times the risk of someone who has only one.

Chances of an attack increase with the magnitude of the risk factor. The individual who smokes two packs of cigarettes a day is at greater risk than the person who smokes one; he, in turn, runs a greater risk than the occasional smoker. The person who is thirty pounds overweight is at greater risk than the one who is ten pounds too heavy. Similarly, the higher the blood pressure, the higher the risk.

Medical researchers have defined the risk factors and propose alterations in lifestyle to reduce the danger from the controllable ones. (The uncontrollable risk factors are a family history of coronary artery disease and being a male.)

Avoiding a Heart Attack

What can you do to reduce your heart attack potential?

1. Stop smoking! Studies show that within one year of stopping smoking, the risk has been reduced to only 10 percent over normal. That 10 percent will disappear completely over the next five to ten years. So throw away those "coffin nails."
2. Control your blood pressure! Have it taken regularly. Take prescribed medicines religiously.
3. Reduce or eliminate the salt in your diet.
4. Reduce or eliminate your saturated fat and cholesterol intake (see: CHOLESTEROL).
5. If you are overweight, take it off, take it off, take it off!
6. Exercise—but see your doctor before starting *any* program. Begin gradually and regularly until your heart muscles and other muscles are in relatively good condition. Any aerobic exercise, such as walking on a regular basis, will help prevent heart attack *(not weight lifting, sprinting, or softball).*
7. Avoid stress. If cousin Albert drives you buggy, stay away from him. If your job is sending you into tailspins but you can't leave it, take "minute vacations" during the day to breathe deeply, think of a serene garden, a movie you enjoyed, a book, a joke.
8. Stop burning the candle at both ends. You are in the middle, you know.

Symptoms of a Heart Attack

There are many different symptoms of heart attack, but the usual warnings are:

- pain, fullness, uncomfortable squeezing or pressure in the center of the chest for more than two minutes
- pain radiating to the neck, shoulders, or arms

Should someone in your household have, or even suspect, a heart attack, take all the actions open to you immediately. SECONDS count!

- Apply CPR (cardiopulmonary resuscitation) and call the paramedics or fire rescue squad.
- Get the victim to the Emergency Heart Care Hospital nearest you as recorded in front of this book. (Emergency Heart Care Hospitals displaying the symbol at left have twenty-four-hour emergency departments meeting the standards of the American Heart Association.)

DO NOT WAIT for other symptoms: severe pain, dizziness, sweating, shortness of breath.

If You're Alone

- Call the paramedics or fire rescue squad or dial "O' for operator and say "Send the paramedics to [*your address*]."
- If you are away from home call the paramedics or ask someone to call them.
- Get to the hospital if one is nearby.

CPR can keep a person alive until an ambulance and medical attention come. Ambulances carry defibrillators that can shock the heart to start it beating again or correct an irregular rhythm. Some hospitals have coronary care units (CCU), where patients are monitored and treated for abnormal heart rate, blood pressure, temperature, and respiration. Medical tests can determine the extent of the disease and assess the severity of the attack.

Medication, therapy, and medical technology unite to help the heart disease patient. New drugs control heart spasms, pacemakers regulate rhythms, and by-pass surgery brings blood to the heart.

Without question, major advances will continue to be made in reducing the toll from heart diseases.

For the address and telephone number of your nearest Emergency Heart Care Hospital, call your local American Heart Association. *Record the number at the front of this book, Emergency Numbers.* The Association will also furnish several booklets and answer questions.

Recommended Reading

The American Heart Association Cookbook, 3rd ed., edited by Mary Winston and Ruthe Eshleman. New York: Ballantine, 1980.

Prevent Your Heart Attack, by Norman Kaplan, M.D. New York: Scribner, 1982.

Stress, Diet, and Your Heart, by Dean Ornish, M.D. New York: Holt, Rinehart & Winston, 1982.

Type A Behavior and Your Heart, by Meyer Friedman and Ray H. Rosenman. New York: Fawcett, 1978.

(See also: ARTERIO- AND ATHEROSCLEROSIS; BLOOD PRESSURE; CARDIOPULMONARY RESUSCITATION (CPR); CHOLESTEROL; EXERCISE; NUTRITION; PARAMEDICS; SECURITY SYSTEMS: INDIVIDUAL; STRESS.)

HOME EQUITY CONVERSION

Here's a plan to put money in your pocket by borrowing on a source where it's stored up—your home. You can arrange for a loan based on the appraised value of your property and take it as monthly income while continuing to live in your house or condo.

The loan is made through a bank or a savings and loan. Interest is charged at the market rate. The loans usually have a five-year minimum and a ten-year maximum term. At the end of the period the borrower has the option of selling the home or refinancing the loan to pay back the original one. If the homeowner dies before the loan is up, the estate is responsible for repaying the loan and any charges.

The money can be used as you like—to meet primary expenses or to make improvements. Some seniors make changes that enable them to continue to live self-sufficiently—adding ramps, bathroom conveniences, or even an elevator.

Equity conversion should be considered only after the social, economic, and physical status of the homeowner and the family is considered, but it's one way to get an assured income if drawing on your home investment doesn't alarm you.

A government booklet describing the ways to turn equity into income may be purchased for $3 from:

Superintendent of Government Documents
U.S. Government Printing Office
Washington, DC 20402

Ask for Y4.Ag 4:H 79/2, *Turning Home Equity into Income for Older Homeowners.*

HOME HEALTH CARE

When Flora B., age seventy-five, broke her knee and hip the orthopedist doubted that she would walk again.

"Oh, yes, I will," asserted Flora.

"She just might," her doctor conceded. "We'll give her a chance."

Flora was sent home and a network of services provided for her. A physical therapist came three times a week. A homemaker/home-health aide assisted her with bathing and did housekeeping chores. Within a year she *was* walking—limping, to be sure, but walking—and taking care of herself and her apartment.

Home health care programs started in Europe in 1892 with England, France, and the Scandanavian countries providing exemplary models. In the U.S. both public and private agencies are now setting up regimens and household help for persons recovering from accidents or illness.

Many specialists may be involved. The attending physician must prescribe the necessary medication, therapy, and care. Physical and speech therapists, part-time nurses, and homemaker-health aides may be called in when needed. A social worker may help. If the services are supplied by a home health care group participating in Medicare and the procedures are in accord with certain criteria, Medicare pays.

The Veterans' Administration and CHAMPUS, the health plan for the retired military, have similar coverage.

Some major medical plans and health insurance policies pay or help pay for the care.

Home health care services can provide the skilled or professional help that may make it possible for someone to remain home during illness or convalescence. You can get help in locating them from the Area Agency on Aging, public health and welfare departments, the United Way, or any group involved in medical care.

The National Homecaring Council sets standards for home health services and publishes a directory of accredited and approved services. Write:

National Homecaring Council
67 Irving Place
New York, NY 10003

Two well-known commercial firms specializing in this care are Medical Personnel Pool and Upjohn Health Care, also known as Upjohn Home Care Services and Homemakers Upjohn.

The Visiting Nurses Association, an eighty-year-old nonprofit agency, also provides a variety of home health services. Fees are based on ability to pay and determined at the first visit. Nobody, however, is ever refused service because of inability to pay.

These and other groups are listed under Home Health Care in the classified section of the telephone directory or under their names.

Caution: Before committing yourself to any of these services determine if they are covered by Medicare, Medicaid, and/or your private insurance. (See also: DISABLED; MEALS ON WHEELS; MEDICAID; MEDICARE.)

HOME REPAIRS

Is your roof leaking? Is your electrical system faulty? Is your bathroom window about to fall out? There just may be a way you can arrange for these or other home repairs within the limits of your budget.

Recognizing that many homeowners cannot afford to maintain their property adequately, the Department of Housing and Urban Development (HUD) established Community Development Block Grant Funds, to be administered by local housing authorities. Within well-defined guidelines the city or county may use the monies in a variety of ways:

- for low-interest loans (3 to 13 percent, depending on family size and income)
- for maintenance and repairs
- for free tool programs (you borrow the tools that will make the job easier)
- for refunds on the cost of certain improvements

The program enables the city to upgrade neighborhoods and prevent slums, and to help struggling homeowners keep up the value of their property and make it more comfortable.

Although these programs are not strictly for senior citizens, they are open to them. Many older persons on low, fixed incomes are eligible for the benefits.

In rural areas the Farmers Home Administration sponsors similar programs.

Sometimes grants are made to cover the labor costs of repairs if the homeowner can pay the costs of the materials out of pocket.

Also, weatherization programs entitle homeowners to low-interest loans or rebates and tax credits.

In Detroit, Maintenance Control for Seniors, a nonprofit organization that managed to survive the 1982 slashing of federal funds, provides employment for retirees, job training for young craftsmen, and a repair service that fills two purposes: alleviating burdensome repair bills for older persons, and preserving turn-of-the-century houses. Similar groups operate elsewhere. Sometimes church or neighborhood teams help older or disabled persons by providing carpentry, painting, electrical work, or other maintenance or repairs.

Should you want to tackle your own repairs, a number of excellent do-it-yourself manuals are on racks in your neighborhood hardware or paint store and on the shelves of your local library. (With renewal you can keep a book four to eight weeks—long enough to get the job done or change your mind.)

The government Consumer Information Catalog lists free booklets or inexpensive books on home repair and maintenance. For a copy of the catalog write:

Consumer Information Center
Pueblo, CO 81009

To see if special programs are operating for the elderly, call your senior center. For information about government programs call your local housing authority, community development office, the Farmers Home Administration, or the Rural Electrification Administration.

HOSPICE

Hospices, first established in medieval Europe to care for the sick and wounded, today are providing the terminally ill with a way to live out their lives among family and friends and to die with dignity.

For the terminally ill to be admitted to home hospice service, their doctors must certify that further treatment will not effect a cure and that life expectancy is six months or less. The patients and their families know the diagnosis.

The ill return to the familiar surroundings of their own homes, where they follow the pattern of their lives, cared for by family members with the support of hospice teams. These teams, composed of doctors, nurses, counselors, social workers, and volunteers, help the family cope with the effects of the illness, providing psychological and spiritual help as well as practical care. The patients are made as comfortable as possible. They are given medication to ease pain whenever they require it, but suffer no tubes, respirators, or mechanical devices. The focus is on the quality of the dying person's remaining months or weeks rather than on extending life.

Should the family not be able to cope, even with help, patients may enter a hospital-type hospice. Here they continue to wear their own clothes, keep some of their cherished belongings, and receive visitors whenever they wish.

The costs of some services at approved hospices are covered by Medicare.

Hospices are found in all sections of the country, and a call to your local hospital should help you locate one near you. The Locator Director, listing all National Hospice Organization providers and a description of each, is published and available from:

National Hospice Organization
1901 North Fort Myer
Rosslyn, VA 22201

(See also: EUTHANASIA; LIVING WILLS.)

HOUSING

Sooner or later you may find that your living arrangements aren't suited to your present way of life: Your house is too big or costs too much to run or you need the money in the equity, or your apartment is too far from essential facilities. Or you want to be closer to your children. Or you simply want to move to a different community.

Your options are wide, limited only by your financial and physical condition. However, before you commit yourself to any move you need to weigh carefully the advantages and disadvantages of each of your options. Be sure to season each choice with a liberal amount of how you *feel* about it. That last part of the equation, your emotional reaction, is the most important factor. Heed it. Many retirees or retired couples move, only to find the grass was greener back home.

Staying Put in Your Own House or Apartment

You know its present pros and cons. Can you prophesy the future?

Will taxes or rent become too high?

Will the neighborhood change?

Will property values go down? (or up?)

Will repairs become a nuisance, an unreasonable expense, or, in an apartment, not be made?

If you are left alone, will your present home be too large, the responsibility too much?

If money becomes a problem, can you get help?

Alternatives

If you own your own home: You may be entitled to tax breaks (see TAXES) and help in making repairs (see HOME REPAIRS).

You may be able to make a sale (and realize some money) on a lease-back arrangement that lets you continue to live there. (See an attorney on this one.)

You may be able to cut down expenses by sharing your home (see SHARED HOUSING).

If you rent: You may be eligible for a rent subsidy (see RENTAL ASSISTANCE).

Another Possibility

Would a cheaper house or an apartment put money in your pocket? If you own the house or condo and sell, would you have a nest-egg left over after you bought a cheaper one? (see TAXES—Capital gains on sale of residence.) If you hope to get the same amenities in a cheaper house, apartment, or condo, you will probably have to move to a different part of town or even different city or state. Will you still have a substantial sum left over after you have paid the cost of relocating?

Making a Move: To an Apartment

A valid argument could once be made for encouraging older people to sell their homes and move into apartments: The landlord would make repairs, maintain the building, and repaint periodically. Rents were stable. If conditions became untenable you could move. No one would have called it paradise, but in retrospect it seems to have been.

Today rents are high, and even if you should qualify for a "Section 8" (rent subsidy) and are protected by rent control, the nagging worry persists, "Will I be able to keep a roof over my head should one or the other be cancelled?" Realistically, it could happen.

You may have more security and will certainly continue to be independent in your own apartment. You can choose the size you want and will have no responsibility for maintenance either inside or out.

However, some buildings are allowed to deteriorate, some are noisy, and many have little storage space. The condition of the halls and common areas is dependent on the manager or superintendent, who may not be competent.

Even under rent control, periodic increases are allowed while your income may stand still. Repairs may or may not be made. Can you be sure that the building will not be converted into a condominium? Then what? If you're thinking about selling your home and trying apartment living, weigh the move carefully.

To a Condominium

Condominums have come to all sections of the country. Those built as new units are usually well designed, but check out the models carefully. Sometimes furniture in the display condo is cut down, Lilliputian-size, to make the rooms look larger.

Condos are cheaper than houses, more fuel efficient (shared walls) but they are less private. You do own your home and get a tax write-off, but you are liable for special assessments and maintenance fees. You must follow the condo association rules, attend the meetings if you want to know what is going on, and may have to ask permission to sell. You may have to pay for improvements you don't even want.

Converted apartment houses or large houses remodeled into condos may suffer from arthritic plumbing, wiring, and heating elements. As co-owner, you are financially responsible if major (or even minor) repairs need to be made. Condominium ownership is *very* tricky, full of possible pitfalls.

Before you buy, get informed. The Department of Housing and Urban Development offers a fifty-three-page booklet: "Questions about Condominiums—What to Ask Before You Buy." For your free copy request Publication No. 567L from:

Consumer Information Center
Department K
Pueblo, CO 81009
Attention: S. James

Your library also has books on condo ownership.

To Co-op Housing

A large house can serve as cooperative housing. In Los Angeles the city's Community Redevelopment Agency purchased and renovated a duplex to accommodate ten senior citizens. Household chores are done cooperatively, each person or couple has a private room, and all share the communal rooms.

Co-op or similar housing gives you companionship, greater security, lower expenses, and someone at hand if you need help. But your private space may be smaller and you may have to conform to a schedule and accept mutual decisions. You have to be flexible to get along with different personalities, but it may beat being alone all hollow.

To a Life-Care Home

Life-care housing offers you a unit (room, apartment, cottage), meals, maid service, planned activities, and comprehensive medical care.

Some life-care centers charge an entrance fee, usually substantial. A few ask no entrance fee but require that the resident's assets over a certain amount be placed in a trust fund. The monthly payments come from the fund. Some may ask for donations from children of the resident.

In a life-care center you will be relieved of much of your housekeeping, can cease to worry about medical care, and are cared for even if your money runs out. But—your quarters may be small, you might not be able to get your entrance fee back if you want to move out, and a change of management can greatly alter the quality of the food, care, and service. If your money is put in a trust fund you lose control of it. Worst of all, some life-care centers, and run by very respectable groups too, have gone bankrupt, leaving the residents without money and without care.

A thorough investigation is in order before you decide this is it. Before you sign a life-care contract, and that's the way it works—be sure about what is covered and what is not. All medical and nursing fees? All meals? Laundry? What further financial demands might be made?

To a Mobile Home

Resist the temptation to call them "trailers" —you're dating yourself. It's rare these days to find a mobile (or manufactured) home that doesn't come equipped with a dishwasher and microwave oven, and that has fewer than two bathrooms. It's still possible to buy a single, a sort of one-bedroom "railroad" apartment, but most mobile homes are doubles, and some, triples; many even have a second story.

Mobile homes are cheaper than houses or condominiums

and are usually well designed, with carpets, draperies, and appliances included. The better mobile home parks have green-belts and recreational facilities that border on the luxurious.

But—you do not own the land; you may have trouble getting conventional financing on your unit and difficulty selling should you want to move. The homes are seldom really mobile. In addition, the rent for your space may be raised periodically. The casual life in the park may or may not appeal to you.

Mobile parks are likely to be far away from shops and cultural and medical facilities.

A tip: A municipally owned park, if you can find one, or a park where the residents have bought the land, will be a better bet.

Out of Your City or State

"Retirement Edens Outside the Sunbelt"
"Where to Retire on a Small Income"

These extravagant promises lured a million elderly retirees to other states from 1975 to 1980. Some of the fervor has cooled, but if you are dissatisfied where you are now, you too may be thinking of moving away.

Reams have been written about American Shangri Las. Unfortunately, if you hope to find such paradises you probably should have gone yesterday. Prices change and the population swells, causing hitherto accurate data to go quickly out of date.

The best way to make a choice of a new location is to make a pilgrimage to check it out—and then arrange to stay there six months or longer to experience the community life and the climate in different seasons.

You may love it. If so, pack up and move—lock, stock and barrel. If not, you still have your home to go back to.

Out-of-the Country

Moving to Puerta Vallarta or Costa del Sol may sound romantic and adventurous but you may be in for culture shock and more adventure than you seek.

A lot of questions arise. Will you find cheaper housing? Will it have the conveniences to which you are accustomed? If you don't know the language, how will you be able to communicate? How will you adjust to different customs? (Or is that part of the fun?) Curriencies fluctuate. Will you be all right if the dollar goes down, down, down? You will certainly broaden your knowledge and have new experiences, but it's well to remember that everybody doesn't always love Americans, and many places in the world are highly volatile politically.

However, foreign climes do attract. At least a quarter of a million U.S. social security beneficiaries collect their checks in other countries. You may decide to be one of them.

Biggest consideration: Your Medicare and some private health insurances do not apply outside the United States.

To Public Rental Housing

Some low-cost public housing is open to elderly people with very low incomes. Because of the shortage of housing for these senior citizens, authorities are making valiant efforts to build new housing or to rehabilitate existing buildings to accommodate them; housing specifically designed for seniors with wider, easily opened doors, elevators, tub grab bars, and many safety features.

In public housing your rent is 25 to 30 percent of youı income. You have a place of your own and no responsibility for outside maintenance or for repairs. But waiting lists are long and you must show your need by disclosing your finances. Much public housing is plagued by crimes, gangs, and deteriorating buildings, and may be noisy as well as unsafe.

If senior housing is available it's a better deal; regular public housing in its present state is a mixed blessing.

To a Retirement Apartment House

Retirement apartment houses sponsored by churches, fraternal organizations, unions, or other nonprofit concerns provide apartments at current rents. If they have assistance from federal funds, some have subsidized low-cost apartments.

Many of the buildings are designed with safety features, including a way to call for assistance if needed. Many serve meals. Some have a beauty shop, a gift shop, or a commissary. Transportation to shopping or the doctor is arranged or provided. Most are security buildings.

But the apartments are often small and the quality of life depends on the management. To get in you must be a minimum age (usually sixty-two), in good health, and if your rent is subsidized, you must show need.

If you don't like it, you can move. That's a plus.

To a Retirement Home

Retirement homes may be owned by profit-making individuals or corporations or by religious, fraternal, or labor groups. You get your meals, a room (sometimes shared), the use of the public rooms, and exposure to a potpourri of activities that you can take or leave, as you like.

Here you can count on personal security and relatively stable fees. You have little or no responsibility aside from keeping yourself and your possessions in order. However, the space you have is small, and sometimes your possessions are not safe. If you have to pay a founders (entrance) fee, it may not be refundable. Since everyone is older, the constant fading away of members is depressing. If you become ill, you will have to go to a hospital or a nursing home.

Shop carefully if you are considering a retirement home; check out the neighborhood shops and recreational and cultural opportunities. You won't want to spend all day, every day, within its walls.

To a Retirement Hotel

Retirement hotels are usually older hotels converted to residential use. For a monthly fee you have a room or suite and maid service. Other services vary from hotel to hotel. Some provide meals and some have doctors who can be called in.

Here you can abdicate all responsibility except paying the bill and taking your clothes to the cleaners. Since these hotels are usually in a central location, you are near the downtown amenities—shops, restaurants, and transportation.

But the buildings are often allowed to deteriorate, you will have to out for all of your meals, and you can be evicted if the owner changes the policy. If you are in a decaying inner city, stepping outside your door may be perilous. If you become disabled, you will have to leave.

To a Retirement Village

Retirement villages sprang up all over in the 1960s and 1970s. The rate has slowed down, but some are still expanding. Since they are planned communities they are usually in rural settings. The housing may be relatively uniform—all single-family units—or varied: houses, condominiums, and apartment houses. Medical and long-term care facilities may be part of the package or an option.

In retirement villages you own your own unit, are responsible for inside maintenance, may entertain whom you please, and sell if you like. Since they are patrolled or guarded, it is easy to lock up and leave. The big ones have their own shops and services and something is always going on: classes, clubs, trips, dances. If that is not enough, you can catch the village bus into town.

On the negative side: Kids, teenagers and young marrieds are not permitted as residents, and there is no guarantee that the fee for outside maintenance and use of pool, putting green, or whatever—which you may or may not use—will not rise. One resident complained of his retirement community: "It stifles individuality."

If you can arrange to stay for a weekend or can sublease for a few months, the pros and cons will begin to appear. It's better than a management tour.

To Shared Housing

We have all shared housing at some stage of our lives—with our families, college roommates, or someone else.

Now shared housing with nonrelatives (even strangers) has entered the scene to help solve the housing problems of seniors. Some programs are federally funded, and others are run with the help of various charities. All bring sharers together.

Sharing one's home allows the owner to keep it and cuts expenses, according to the number of people involved and the agreements made.

Sharing requires great cooperation and fair play. Finding the right person or persons is not easy, nor is adjusting to the habits and tastes of strangers. It involves giving up a measure of independence for all, and that is not easy either.

One big stumbling block to the concept is that more people own homes than are willing to give them up and move in with others.

A directory of shared housing opportunities in 100 communities (not necessarily yours, so inquire before you invest) is available from:

Shared Housing Resource Center
6344 Green Street
Philadelphia, PA 19144
Cost: $3.50 in 1983

An in-depth treatment of the dynamics of finding a "sharer," including a comprehensive list of questions on the nitty-gritty problems of cooperation—who takes out the trash, what temperature is comfortable for you, and so on—is part of Dr. Barbara Stanford's book, *Long Life and Happiness,* $7.95 postpaid from:

Long Life Center
1140 Iris Street
San Luis Obispo, CA 93401

I

ID CARDS

What do you use for identification if you no longer have a driver's license? Recognizing this need, many state motor vehicle departments issue senior citizen identification cards. Proof of age is necessary. Acceptable documents include: birth certificates, passports, visas, baptismal certificates, and expired or out-of-state driver's licenses. The charge for the ID is low, usually about $3.

To check on the place and time to get your ID card, call your local senior center or check with the motor vehicle department.

IMPOTENCE

Temporary, chronic, or permanent impotence sometimes comes with age, but it should not be thought of conclusively as age-related. It can be caused by accident or surgery, or by a degenerative disease, such as diabetes, arteriosclerosis, and chronic kidney failure. In these cases it may be irreversible. But when it is caused, as it may be even in young men, by alcoholism or by medications (notably some of those used to treat high blood pressure and depression), then it is curable.

Psychotherapists believe that impotence in older men is as often psychological as physical. A competent urologist with a specialty in male sexual problems can determine which it is. If hormonal, it may be curable by medication. If it is caused by permanent damage to the nerves or blood vessels, a penile implant or prosthesis, surgically inserted, can resolve the sex problem. Both a semirigid rod prosthesis and an inflatable penile prosthesis are available to make intercourse possible again. Surgery must be performed by a urologist. Healing may take as long as a month. Most insurance companies will provide coverage. (See also: SEX.)

INFORMATION AND REFERRAL (INFO LINE)

"My social security check didn't arrive. What shall I do?"
"Do I qualify for SSI (Supplemental Security Income)?"
"I am being evicted. Where can I find an apartment?"

If you have a similar question or one about a service open to you, call Info Line. Mandated by a federal law providing that all older people, no matter where they live, "must have reasonable access to...services in the community," Info Line strives to link those who need help with services and opportunities in the community.

In many places Info Line is operated by the Area Agency on Aging; in others by a local public or volunteer organization. Information and Referral will not only, as the name implies, give you information, but will also refer you to the proper place to get help. The counselor may even make an appointment for you and check back later to see if your problem has been resolved.

If Info Line or Information and Referral is not listed in your phone directory, call the Area Agency on Aging or a senior center for the local number. Recording it under Emergency Numbers in the front of this book will save time when you need help or the answer to a burning question.

INSOMNIA

From earliest times, the virtues of sleep have been extolled in literature, and the agonies of wakefulness deplored. Causes of insomnia have been analyzed and palliative measures suggested, but no magic cure has been found.

Some insomniacs toss and turn, fidget and seethe, while trying vainly to fall asleep. Others drop into slumber quickly and easily, but wake frequently during the night; or wake for good well before dawn, regardless of the time they went to bed. Among the causes of these sleep disorders are:

- irregular sleep schedules or daytime catnaps
- lack of exercise
- caffeine (in tea, coffee, many soft drinks, Anacin, Empirin, etc.)
- chronic use of tranquilizers, sleeping pills, or alcohol
- smoking before bedtime
- diet pills, which contain stimulants
- certain medications (steroids, hormones, asthma drugs, etc.)
- chronic anxiety or depression

If anxiety or depression continues for a long time after any loss, or if it is habitual, psychotherapy can help. The therapist may recommend that an antidepressant be prescribed.

If your trouble is falling asleep, do only relaxing things before bedtime. *Don't* start cleaning closets or balancing your books in the evening. These measures may help:

- tranquilizing techniques such as deep breathing, self-hypnosis, meditation, visualization, biofeedback, yoga
- a high-carbohydrate snack and tryptophan (available in health-food stores), warm milk, calcium pills, or, occasionally, two aspirins
- reading something 'heavy' —history, philosophy, essays, etc.

If you wake frequently during the night, you can also benefit from any of the above. Or determine to enjoy being awake: Have a radio or a cassette deck on your bedside table, using earphones if you have a roommate. Some fine relaxation cassettes are almost hypnotic in effect.

Alternatively, you can get up and work for a while, or write—letters, a journal, anything. Some people get their most productive thinking done during the night.

It may be that your biological pattern isn't synchronized with the work-sleep pattern in your time zone. If you're a night person, don't struggle to sleep before you're ready. If, on the other hand, you find it hard to stay awake after 8:00 P.M., try to schedule your social life around lunches and brunches instead of dinners, and matinees instead of evening performances.

Although seven to eight hours a night is generally considered the norm, individuals differ greatly; some manage well on as few as four or five hours. As you age, you generally need less and less sleep, but worry more and more about sleeplessness. Insomnia can, after all, be a minor problem if you don't have to go out to work or drive the following day.

If, however, your sleep problems are truly severe, seek out a sleep clinic. If your physician or local hospital doesn't know of any, write for a list of clinics in your area to:

Dr. William Dement
Association of Sleep Disorders Center
Stanford University School of Medicine
Palo Alto, CA 94305

or

Peter Bent Brigham Sleep Clinic
721 Huntington Avenue
Boston, MA 02115

Recommended Reading

The Complete Book of Sleep, by Dianne Hales. Reading, MA: Addison-Wesley, 1981.

Biofeedback: Turning on the Power of Your Mind, by Marvin Karlin and Lewis M. Andrews. Philadelphia: Lippincott, 1972.

A Good Night's Sleep, by Jerrold S. Maxmen. New York: W. W. Norton & Co., Inc., 1981.

Recommended Cassette Tapes

"Self-Management Techniques for Controlling Insomnia," with self-instruction manual, by Richard R. Bootzin, Ph.D. Available from:

BMA Audiocassettes
200 Park Avenue South
New York, NY 10003

"The Sleep Tape," by Emmett E. Miller, Ph.D. (Includes "Putting the Day to Rest" and "Escape from Insomnia.") With instructions for optimum use. Available from:

Emmett E. Miller Tapes
P.O. Box W
Stanford, CA 94305

Ask for list from:

ISHK Book Service, Dept. T-5
P.O. Box 176
Los Altos, CA 94022

(See also: STRESS; YOGA.)

INSURANCE

You retire, turn sixty-five, are widowed or divorced and, woosh, your insurance needs and coverage change overnight! You find you have too much, too little, or none at all of—life, automobile, health, fire, homeowner's or renter's insurance. Or you have an income-protection policy but now have no job-related income to protect.

Do you have too much insurance?

Life Insurance. Do you still have dependents? Will your life insurance be needed to support a spouse, a son or daughter launching a career, a grandchild without funds for college, or to cover inheritance taxes? If not, would you benefit by cashing in your policy or changing it to an annuity? (While you are thinking about life insurance, are the beneficiaries on your policies up to date?)

Automobile Insurance. Are you driving less? Ask your agent about discounts that reflect your changed lifestyle, safe record, completion of the AARP driving course.

If you are a two-car family can you reduce insurance costs by eliminating one car?

Are you paying more for collision insurance than your car is now worth? Would a higher deductible reduce your premiums and still give you coverage for any loss you couldn't handle? Have you comparison-shopped for insurance? Some companies' rates are lower by as much as $20–$40–$80 or more a year. You want a good company, though—one that has an A or A+ (excellent) rating. Ask your agent (if he or she doesn't handle your auto insurance!) or ask the reference librarian for *Best's Insurance Reports* and look it up yourself. And you want a company that guarantees in writing it will not drop you because of age if you have accidents.

Income Protection Policy. Don't forget to notify the company of your retirement date. A refund may be due on your last premium.

Do you have too little insurance?

Health Insurance. Frequently tied to a job or a spouse's job, health insurance may end when the job ends or marriage is terminated, by death or divorce. If your medical coverage comes from your spouse's job, or former job, you need to know:

- If your spouse dies, will you continue to be covered?
- If your spouse dies, can you subscribe for the medical coverage without an examination? (If the coverage will not continue, or an examination is required and you have no health problem, you need additional coverage *NOW before a change in your physical condition makes it difficult or impossible to get insurance.*

Do you need health insurance if you have Medicare? *Yes, indeed,* unless you own a half-interest in Chase Manhattan Bank.

- If you already have health insurance, keep it if it covers what Medicare does not. Now that you are on Medicare, you may get it cheaper.
- If you have job-related health insurance that stops when you retire, see if you can convert it to an individual policy. Compare its costs, benefits, and reliability with those of other insurance companies.

(See also: HEALTH MAINTENANCE ORGANIZATIONS (HMOS); MEDICARE; MEDI-GAP INSURANCE.)

Homeowner's or Tenant's Insurance. Have you increased the coverage in your homeowner's or tenant's insurance to keep pace with the increased cost of houses and home furnishings? In case of fire or theft, does your insurance pay *replacement* costs?

Now is a good time to review your policy to make sure it covers all the risks and disasters that may be a threat to your home, but no more. By tailoring the policy to your location and situation you can save money.

Deductibles save money on homeowner's and tenant's policies also. If you raise the deductible from $100 to $500 your premium may be substantially decreased.

Too much insurance means money down the drain; too little—should illness or disaster strike—sweeps it away even faster. Placing yourself in the center of this economic teeter-totter isn't easy.

Further Tips

- Comparison shopping pays off for all insurance, not just automobile coverage.
- Try your credit union or professional organization for insurance. Frequently premiums are cheaper.
- Look into Federal Crime Insurance (sold by the Federal government in 28 states) if you can't get home or apartment insurance against burglary or if it's too expensive. It's low cost and can't be cancelled regardless of the number or size of claims you make. To qualify, you must install approved locks on outside doors and windows. For information call any licensed property agent or broker or:

Federal Crime Insurance Program
P.O. Box 41033
Washington, DC 20014
Tel. 1–800–638-8780
(In Washington, DC and Maryland
call [301] 652-2637.)

Do you have any kind of a complaint connected with insurance? Call your state insurance commission at your state capital.

Collecting Insurance

If you are the beneficiary of a policy you can usually claim the insurance by filling out a simple form supplied by your agent or the insurance company. The address is on the policy. Attach a *copy* of the death certificate and return it to the company. Companies usually pay within a week or ten days.

In a few states, state tax authorities must issue a release before the company can pay if the policy is for a fairly large sum of money. Payment will then take longer.

INTERNATIONAL EXECUTIVE SERVICE CORPS (IESC)

"ASK YOUR RETIRED EXECUTIVES TO WORK HARD IN A STRANGE PLACE WITH NO PAY," reads an ad in the *Wall Street Journal.* Donald M. Kendall, Chairman of the Board and CEO of Pepsico, asks other firms to support the International Executive Service Corps, a nonprofit organization that sends retired executives to help companies in developing nations, usually for a period of two to three months.

Although no salary is paid, both the volunteers and their spouses receive travel expenses and generous per diems.

IESC has completed 8500 projects in seventy-two countries, according to the ad, which is directed to companies rather than individuals, although individuals may apply. Here's a great chance to feel useful again, and to try a new life in a new place for a limited time.

For further information call (212) 490–6800 or write to:

IESC
622 Third Avenue
New York, NY 10017

L

LANDLORD/TENANT RELATIONSHIPS

Senior citizens are the darlings of landlords. They are not in the habit of giving wild parties or playing the hi-fi to 2 A.M. at full blast, and they pay their rent on time. Relationships between senior tenants and landlords are not always rosy, however. The landlord may not provide adequate heat or fail to make repairs; the tenant may let an obstreperous grandchild roller skate up and down the halls or insist on improvements the landlord is either unable or not required to make. Explosive situations sometimes develop when this happens, and neither side benefits.

The tenant is entitled to have conditions affecting his safety and comfort corrected, and the landlord is certainly within his rights to halt tenant actions that are detrimental to others or the property, or in violation of the terms of the rental agreement.

Both landlord and tenant have responsibilities spelled out in state and local housing codes. These are usually enforced by local agencies such as the housing department, the health department, and, for conformity to fire regulations, the fire department.

In general, landlords are responsible for keeping the building structurally sound, making sure the plumbing and heating work, the roof doesn't leak, and keeping mutually used areas, such as hallways and elevators, clean and safe.

Tenants are responsible for taking reasonable care of their premises, replacing or repairing anything they break, and paying the rent on time.

Both parties must comply with the terms of the lease or rental agreement. For this reason, such an agreement is an important part of good landlord/tenant relationships.

The Rental Agreement. Before you sign your lease or rental agreement make certain it reflects conditions you expect the landlord to live up to and that you find acceptable. The U.S. Department of Consumer Affairs gives some general guidelines that apply almost everywhere and are generally encouraged by responsible landlords.

Before You Rent

- Find out what your renter's rights are. Many local housing authorities or consumers' offices publish a guide for renters. Study it before signing a renter's agreement or lease.

- Read the agreement or lease carefully. Discuss any clauses that are unsatisfactory to you, and bargain to change them.
- Check the property carefully, noting dirt, chipped paint, broken faucets, windows or doors. Make sure the appliances are in working order. List any problems that need to be corrected under the title "Problems that are to be corrected by (___ date)." Date the list and have the landlord sign it. This may seem like a time-consuming task, but it may help you get the repairs needed, and, should you move, enable you to get back your security deposit.

Establishing Good Relations. Live up to your part of the agreement. Be complimentary if the property is kept in good repair, made attractive, or improved. Thank the manager or landlord for efforts to make you more satisfied and comfortable.

Problems after Renting. Reasonable tenants and landlords will curb actions or correct conditions if requests are reasonable, but not all tenants nor landlords are reasonable. Where the housing market is tight the landlord has the upper hand, just as the tenant does when vacancies abound and rentals go begging. Some rent-control laws, which remove rent ceilings only when vacancies occur, have prompted unscrupulous landlords to neglect repairs and harass tenants, hoping to make them move. Some undesirable tenants, taking advantage of laws to protect them from eviction, abuse the property or their neighbors' privacy or let their rent payments fall behind. Little short of legal action can introduce justice when this happens, and sometimes that fails.

But landlord/tenant issues are not, fortunately, always so grave. What can be done about lesser matters? When complaints about midwinter 50-degree heat, for example, or leaking pipes go unheeded, what can you do?

Step 1. Talk to the landlord or manager again. He may have forgotten your request or misplaced your note. Remind him of your previous complaint. Ask him when he thinks he can make the repairs or to let you know when a workman will be coming. Allow a reasonable time for action.

Step 2. In a dated note or letter remind him that you have called the leak or the broken window to his attention before. *Keep a copy.* If your building has a manager, send a copy to the owner as well as the manager. Again, allow a reasonable time for action.

Step 3. Reread your renter's guide to:

- determine your rights
- know what can be done and where to call to state your case

Step 4. If other tenants are having similar problems, draw up a petition stating the case. Sign it; have all the other tenants sign it. If some won't, try for a majority, but *all* is better. Photocopy it and give it to the landlord.

This might be the time to encourage the landlord to meet with the tenants. If he is willing, put everyone on his good behavior and let each side hear the other out. Be open to compromise if the issue is not one threatening your health or safety.

Step 5. If the problems are not resolved it is time to turn elsewhere. Your renter's guide should tell you where to call.

If you do not have a renter's guide, many cities have a mediation board to open lines of communication between landlords and tenants when disputes arise over unresolved problems. This board is part of a housing authority or housing programs office. Look for it in the telephone directory under your local government heading or call Information and Referral (Info Line).

LEG PROBLEMS

Many older people suffer from leg cramps in the night. Stretching, massaging, or applying heat may help. Avoid sleeping on your back or stomach. If nothing you can do in bed relieves you, get up and try the following exercise, recommended in a letter to the *New England Journal of Medicine:*

With shoes off, stand 2–3 feet from the wall, facing it; lean forward, with hands against the wall and heels remaining on the floor, until you get a pulling sensation in the calf muscles. Hold for 10 seconds, relax for 5, then repeat a few times. Repeat the exercise three times a day until your leg cramps disappear; if they recur, go back to the routine.

If the cramps persist see your doctor to make sure there's no underlying medical problem. He may find a calcium or vitamin deficiency and prescribe added amounts in safe dosages.

Varicose Veins

Whether you already have them or want to prevent them, these measures will help:

- Use footstools when sitting.
- Elevate the legs above the heart when possible.
- Don't sit or stand still if you can help it; move legs as much as possible, even when sitting.
- Don't sit with knees crossed.

And remember, standing (not still) or walking just one hour a day will help keep the long bones of the legs strong.

LEGAL AID

Need help in fighting an eviction notice? In settling a dispute with a creditor? In establishing your eligibility for veterans or other benefits? In determining your rights under rent control, or your rental agreement? If you need legal advice or action, and your income is limited, Legal Aid may come to your rescue.

Some 225 communities across the country have Legal Aid offices. Clients may be referred by social service agencies, employers, courts, and other legal sources. They may hear of the helpful agency through publicity. The assistance Legal Aid gives is dictated by the situation.

Legal Aid is a federally funded program, one of a series to help the poor, passed by Congress in the 1960s. That laws should apply equally to everyone is a basic American principle. Unfortunately, those who most need the protection of the law are sometimes unable to pay attorneys' fees. In criminal cases or disputes between people, they don't. This is where Legal Aid comes in. (Because of budget cuts in its federal funding in 1983, the agency has had to reduce its services, but its dedicated operators continue to provide all the help they can.)

Other groups that provide free legal advice and counseling for persons unable to pay vary from city to city, but the following may operate in your community. Check in your telephone directory or inquire at Family Service or a senior center about city or county bar associations, Grey Law, Jewish Legal Services, neighborhood justice centers.

Call to determine if you are eligible and to make an appointment.

LIBRARY SERVICES

If you can no longer go to the library, the library will probably come to you. Most systems now encourage volunteers to visit shut-ins, learn their reading tastes, and bring them books and magazines on a regular basis. Other libraries offer books-by-mail service; you order from a given catalog and return books in the same container, post-free. Bookmobiles visit senior centers and retirement communities and homes.

For those with vision problems, libraries have large-print books and audiocassettes of novels, short stories, and plays. For those who can't read even large print, Library of Congress has an enormous collection of talking books; ask your local librarian how to get in touch.

Even those who have used libraries all their lives may not realize all the help they can provide. Reference librarians will either find the answer to almost any question you can think of or will guide you to books where you can find it. They can tell you whom to call for social services or senior facilities, and how to write to your government representatives for information or to make your opinions known. Many reference librarians are imbued with the spirit of Sherlock Holmes: Find the explanation, the answer. *Please disturb* is a statement of the dedicated librarian's creed.

Many libraries also have movies, lectures, videotapes, and records; and all have current newspapers and magazines to keep you up to date without the cost of a subscription. In *Consumer Reports* you can check out prospective purchases, from food to furnaces, from antacids to automobiles. And if you are or want to become a do-it-yourselfer, you can find how-to books on just about everything from changing a washer in the kitchen sink to placing ships in bottles.

Today's libraries differ greatly from those of our youth, when we whispered and tiptoed around for fear of incurring the wrath of the librarian. They are pleasantly decorated, air conditioned, have inviting facilities, with easy chairs and tables for your comfort and convenience—good places to spend an afternoon if your home is uncomfortably hot or cold, or even if it isn't. (See also: BLIND, SERVICES FOR THE.)

LICENSES

Before you pay full price for a dog, fishing, or hunting license ask about senior citizen privileges. You may be entitled to a discount or even a free permit. The usual places where you buy your license can tell you.

LIVING TRUSTS

Can you safeguard your estate from probate, and the delays and expenses involved, by setting up a "living trust"? A best seller of some years back suggested that this is the way to do it. Does it work? Well, yes and no.

In California, for example, you can have your attorney draw

up papers that put your assets in a trust with you as the trustee of your own estate until your death or incompetency. You pay the fee, pick up the document and squirrel it away in your safe deposit box. You can name another trustee to take over when you die. Should you want to change the terms of your trust, perhaps drawing money out of the sums you have put in, you can revoke part of the trust. It's a little like being your own grandpa. When you die, chances are your estate will escape probate, if your affairs are in good order. But in some other states the trust is treated as a will and must be probated.

If probate is avoided, will the estate be immediately available to the heirs? Even with the best of planning, no. All states have a period of time before assets are distributed during which creditors may make claims and any challengers may file.

Your trust may be the simple one with you in charge, or an elaborate arrangement between you and a trust company or the trust department of a bank. You go so far as to give up the responsibility of managing your assets and have the bank or trust company manage them for you, making investments, keeping accounts, preparing tax reports, and paying the income to you or anyone you designate. You can be carefree. You may be speeding toward Istanbul on the Orient Express but your dividend checks are still deposited and your business affairs handled.

Along with the day-to-day supervision of your assets, a trust managed by a financial institution has other advantages. If you become ill, your assets will continue to be handled as you have instructed. When you die, the bank or trust company with its experts in state and federal taxes and probate law can guide your estate through probate. If there is probate, this usually speeds it up. All of this tailor-made management is not, of course, free. The bank or trust company collects fees based on the size of the estate.

Trusts may be revocable or irrevocable.

In a revocable trust you reserve the right to change the trust and to resume control of your assets. Here the assets are still legally yours for tax purposes. It is this trust that has run afoul of the courts and been treated as a will.

In an irrevocable trust you give up the right to the property involved. You ordinarily cannot retrieve it. This kind of trust is often used in estate planning and may save taxes, but it should be used only after the greatest consideration and a firm decision that you won't need or want the property back.

Even though trusts have sometimes been considered as wills, they do not take the place of a will. When you put your trust agreement in your safe deposit box or leave it with the trust company or bank, a copy of your will should be with it.

LIVING WILLS

The name may be misleading but the purpose of a living will declaration is not: It is a formal written statement to your family, physicians, lawyers, and medical facility that you do not want to be kept alive by artificial means if you suffer an illness or injury that your doctor considers incurable and terminal.

According to the Society for the Right to Die, which publishes the living will declaration reprinted here, "Common law assures the individual's right to refuse treatment, even life-sustaining treatment."

In recent years this right has been challenged in cases that have made front-page news. In 1983 two California physicians were charged with murder when, with the consent of the family, they withdrew artificial life-support systems from a comatose patient. California has both a Brain Death Law and a Natural Death Act that recognize a living will declaration but the patient had not made one. The doctors were finally acquitted, but not before they and the family had undergone protracted trauma.

The right to die frequently comes into conflict with the dedication of the medical community to sustain life and the responsibility of the civil authorities to enforce laws. Sometimes families of the hopelessly ill or injured go to court to try to force discontinuance of artificial life-sustaining measures. In this event, according to the society, "The courts, as a general principle, try to determine what the incompetent's wishes would be if he were capable of stating them." The living will makes these wishes clear.

If your state has a right-to-die law, a specific form may be required for the living will. If not, the living will declaration given here will serve as important evidence of your wishes to your doctor and family.

The society suggests that you:

- Sign it, date it, and have it witnessed.
- Discuss it with your doctor and add a copy to your health record.
- Discuss it with your family and give a copy to the person who may some day have to make treatment decisions on your behalf.
- Keep a copy readily available. Review, initial, and date it at regular intervals—perhaps once yearly—to show that it still represents your wishes.

The society can give you information on the status of right-to-die laws in your state and the correct forms. Joining the society or making a small donation will help continue its work. Membership ($10) entitles you to a wallet-size living will membership card, a

Living Will Declaration Form

LIVING WILL DECLARATION

To My Family, Physician and Medical Facility

I, ______________________________, being of sound mind, voluntarily make known my desire that my dying shall not be artificially prolonged under the following circumstances:

If I should have an injury, disease or illness regarded by my physician as incurable and terminal, and if my physician determines that the application of life-sustaining procedures would serve only to prolong artificially the dying process, I direct that such procedures be withheld or withdrawn and that I be permitted to die. I want treatment limited to those measures that will provide me with maximum comfort and freedom from pain. Should I become unable to participate in decisions with respect to my medical treatment, it is my intention that these directions be honored by my family and physician(s) as a final expression of my legal right to refuse medical treatment, and I accept the consequences of this refusal.

Signed______________________________ Date______________

Witness ____________________ Witness ____________________

DESIGNATION CLAUSE (optional*)

Should I become comatose, incompetent or otherwise mentally or physically incapable of communication, I authorize ______________________________,

presently residing at ______________________________
to make treatment decisions on my behalf in accordance with my Living Will Declaration. I have discussed my wishes concerning terminal care with this person, and I trust his/her judgment on my behalf.

Signed______________________________ Date______________

Witness____________________ Witness____________________

*If I have not designated a proxy as provided above, I understand that my Living Will Declaration shall nevertheless be given effect should the appropriate circumstances arise.

Used with the permission of the Society for the Right to Die.

subscription to the newsletter, and information on legislative progress across the nation and around the world. Write:

Society for the Right to Die
250 West 57th Street
New York, NY 10107

Signing a living will is strictly voluntary; you can easily revoke the document if you change your mind.

Record the location of your copy in the space provided in the MEDICAL RECORDS and RECORD KEEPING sections of this book. (See also: EUTHANASIA; MEDICAL RECORDS; RECORD KEEPING.)

LOCAL SENIOR GUIDEBOOKS

Someone in your area—an elected official, a radio station, a newspaper—has almost certainly compiled a handbook or survival guide for senior citizens. Snoop around until you get one. In it you'll find local agencies for services described in this book. Using it is easier than groping through the telephone directory. Keep it with this book as an additional tool for enhancing the quality of your life.

LONELINESS

People need people. Nobody has classified loneliness as a disease yet, but evidence is mounting that it's an important factor in death from heart problems and other causes. All things being equal (according to studies at the University of Michigan and the University of California at Berkeley) mortality rates are higher for those in social isolation. In the Michigan study, the health, work, marital status, close personal relationships, leisure time activities, and organizational involvement of 2,754 adults were tabulated. Those with the lowest level of social contacts had from two to four times greater risk of dying.

Men appear to suffer more than women from the lack of human relationships. One study found that men living alone have a mortality rate 94 percent higher than married men. (*Psychology Today,* January 1977, p. 22).

Those who live alone—the single, divorced or widowed—seem to be more vulnerable to stress and anxiety, conditions that cause wear and tear on the heart. Research shows that loneliness disrupts normal hormone secretion, causes changes in the body's nervous system, and alters its response to drugs. ("Biology of Loneliness: Isolation vs. Our Brains," *Science Digest,* December 1973, pp. 36–41.) Prolonged loneliness can cause drastic personality changes.

Older people have no corner on loneliness, but the components of their lives are likely to leave them more open to it. Friends move away, loved ones die, work contacts are lost with retirement, and the energy to seek new experiences may be at a low level.

"Human contact," says Dr. Bert Forer, clinical psychologist," is more conducive to good health than medication is."

If loneliness is undermining your health, what can you do to get back into contact with others?

The simplest way is to look up old friends, but that may not be possible and you may have to make new friends. That won't be as easy, but the rewards will justify the efforts. Do you belong to any groups? A church? Friendship depends on mutual interests. If you don't belong to any organizations, find some groups that represent your interests. Try adult education classes at the high school or classes at the community college or the university. Are there sports you once enjoyed? Short of pole vaulting you can probably get in shape and get involved again. (There's a skiing club for those over seventy that takes to the slopes regularly.)

Can you take a part-time job, get a roommate, share your home, or move into shared housing? Try the senior center, the neighborhood parks. People make friends at center-sponsored dances, crafts classes, luncheons, or on trips to Las Vegas or Atlantic City.

Others need and desire love and friends, too. Your efforts won't continue to be one-sided. You will find those other people who need people. (See also: CALL-A-DAY; EDUCATION; EMPLOYMENT; PETS; VOLUNTEERING.)

LONGEVITY

Tithonus, loved by the goddess Aurora, asked for and was granted immortality; but he forgot to ask for eternal youth and vigor, and life became so insupportable that she changed him into a grasshopper.

According to the song, Methuselah lived 900 years; according to the Bible, he died at age 969.

Ponce de Leon and others searched in vain for the fountain of youth, once supposed to be in the Bahamas.

Dorian Gray kept a picture in the attic that grew old for him. He retained his youth and beauty till he stabbed the picture and died of the wound.

In Aldous Huxley's *After Many a Summer,* a character is still alive and sexually active at age 200 thanks to a diet of raw carp entrails.

From earliest times, people have sought magical substances to keep them youthful and ensure longevity. Nowadays they often turn to dietetic regimens—some sensible, some very far-out. The macrobiotic people claim that their diet is the only answer. The Adelle Davis and the Rodale books, and Jethro Kloss's *Back to Eden,* have sold in enormous quantities.

Although heredity seems to be a major component of longevity, many people are convinced that modification of diet will extend their lifespan and improve their health. And they are right, according to the experts, except that diet is not the only factor.

Claims of remote, incredibly long-lived people such as the Hunzas in the Himalayas and the Vilcabambas in Southwest Ecuador, some supposedly into their 130th or 140th year, are found, when scientifically investigated, to be either untrue or unprovable. Nevertheless, isolated individuals make it past the hundred mark in good health, and in certain areas an unusually high percentage of people live to a very old age.

Among the factors for longevity compiled from many studies are:

- a low-calorie, low-fat diet consisting largely of fresh fruits and vegetables, grains, and low-fat milk products
- a considerable amount of daily physical activity and exercise
- a continuing regular work schedule, which gradually slows down, but doesn't cease
- positive thinking
- no smoking
- a stress-free life style

So, to live to be 100 or more: Remain or get thin; reduce considerably the amount of fat, meat, and salt in your diet; don't smoke; keep working; avoid stress and depression; and exercise regularly and aerobically.

If you have lots of money, consider the Pritikin Longevity Center in Santa Monica, California. For thirteen or twenty-six days you can live, eat, exercise, and learn at this large beachside health center. The staff of ten physicians (including cardiologists and endocrinologists) will give you a complete physical, work out an individualized program of diet and exercise for you, and monitor you during your stay. Lectures, workshops, and cooking classes will teach you to continue on your own.

If you can't afford the price but would still like to follow the strict Pritikin regimen, you can learn the details from his two books.

The American Longevity Center is a new public-participation, nonprofit organization "whose aims are to significantly accelerate progress in those areas of medical research most relevant to longevity." They raise funds for research, sponsor lectures, and send newsletters to members; that of June 1983, for example, included articles on prevention of cancer, heart attacks, and stroke, and ten tips on living to be 100. On the center's board are leading research professors and ten Nobel Prize winners.

For further information or membership, write to:

American Longevity Association
330 South Spalding Drive
Beverly Hills, CA 90212

Recommended Reading

The Pritikin Program for Diet and Exercise, by Nathan Pritikin. New York: Grosset & Dunlap, 1979. Also available in paperback.

The Pritikin Promise, by Nathan Pritikin. New York: Simon & Schuster, 1983.

The Methuselah Factors: Strategies for a Long and Vigorous Life, by Dan Georgakas. New York: Simon & Schuster, 1980.

M

MAIL-ORDER SHOPPING

No other kind of shopping beats mail order for convenience. If you can't get to stores or lack the interest or energy to plug from one shop to another, mail order brings the marketplace to you. In the comfort of your own home you can browse through the catalogs and make out your orders. Drop them in the mailbox and in a week or two United Parcel or the postal service will bring your purchases to your door. To speed up service some catalog houses have twenty-four hour 800 numbers. Order at midnight if you like, as long as you use your Visa, American Express, or other plastic entrance to instant credit. (*Tip:* if your order is substantial, sending a check instead of charging to your credit card may delay your transaction; some firms wisely wait for checks to clear.)

Catalog shopping saves time, effort, and gasoline, but it isn't necessarily easier on your pocketbook. Shipping charges, often bearing little relation to the weight of the order, add to the cost. And if the skirt is too tight or the callus remover doesn't vibrate, you are stuck with the return postage.

You may encounter other difficulties—undelivered merchandise, delays in getting refunds, or, worst of all news that the company has gone bankrupt.

Each year the U.S. Postal Service receives about 30,000 complaints, and the Council of Better Business Bureaus says mail order problems have been their number-one consumer complaint for the last decade.

But millions of transactions proceed without a hitch. Most firms are reliable, do their best to supply you with good merchandise (some of it sensational) and carry on their business in a totally ethical manner. Many have been in business for decades. You can help make your mail order shopping successful by:

- dealing with well-known, reliable firms.
- reading the product description carefully.
- paying by check, money order, or credit card, so you have a record.
- keeping a record, such as the one shown on the sample form so you can follow up an order.
- knowing the company policy on refunds and exchanges. Some have a strict ten-day or thirty-day limit others are open-ended.
- keeping your postal or United Parcel receipt until you receive your refund or exchange on returned merchandise.

Mail-Order Record Form

Date	*Name & Address of Company*	*Page*	*Catalog Number*	*Items ordered Description*	*Price*	*Paid by*

Subtotal ______
Sales Tax ______
Shipping Charges ______
Total ________

Handling Problems

Unsatisfactory Merchandise. Send it back by certified or insured mail or a shipping service that insures your package and keeps a record of delivery.

In the package enclose:

- invoices you received
- a note explaining your dissatisfaction and the method you used to pay—check, money order, or credit card
- a request for an exchange or a refund

Late Deliveries. Notify the company. By law the company must ship your prepaid order within thirty days or notify you of the reason for the delay. At this time it must give you a chance to cancel on an easy *no-cost-to-you* form. (Cancellation *must* be in writing.) Upon cancellation the company must send your full refund within seven working days. If your order was charged, you must get credit on your next bill (exceptions: C.O.D., magazine subscriptions, photo finishing, and growing plants).

Damaged Items. If the package is damaged, refuse it. Write REFUSED on the unopened package. It will be returned to the seller without additional postage UNLESS you signed for it as a COD or insured or registered mail. If you opened it, send it back by certified or insured mail, enclosing a note explaining the problem.

Late Refunds. Notify the company. If you get no action, notify the Consumer Inquiries section of the Federal Trade Commission (address follows).

Unordered Merchandise. Consider it a gift. You have no obligation to return it or pay for it.

Stopping Credit Card Payments in Disputes. If your credit card is not issued by the seller, you can stop payment. Notify the company that issued the card. The company will inform you of the law regarding stopping payment. If the problem has not been settled within two billing cycles, contact the card company again.

Most firms want your repeat orders and are eager to settle disputes. However, if you don't get results within a reasonable time, contact the appropriate agency. Include details, a copy of your canceled check, charge, or credit card statement, and all correspondence concerning the transaction.

Mail fraud or misrepresentation
Local Postmaster or Chief Postal Inspector
U.S. Postal Service
Room 3517
Washington, DC 20260–2100

Undelivered merchandise and mail order delay
Consumer Inquiries
Federal Trade Commission
Washington, DC 20580

MARRIAGE AND RETIREMENT

After forty years of a happy marriage you're suddenly at each other's throats. He's underfoot—all day long. You know how that woman felt who characterized retirement as "half as much money and twice as much husband." After you've run your own kitchen all of these years, he's in there telling you the gas is too high or you have too much soap in the dishwasher. Why doesn't he go fix the faucet in the service porch or just take a walk around the block?

She's still at work all day long while you're stuck with the housework. Hardly your idea of what retirement should be, and where's the left-over turkey you are supposed to have for lunch? Be nice to surprise her by making dinner but cooking has never been one of your talents.

Retirement of one spouse or both brings a change in lifestyle for both partners. She finds fixing lunch for two a bore. He launches into neglected household repairs and finds them a bore. Although his coming home fifteen minutes later from work never bothered her before, she worries now if he goes out by himself. She was happy doing the gardening before, but she resents it now when he doesn't help, and even more when he "weeds out" the petunias. He checks on the food prices at the market, but goes bonkers with a new car. She wants to move; he prefers the old neighborhood.

Planning in advance of retirement can smooth the way. Some employers engage preretirement planners to help the retiring employee. Unions give step-by-step advice about benefits, taxes, and sources of help. These sessions are largely financial.

Sometimes the emotional adjustment is discussed, introducing strategies for recasting an existing life pattern. What does each spouse want from retirement? What does each hope to achieve that is creative or rewarding in terms of increased skills, assistance to others, pursuing unrealized ambitions? Painting the house, repairing the roof, redecorating the guest room is not enough. Retirement gives time to set up long-range goals, to reach for a dream.

Take time to plan. What can you do together that has been impossible until now? What will you continue to do apart? How will you maintain business friendships? Make new friends?

Income gets star-billing in setting the stage for this new phase in the marriage. What can you afford? Not afford? How can you insure your security?

Planning together involves couples in a procedure they followed in the early days of their marriage, working jointly to establish a satisfying alliance.

Because of the strain retirement places on many marriages, workshops and classes have been introduced by some psychologists. Couples learn to meet the challenge of their new life rather than let crises develop. If you simply can't face this shift in your life, see if you can locate such a class. Try a mental health center or call your county psychological association, or be a do-it-yourselfer at your library, where you'll find a shelf or more of books on retirement. Some are deadly, some neolithic. But some are sprightly and loaded with how-to-make-the-most-of-it pointers, so keep digging. Choose what will work for you.

MEALS ON WHEELS

Because people usually eat better when they are with others, federal funds for senior nutrition programs are used primarily for group meals. However, many communities have programs to deliver lunch or dinner to the homes of older people who have difficulty preparing their own. This Meals-on-Wheels service is usually sponsored by a public or a nonprofit organization. Volunteers deliver the meals. Since each volunteer has only a few stops, the meal can be delivered hot at the luncheon or dinner hour.

Meals on Wheels developed after a survey of the National Council on Aging revealed that many older persons are unable to get out to do adequate marketing or do not feel up to preparing a proper meal. The law requires that the meal delivered must provide one-third of the daily food requirements. Menus must be approved by the state nutritionist.

The site of food preparation and the quality of the food vary from place to place, depending upon the funds and volunteers available and the expertise of the current cook.

The program is open to any older people who are physically disabled and confined to their homes, temporarily or permanently. In some places those on special diets can request them. Charges, always low, are based on ability to pay. Needy older people pay nothing.

Local directories for senior citizens often list the organizations that home-deliver meals.

Your senior center, information and referral service, or Area Agency on Aging can tell you if a Meals-on-Wheels program is operating in your community and where to call if you or someone you know needs this assistance.

Complaints

In this imperfect world nothing is 100 percent on target all of the time. If you are a recipient of Meals-on-Wheels and have a complaint, talk to the nutrition director first. If you are not satisfied, contact the senior center administrator. As a last resort, take your problem to higher levels—the Area Agency on Aging or the state inspector of the program. Your state elected representative will help you find the proper person.

MEDICAID

Medicaid, cofinanced by the federal, state, and some local governments, pays hospital and medical costs for certain groups of needy and low-income people. The program varies from state to state. In all states, however, coverage is extended to needy and low-income individuals who are over sixty-five or blind or disabled, to some children, and to families with dependent children.

In all states those entitled to Supplementary Security Income (SSI) are covered. Some states cover low-income people as well. Many states pay for such additional services as dental care, eyeglasses, and preventive and rehabilitative care.

Some people are eligible for both Medicare and Medicaid,

Medicaid covering the deductible on hospital and doctor bills and other charges Medicare doesn't pay.

Medicaid details can be obtained at the local welfare office. (See also SUPPLEMENTAL SECURITY INCOME [SSI])

MEDICAL ID CARDS

Are you highly allergic to certain medications? Or to bee stings? Do you wear contact lenses? Are you a diabetic, an epileptic, or a heart patient? Do you have any problem that necessitates regular medication? What if you were in an accident or became unconscious and medical attendants had no way of knowing this essential information? Might you die or be seriously injured because they were unaware?

If there is *anything* that others should know about you in the event that you are temporarily incapacitated, you should have easily recognizable information about your condition on your person. In an emergency room you may be too sick or confused to remember your allergies or chronic medical problems.

For a reasonable fee, you can get an emergency medical card or a metal tag from a number of different organizations, all of which will send brochures on request. Among the best known are:

Medic Alert Foundation
P.O. Box 1009
Turlock, CA 95381
Tel. 800–344–3266 except in California, Alaska, or Hawaii, where it's 209–668–3333.

Medic Alert supplies a bracelet or necklace with tag in stainless steel, sterling, or gold. Prices differ, of course.

Medical Identification Data Corporation
1119 Springfield Road
Union, NJ 07083

This group supplies a crimson plastic credit-sized ID card, durably embossed on both sides with all essential information, and Awareness stickers ("I carry medical ID") to affix to your windshield, office phone, driver's license, or wherever appropriate.

Heart Chart, Inc.
P.O. Box 221
New Rochelle, NY 10804

Specifically for heart patients, these cards hold your latest EKG as well as other medical information.

American Medical Association
Emergency Medical ID Card
536 North Dearborn Street
Chicago, IL 60610

The AMA will send a single card free, to be filled out by you.

American Diabetes Association
One West 48th Street
New York,NY 10020

This free card gives instructions for a diabetic condition only.

MEDICAL RECORDS

A record of your medical history will save time and trouble if you have to consult a new physician. It may also prevent your having to repeat previous tests and procedures at needless expense. If your doctor or insurance agent doesn't have a booklet for recording the details of your medical history, use the following form, one for yourself and one for each member of your household.

Medical History Form

*MEDICAL HISTORY OF*________________ *Date of Birth*________ *Blood Type*___

SPECIAL DRUG REQUIREMENTS

Condition	*Drug*	*Dosage*	*Frequency*

ALLERGIES

Food	*Drug*

IMMUNIZATIONS

	Dates of Shots
Flu	

Tetanus ______________________________

CONTAGIOUS DISEASES: Circle the ones you have had and give the approximate date in the space following the disease.

chicken pox	____	*mumps*	____	*typhoid fever*	____
diphtheria	____	*pneumonia*	____	*typhus*	____
German measles	____	*polio*	____	*Others:*	____
hepatitis	____	*rheumatic fever*	____	________	
malaria	____	*scarlet fever*	____	________	
measles	____	*tuberculosis*	____	________	

HOSPITALIZATION RECORD

Date	*Hospital*	*Reason*	*Doctor*

CHECKUPS, MEDICAL

Date	*Doctor or clinic*	*Tests or examinations*	*Results*

CHECKUPS, DENTAL

Date	*Dentist or clinic*	*Treatment*	*X-rays*

CHECKUPS, EYES

Date	*Doctor or clinic*	*Examination*	*Diagnosis*	*Treatment*

GLASSES

Date *Prescribing ophthalmologist* *Copy of prescription* ____ *(attach here)*

____

____

PRESCRIPTIONS

Date	*Prescription number*	*Pharmacy*	*Physician*	*Drug instructions*

MEDICAL INSURANCE POLICIES

Coverage	*Company*	*Policy No.*	*Premium*	*Date due*	*Agent*

I have________do not________have a Living Will Declaration.
If it is not appended here it can be found____________________

Two excellent booklets to help you keep tabs on your medication and prepare for appointments with your doctor are free from:

National Clearinghouse for Drug Abuse Information
Room 10A-53
Fishers Lane
Rockville, MD 20857

(Don't let the name discourage you. It's part of the Food and Drug Administration.) Ask for: *Use Your Medicines Wisely: A Guide for the Elderly* and *Passport to Good Health.* This is a pocket-sized eight-page booklet you can carry with you; it has space for emergency medical information and your medication record.

MEDICARE

The first line of defense against hospital and medical bills for the elderly is Medicare. Although the coverage is inadequate, requiring patients to pay increasingly high initial fees and deductibles at both the hospital and doctor's office, the system has greatly broadened the scope of medical care for those over sixty-five. Questions commonly asked about Medicare follow.

What does Medicare cover? It has hospitalization insurance (Part A) and medical coverage (Part B).

How do I get Medicare? Anyone over sixty-five who receives social security or railroad retirement checks is automatically covered by Part A. If you want Part B, however, you must enroll. For Part B the monthly premium is taken out of your social security or railroad retirement check.

If you don't get a pension from either of these sources you

can still get Part B by paying the monthly premiums. If you want the coverage to start when you are sixty-five, apply at the social security office three months before your birthday.

How do I get my Medicare card? When you are covered you will be sent your card showing the kind of coverage you have and the date it starts and your claim number. This is the number, plus any letter that follows it, that you must use on all claims and correspondence. Carry your card with you and present it when you receive services Medicare can help pay for.

You will also receive a copy of *Your Medicare Handbook,* explaining the coverage in detail. If you don't get one or lose it, you can get a copy at any social security office. (This is also where you apply for a duplicate card if you should lose yours.)

How much does Medicare pay? For most services Medicare pays 80 percent, *but* this is of the *approved* charges. Approved charges may be lower than the bills you receive. (See MEDI-GAP INSURANCE.)

How do I collect? If your doctor, the hospital, or supplier of services (therapist, part-time nurse, etc.) is willing to accept the approved payment, he or she submits the claim. If not, you must submit it on the form called *Request for Medicare Payment.* Most doctors' offices and all social security offices and Medicare carriers have it. Instructions on how to fill it out are on the form.

What if I can't figure out how to fill out the form? AARP and other organizations have trained older persons who will assist others in their communities with Medicare claims and appeals. Your Area Agency on Aging or senior center will tell you how you can get their help.

How can I find a doctor who will settle for Medicare's payment? You can get a directory of doctors who have filed more than 100 Medicare claims and have accepted the Medicare payment at least 10 percent of the time (not a very high percentage) at all social security offices and Part B insurance carriers. Look for the address of the carrier on the Part B Medicare payment claim form. Some senior centers have lists. If the center doesn't have a directory, ask the director to get one for you.

What do I do if I feel my claim is not handled fairly? Get the leaflet "Your Right to Question Your Medical Insurance Payment" at the social security office. Follow the step-by-step directions for appealing. Don't be reluctant to appeal. You can win and have less to pay if your case has merit *and* you will be doing others a favor, showing someone is willing to fight if the system short-changes him.

Medicare is under fire from many directions. Before you join the doomsayers, question their motives, the source of their information, and the astronomical rise in hospital and medical care charges. Other countries have had successful systems for many more years than the U.S. and make them work without overburdening their older citizens.

Word of caution: Except for special Canadian border cases, Medicare doesn't cover illness or injury outside the United States.

(See also: MEDICAID; MEDI-GAP INSURANCE.)

MEDI-GAP INSURANCE

Medicare works best when you don't need it. You wheel along secure in that comfortable feeling that should you have any medical expenses, they will all be taken care of.

Then the bubble bursts. You are rushed to the hospital and the instant you are admitted you discover that the first big chunk of the bill is yours to pay. Or stomach pains send you scurrying to the doctor. Now you find that Medicare medical coverage has a deductible. Also, this bill is *all* yours since the fee doesn't exceed that deductible.

Medicare coverage has gaps big enough to drive a twenty-mule team through, handily. And the gaps are not limited to those initial fees. In fact, Medicare covers only about 45 percent of the cost of your medical care. Unless you are willing to court financial disaster, you need additional insurance.

Now comes the insurance maze to penetrate; what kind of supplementary insurance should you buy?

Types of Private Health Insurance

The following types of insurance have the broadest coverage.

Medicare Supplement pays some or all of Medicare's deductible and copayments. Some policies *may* pay for some services not covered by Medicare. Most Medicare supplements pay nothing for services that Medicare finds unnecessary.

Catastrophic or Major Medical Expense policies help cover the cost of serious illness or injury, including some health services not covered by Medicare. They usually have a large deductible and may not cover Medicare's deductibles and copayments.

Health Maintenance Organizations give both health care and service. You pay a membership fee and go to the HMO doctors. HMOs have their own hospitals or are affiliated with one. Services are prepaid or have a small fee. Medicare deductibles and copayments are covered.

The following coverages are limited and are not substitutes for Medicare supplement, catastrophic, major medical expense policies or HMOs.

Nursing Home Coverage policies pay a specified daily amount for care in a skilled nursing facility. They seldom, if ever, include intermediate care, rest care, or custodial care. (Most people in nursing homes are receiving custodial care, the most needed coverage.)

Hospital Confinement Indemnity Coverage pays a fixed amount for each day you are in the hospital up to a certain number of days. Some policies cover some surgical benefits or confinements in a skilled nursing home. Premiums usually remain the same, but payments do also.

Specified Disease Coverage policies cover you for a single disease, such as cancer. Benefits are usually limited to a fixed amount for each type of treatment. The value of the coverage depends on your chances of getting the disease. The benefits do not fill the Medicare gaps.

If you are still employed or belong to an association that offers it, you may get group insurance.

Employer Group Insurance covers those who are employed. Some employer group insurance can be continued after retirement or converted to a satisfactory Medicare supplement policy when you reach sixty-five. This insurance has the advantage of having no waiting period or preexisting condition exclusions.

Association Group Insurance is offered by organizations to their members over sixty-five. The worth of the coverage depends on the benefits. The rates may be low but so may the coverage.

Buying Supplemental Health Insurance

Before you buy:

1. Review your Medicare benefits and those of any other insurance you have
2. Get a clear picture of the coverage you need.
3. Study the types of private health insurance to see which kind will give that coverage.
4. Compare the coverage and costs. (Use the charts on pages 148 and 149 to compare coverage.)
5. Get the answers to the following questions:

Will the policy cover health problems you already have? Don't be misled by the blurb "no medical examination is necessary." Sure, not to sign up, but does the fine print exclude "existing conditions"?

Medicare: Hospital Insurance and Medical Insurance—Covered Services

MEDICARE (PART A): HOSPITAL INSURANCE — COVERED SERVICES PER BENEFIT PERIOD (1)--1984			
Service	Benefit	Medicare Pays	You Pay**
HOSPITALIZATION Semiprivate room and board, general nursing and miscellaneous hospital services and supplies.	First 60 days	All but $356	$356
	61st to 90th day	All but $89 a day	$89 a day
	91st to 150th day*	All but $178 a day	$178 a day
	Beyond 150 days	Nothing	All costs
POSTHOSPITAL SKILLED NURSING FACILITY CARE... In a facility approved by Medicare. You must have been in a hospital for at least 3 days and enter the facility within 30 days after hospital discharge. (2)	First 20 days	100% of approved amount	Nothing
	Additional 80 days	All but $44.50	$44.50
	Beyond 100 days	Nothing	All costs
HOME HEALTH CARE	Unlimited as medically necessary	Full cost	Nothing
HOSPICE CARE	Two 90-day periods and one 30-day period	All but limited costs for outpatient drugs and inpatient respite care.	Limited cost sharing for outpatient drugs and inpatient respite care.
BLOOD	Blood	All but first 3 pints	For first 3 pints

*60 Reserve Days may be used only once, days used are not renewable.
**These figures are for 1984 and are subject to change each year.
(1) A Benefit Period begins on the first day you receive service as an inpatient in a hospital and ends after you have been out of the hospital or skilled nursing facility for 60 days in a row.
(2) Medicare and private insurance will not pay for most nursing home care. You pay for custodial care and most care in a nursing home.

MEDICARE (PART B): MEDICAL INSURANCE — COVERED SERVICES PER CALENDAR YEAR			
Service	Benefit	Medicare Pays	You Pay
MEDICAL EXPENSE Physician's services, inpatient and outpatient medical services and supplies, physical and speech therapy, ambulance, etc.	Medicare pays for medical services in or out of the hospital. Some insurance policies pay less (or nothing) for hospital outpatient medical services in a doctor's office.	80% of approved amount (after $75 deductible)	$75 deductible* plus 20% of balance of approved amount (plus any charge above approved amount)**
HOME HEALTH CARE	Unlimited as medically necessary	Full cost	Nothing
OUTPATIENT HOSPITAL TREATMENT	Unlimited as medically necessary	80% of approved amount (after $75 deductible)	Subject to deductible plus 20% of balance of approved amount
BLOOD	Blood	80% of approved amount (after first 3 pints)	For first 3 pints plus 20% of balance of approved amount

*Once you have had $75 of expense for covered services in 1984, the Part B deductible does not apply to any further covered services you receive the rest of the year.
**YOU PAY FOR charges higher than the amount approved by Medicare unless the doctor or supplier agrees to accept Medicare's approved amount as the total charge for services rendered. (See page 13.)

What are the maximum benefits in *dollars* and *days?*

Do you have the right to renew? Beware of policies that let the company refuse to renew. Some policies guarantee renewal for life or are renewed automatically. That's even better.

Have you been given an easily understood summary of the policy? (If you buy, keep it.)

Will you be given a trial period to look over the policy with the option of returning it for a refund?

Does the company have a good rating? Consult Best's Insurance Reports at your library or call an agent (not the one you are doing business with).

Is the agent licensed? A business card is not a license.

Private Insurance Checklist for Expenses Not Covered by Medicare
Note: This Medicare information is for 1984. It will change from year to year. For a more detailed and current explanation of Medicare and its benefits, obtain a free copy of *Your Medicare Handbook* from your local social security office.

PRIVATE INSURANCE CHECKLIST

WHAT YOUR CURRENT INSURANCE WILL PAY	WHAT PROPOSED INSURANCE WILL PAY
If you are considering buying insurance, use the chart on the left and this checklist to help you decide. If you are buying from an agent, ask him or her to help you complete this checklist.	

EXPENSES NOT COVERED BY MEDICARE
Medicare does not cover certain kinds of care. Most private insurance does not cover them either. Among them are:

- Private duty nursing.
- Skilled nursing home care costs (beyond what is covered by Medicare).
- Custodial nursing home care costs.
- Intermediate nursing home care costs.
- Physician charges (above Medicare's approved amount)
- Drugs (other than prescription drugs furnished during a hospital or skilled nursing facility stay).
- Care received outside the U.S.A., except under certain conditions in Canada and Mexico.
- Dental care or dentures, checkups, routine immunizations, cosmetic surgery, routine foot care, examinations for and the cost of eyeglasses or hearing aids.

FOR ADDITIONAL HELP...
If you need additional help or advice on Medicare benefits or eligibility, contact your nearest Social Security office or the Health Care Financing Administration.

For information on private insurance to supplement Medicare, check your State Insurance Department or State Consumer Protection Agency.

If you bought or are considering buying a health insurance policy, the company or its agent should answer your questions. If you do not get the service you feel you deserve, discuss the matter with your State Insurance Department.

And remember:

- Don't buy more policies than you need.
- Don't pay by cash. Pay by check or money order made out to the company, not the agent.

Insurance Counseling

Call your senior center, the Area Agency on Aging, or Information and Referral to find a class, a lecture, or individual counseling on buying Medi-gap insurance.

Senior citizen newspapers or newsletters periodically publish comparison charts of policy coverage. It will be worth the effort to track a current one down. The more you know, the more you can protect your interests. Using the chart on page 149 will help you make comparisons between policies you consider to supplement your Medicare coverage, shown on page 148.

MEMORY LOSS

The notion persists that memory deteriorates with age. Research reveals no firm answers as to just what happens to our ability to recall as we grow older. Seniors seem to perform less well on memory tests if they are under time pressure, but as well as younger people if they have enough time. A small percentage of people show severe memory loss at sixty-five, the percentage increasing with age, but only up to 20 percent at age seventy-five.

We can expect some memory loss for recent events as we get older. (We remember our youth well enough!) Our retrieval systems are not so quick and efficient as they used to be; but usually it's an annoyance rather than a serious problem. We may forget that we opened the refrigerator to get a Coke, but if someone's having an angina attack, we don't forget that we went to the medicine cabinet for nitroglycerine.

Studies indicate that people who use their minds regularly do better on memory tests than people who don't. One researcher believes that our dendrites (the branching ends of nerve cells) dwindle with age, but that using the mind helps stimulate the dendrites and slows down the loss. People in old-age homes that have no programs to keep the occupants involved frequently drift into senility. The lack of stimulation may well have accelerated the deterioration.

In *Learning, Memory, and Aging,* the National Institute on Aging suggests that part of the problem may be that we just get out of the habit of concentrating as much as we used to.

Well-organized executives and successful students, for example, don't trust to chance or memory. They simplify and systematize their surroundings. They have a place for everything and everything in its place. They concentrate on one problem at a time, make notes of appointments, make lists, and assign certain tasks to certain hours.

Some things are more important than others. (Some things are better forgotten!) Write down what you need to remember in an appointment book or on a big calendar. Don't try to do more than you can handle—that's a sure ticket to confusion and forgetfulness. Don't let your slowed-down pace of remembering names or facts upset you. Give yourself time.

And stop worrying about losing your memory. Some of it may go, but most of it will remain.

Now, if we can just remember where we put the list of helpful books....

Recommended Reading

How to Develop a Super-Power Memory, by Harry Lorayne. New York: New American Library, 1974.

Instant Mind Power, by Harry Lorayne. No. Hollywood, CA: Newcastle, 1980.

A Memory Retention Course for the Aged, ($4.00 + postage) and *Facts and Myths About Aging* (free) by the National Council on Aging.

Address for the last two:

National Council on Aging, Inc.
600 Maryland Avenue SW
Washington, DC 20024

MENTAL HEALTH

Mental health problems have always existed within all segments of the population. They used to be handled mostly within the family or community, but in our urban, mobile society they often go undetected and without proper care. Mental problems of older people are often looked upon as symptoms of old age when in fact they are ordinary mental problems that can be treated just as successfully as with younger people.

Common symptoms of mental illness are continuing anxiety, depression, apathy, lack of interest in anything or anybody. Other symptoms are helplessness, lack of responsibility, excessive worry about health, moodiness or belligerence, and excessive or unwarranted suspicion (paranoia).

Fortunately, help is available. The important thing is to seek it; the problem won't go away by itself. Start with your family doctor, who will know what resources are available in the community. Community mental health centers funded by the federal government can give help or direct you to counselors or self-help groups such as Neurotics Anonymous, the American Schizophrenia Association, and Recovery, Inc. Your county Mental Health Association or local Family Service can also give referrals.

Depending on the capacity of your purse and the severity of your problem, you will be directed to a psychiatrist, a psychologist, a marriage and family counselor (MAFC), or a psychiatric social worker.

Remember that mental health problems are not anything to be ashamed of, any more than physical health problems. Do not hesitate to seek help.

For further information write to:

Family Service Association of America
44 East 23rd Street
New York, NY 10010

National Association for Mental Health, Inc.
1800 North Kent Street
Rosslyn, VA 22209

For their pamphlets "Mutual Health Groups" and "Consumers Guide to Mental Health Services," or for general information, write to:

National Institute of Mental Health
Public Inquiries
5600 Fishers Lane, Room 11A21
Rockville,MD 20852

MONEY TROUBLES

"Money makes the world go 'round," but how can you make your world spin if your income lags behind your necessary expenditures?

Comfortable retirement requires more than social security. Even social security and a private pension, if it is low or doesn't keep pace with rising prices, need to be supplemented with personal assets. If you've been able to save or make investments or set aside some tax-sheltered funds through an IRA (Indvidual Retirement Account) or the Keogh plan, you have added resources, but are they enough? If you haven't been able to save, and you don't have a private pension, where do you look for income?

Social Security. If you are not eligible now for social security, could you qualify with more work credit? Find a part-time job to add the necessary quarters for you to qualify for minimum social security and its Medicare benefits.

Pension. If you worked where you might have received a pension, have you checked to see what your status is? (See: PENSIONS.)

Employment. Can you get full- or part-time employment? Can you baby-sit, house-sit, do odd jobs, or not-so-odd jobs, selling, consulting? Keep in mind that unless you are over seventy, earning more than a specified amount reduces your social security, so buzz to the calculator to see at what point working may not pay. (See: EMPLOYMENT; SOCIAL SECURITY.)

Rentals. Can you share your home, or rent a room, a garage, storage space in your garage, basement, or yard? (See: HOUSING.)

Home Equity Conversion. Do you have equity in your home? That equity can be turned into income. (See: HOME EQUITY CONVERSION.)

Sales. Do you have valuables you can convert to cash—jewelry, art objects, antiques? (Get appraisals first.)

Can you sell your house, buy one for less, and invest the profit? You have a one-time capital gain exemption of $125,000, you know. Be careful about selling and renting, though. (See: *Housing*) For a one-shot boost to your resources, try a garage sale, getting rid of anything and everything that is no longer useful to you, except for items of suspected worth that should be appraised. (Appraisers are listed in your telephone classified section.)

Family Assistance. Can a member of your family lend a financial hand: pledge a monthly check, or agree to pay one monthly expense, such as the telephone bill? Are there several who could contribute?

Community Assistance. Are you eligible for old-age assistance or Supplementary Security Income? (See: SSI.) Does your religious affiliation, labor union, or community have assistance programs? (See: SENIOR CENTERS.)

Can you get rental assistance? Medicaid? To find sources of help, contact one or more of these agencies:

Department of Social Services
Area Agency on Aging
Housing Authority
Welfare Department

Stretching It

Ten Commandments

1. Comparison shop for everything—goods and services.
2. Check consumer publications, especially *Consumer Reports,* for quality and cost comparisons. Ask for it at your local library.
3. Before you engage doctors, lawyers, and other professionals, ask what their fees are and what specific services they will give you.
4. *Pay cash* or pay your charge account or credit card bills on time so you aren't stuck with the interest.
5. Think before you spend. For large purchases, overnight is a good idea. (Impulse shopping puts money in someone else's pocket and junk in your closet.)
6. Buy when the price is right. Learn the time of year to expect sales on what you want.
7. Know what you really need before you start out—list-shop. Take advantage of coupons, even double coupons, when grocery shopping.
8. Adjust your expenditures to your present income. You don't *have* to buy expensive gifts for your children, relatives, or friends. You don't *have* to wear the same quality of shoes and garments you could afford before, or drive a gas-guzzling car. You don't *have* to eat at the same restaurants or see all of the latest movies or shows.
9. Look for discounts—everywhere.
10. Repair if cheaper, replace only if necessary.

(See also: BARGAIN HUNTING; DISCOUNTS; INSURANCE.)

MYTHS

The problem with myths is that they often are widely accepted as truth. The following myths about aging and older people are as persistent as a bad case of hay fever in ragweed season.

Myth: Aging is a disease.
Fact: Age and other factors, some congenital or inherited, increase the chances for getting certain diseases; but aging, with the changes that accompany it, is not the disease.
Myth: Senility is an inevitable consequence of aging.

Fact: Research has established that senile dementia—serious confusion and forgetfulness—is a neurological disorder affecting only a small proportion of the elderly.

Myth: Intelligence declines as one gets older.

Fact: Research shows that the majority of people maintain their intellectual level or improve as they grow older. After age eighty, some show a decline, but others continue to improve.

Myth: Older women are wealthy.

Fact: Three times as many elderly women as men live in poverty. In 1973, 14 percent of the women over sixty-five had *no* income. Only 3 percent of all householders (men and women) over sixty-five had incomes over $50,000.

Myth: Older people prefer to be with older people.

Fact: In a Hunter College study based on a 1975 Harris survey, 75 percent of the older people preferred to be with people of all ages.

Myth: Old age begins at sixty, sixty-five, seventy...

Fact: No chronological cut-off determines when a person is old. To establish one arbitrarily categorizes individuals. When is a person old? What counts—his physical or mental ability or life expectancy? Age sixty-five was chosen by Bismarck in Prussia in the 1880s as the age when pensions began because it was actuarially sound—few people lived beyond that age so not many would be collecting.

Myth: Seniors take unfair advantage of Medicare.

Fact: That's pretty hard to do, since Medicare on the average pays only 45 percent of the medical expenses of senior citizens. The individual or his insurance must pay the other 55 percent. It's hardly a good idea to go for unneeded medical treatment.

Myth: Older people are forgetful.

Fact: Forgetfulness is normal at all ages. When an older person forgets he is likely to say "I must be getting old," forgetting that he also forgot when he was young.

Myth: Most old people are alone, neglected.

Fact: On the contrary, 80 percent of the older people in the United States live with someone else.

Myth: Older people are asexual.

Fact: Don't you believe it. Absence of partners makes many so, but it is not the choice of most.

Myth: Most old people are in rest homes.

Fact: Actually, only about 5 percent are.

Myth: Older workers are less capable than younger workers.

Fact: The older worker is a better investment for the employer than a younger one, having less absenteeism, fewer on-the-job accidents, and equal efficiency.

N

NATIONAL ASSOCIATION FOR THE VISUALLY HANDICAPPED (NAVH)

More than 11 million people in this country are only partially sighted. They can get around without aid and perform many tasks, but they usually can't read, drive, or recognize people unless very close. Some of these, having certifiably lost 70 percent of their vision, can be considered legally blind. But not all.

NAVH is the only national agency devoting its entire program to the visually impaired. This nonprofit membership organization offers large-print materials, optical aids, emotional support services, counseling, and workshops for the partially seeing, their families, and professionals.

For further information and membership, write to:

National Association
for the Visually Handicapped
3201 Balboa Street
San Francisco, CA 94121

NATIONAL HEALTH INFORMATION CLEARINGHOUSE (NHIC)

Many people have health questions but don't know where to go for the information they need. For example, a person may want to know about high blood pressure, physical fitness, or certain medications.

NHIC, a central source of information and referral for health questions, is a service of the Department of Health and Human Services. It identifies groups and organizations that provide health information to the public. Its staff will determine which of these can best give you an answer. A staff member contacts the resource, which responds directly to you. NHIC itself provides only general information and referrals; it can't give medical advice, diagnose, or recommend treatment. However, it maintains contact with health educators and resources across the country and so is kept abreast of the most recent changes in the health field.

The agency contacted by NHIC may or may not respond as

quickly as you'd like, so if speed is essential, you might want to get its number and call directly.

Since toll-free numbers are frequently busy for long stretches of time, you may need patience; but once you get through, you'll find the staff warm, friendly, and eager to help you. Their telephone numbers are

1–800–336–4797 (toll-free)
(703) 522–2590 (in Virginia)

If you wish to write your query:

NHIC
P.O. Box 1133
Washington, DC 20013–1133

NATIONAL MEMBERSHIP ORGANIZATIONS

See chart on page 158.

NEW DIMENSIONS

To friends who question, "What do you do with all that free time?" most retirees can only reply, "What free time? I'm busier than I've ever been." But just in case you want to break out of the old familiar patterns and explore a new dimension, try one of these:

Art. Do you have a secret feeling that you could do as well as Grandma Moses? Or even Matisse or Mondrian or Jackson Pollock? Sketching, painting, and sculpting classes attract retirees. Your senior center, adult school, or community college will have classes.

If you don't feel creative but want to learn more about art, past or present, enroll in an art history class and attend museum lectures. Join architectural tours; haunt galleries. Specialize after you've learned what you like best.

Crafts. Interested in sewing, woodworking, ceramics, jewelry making, enamelling? The possibilities are limitless. Look for classes; start reading the crafts books and magazines on the library shelves.

Music. Slots are open in church choirs, barbershop quartets,

National Membership Organizations

ORGANIZATION	*ADDRESS*	*PURPOSES*	*SERVICES*	*PUBLICATIONS*
AARP American Association of Retired Persons Membership: 14,000,000 Modest membership fee.	National headquarters: 1909 K St. NW Washington, DC 20049 Membership 215 Long Beach Blvd. Long Beach, CA 90801	Equitable treatment for those over 55 Gain benefits and secure rights for senior citizens.	Among others: pharmacy service, mail order and at centers: health care plan health education auto insurance hotel/motel, auto rental discounts Tax Aid program (see TAXES)	*Modern Maturity,* bimonthly magazine "AARP News Bulletin," Better Retirement Guides (many—excellent—free to members, write for list.) All publications free with membership.
Gray Panthers Open to all ages Dues on two levels, national and local, both moderate.	3635 Chestnut St. Philadelphia, PA 19104 For local chapter see telephone directory	To bring social change: greater human freedom, justice, dignity and peace. Help eliminate the poverty and powerlessness of old.	Organization is dedicated to social change rather than services to individuals. Instrumental in removing mandatory retirement laws.	"The Network," a newsletter published several times during year Bibliographies of recommended readings Assorted pamphlets Newsletter with membership.
NAMP National Association of Mature People Moderate dues	2212 NW 50th St. Box 26792 Oklahoma City, OK 73126	Promotes welfare of older people through influencing state and federal legislative bodies.	Among others: health, auto and life insurance financial guidance pharmacy service, mail order discount buying assistance	*Best Years* quarterly magazine "NAMP News" quarterly newsletter (free) Special-interest bulletins

NASC National Alliance of Senior Citizens Membership: 150 regional groups Moderate dues	Box 40031 Washington, DC 20016	To inform the public of the needs of senior citizens	Compiles statistics about seniors. Maintains a library for political research. Represents senior causes before state legislatures and Congress. Maintains a Golden Age Hall of Fame, honoring outstanding service to seniors.	*Senior Independent,* bimonthly magazine *Senior Services Manual,* an annual Publications free with membership
NCSC National Council of Senior Citizens Membership: 4,000,000 3800 Senior Citizen Clubs Moderate dues	1511 K St. NW Washington, DC 20005	Through public-relations activities promotes welfare of senior citizens. Fact-finding and analysis of issues.	Among others: supplemental Medicare insurance prescription drug service furnishes films on senior topics travel planning assistance workshops and educational programs	*Senior Citizen News,* monthly newspaper (free)
NSSA National Senior Sports Association Moderate dues	1900 M St. NW Washington, DC 20036	Encourages physical and emotional health through sports.	Bargains in resort areas for golfers, bowlers, fishing, tennis, etc., enthusiasts. Discounts on sports clothing and equipment.	*Senior Sports News,* monthly

National Membership Organizations (continued)

ORGANIZATION	*ADDRESS*	*PURPOSES*	*SERVICES*	*PUBICATIONS*
OWL Older Women's League Moderate dues	3800 Harrison St. Oakland, CA 94611 or 1325 G St. NW Washington, DC 20005	Dedicated to the welfare of older women.	An advocacy group, seeks to organize older women and their supporters to effect changes in public policy and to change the image of the older woman.	*Owl Observer*, newspaper Pamphlets and monographs on special problems of older women: pension, health care, divorce, etc.
Senior Sports International Association Moderate dues	5670 Wilshire Blvd. Suite 360 Los Angeles, CA 90036	To encourage all adults to exercise regularly To give recognition to adult athletes in every sport at every age level. To increase international understanding	Organized Senior Olympics first held in 1970. Organizes competition in sports for all age groups among seniors.	*Senior Sports*, quarterly magazine included with membership.
ISCA International Senior Citizens Association Membership: Life membership is expensive; yearly individual dues nominal. Organizations or groups may join. Dues vary with group. Age requirement: 50	11753 Wilshire Blvd. Los Angeles, CA 90025	To provide coordination on an international level to safeguard the interests of senior citizens around the world. To establish educational and cultural communication with older persons throughout the world.	ISCA is affiliated with senior organizations in other countries. Holds international meeting (Hong Kong, 1984).	"ISCA News," quarterly newsletter included in membership.

choral groups, and amateur musicals. Your basso profundo or lyric soprano may be very much needed.

Or try an instrument—one you played before, or a new one. Looking for an easy one? The recorder, the flute-like Irish penny whistle, the harmonica, the ocarina, and the portable synthesizer give ample reward for little effort and limited investment.

If you play an orchestral instrument, try the Music Minus One records; these give you a chance to play along with a piano accompaniment, a string quartet, or even a symphony orchestra. Ask about them at your local music store.

Or just deepen your enjoyment with a class in music appreciation or history.

Dancing. Ballroom, folk, and square dancing are all excellent exercise as well as fun. Join a class at the YMCA or YWCA, an adult school, a dance club, or a senior center. You don't have to be Fred Astaire or Queen of the Starlight Ballroom to enjoy the benefits of ballroom dancing, and folk dancing can extend your friendships throughout the world.

Birding or Birdwatching. Seeds, nuts, fruit parings, and suet outside your window will bring a variety of birds even if you live in the city. Learn their names. You might want to go farther afield and look for different birds in different habitats—city parks, marshland, wooded areas, and so on.

If you're hooked, you'll want a pair of binoculars and a good field guide. *Birds of North America,* by Robbins, Bruun, and Zim, is available in paperback. *National Geographic* also puts out an excellent guide to field identification.

For local field trips, related events, and information, get the name and number of your local birding group from:

The National Audubon Society
950 Third Avenue
New York, NY 10022

Gardening. Try an herb garden on the windowsill, a strawberry barrel on the balcony, or your own vegetables in the community garden if you don't have your own back yard. For valuable hints and companionship, join the local garden club. If you want to specialize, you can find an orchid society, a cactus club, a group of African violet aficionados. A nationwide project of the National Association for Gardening publishes a newsletter of practical, effective gardening tips. For a free copy and information about membership, write to:

Gardens for All
Department P
180 Flynn Avenue
Burlington, VT 05401

Golf. Borrow a six-iron and search for a class and a driving range. Golf can become a passion. The paraphernalia and green fees are expensive, but you can play till you're 101.

Gourmet Cooking. Become the neighborhood Julia Child or Galloping Gourmet. Dig into cookbooks and magazines from the library. Watch the newspapers for gourmet or ethnic cooking classes. Join with interested friends for potluck gourmet feasts, or try out restaurants with unusual menus.

People-Watching. This leisure activity requires no investment and very little energy. Just get yourself to a park, a shopping center, or anywhere and observe the passing parade. You'll find yourself speculating about relationships and destinations, or wondering where she got that Mad Hatter hat. If you want to specialize, visit the stock exchange, courtrooms—use your imagination!

Games. Resurrect the old ones: Monopoly, checkers, cribbage, backgammon, Scrabble. Join a chess or a duplicate bridge club. If you like word games, look for Boggle and Perquackey in the games section of a toy or department store. Try One Enchanted Evening or Dungeons and Dragons, or go electronic with TV games.

If solitaire is your secret vice or solace, get the U.S. Playing Card Company's *150 Ways to Play Solitaire.* Try Hit and Miss, Streets and Alleys, Idiot's Delight. (Are they trying to tell us something?) Write to:

U.S. Playing Card Company
P.O. Box 12126
Cincinnati, OH 45212

Winemaking. Make and bottle wine—under your own label, of course. A closet or a corner of the service porch is adequate for your winery. Check your library for an instruction book.

Prefer just being a connoisseur? Find a wine-tasting class: check your newspaper or ask your wine merchant. Join a wine tour, in this country or abroad.

New-dimension possibilities are endless. You might, for example, join a writers' group and write a book for senior citizens—a book on hobbies, perhaps.

NURSING HOMES

Not everyone winds up in a nursing home, but some of us will: approximately 8 percent of the seventy-five to eighty-four age group live in such facilities. That is roughly one out of twelve; so it's a good idea to explore the options you (or those responsible for you) will have if you can no longer look after yourself. Remember that the situation could come up suddenly rather than gradually, following a stroke, perhaps, or a broken hip.

Some of the options depend on your physical, financial, or family situation.

Can you stay in your own home? Get information about services that may give you this alternative from the Area Agency on Aging, Family Service, a senior center, or your physician or clergyman.

One common solution is to move in with one of the children. Many people are uncomfortable with that arrangement, but not everyone. It's best if there is a room just for you and someone willing to stay home with you (see GRANNY FLATS).

The National Advisory Council on Aging says:

> Inappropriate placement of older persons in institutions reflects medical custom and the unavailability of other services and facilities, rather than a careful decision on the part of the older person or his family. Where home care programs are limited, institutionalization is often the only option available.

In other words, people are beginning to look for alternatives because nursing homes are expensive and in general do not have a good reputation. The Council goes on:

> ...Though excellent care is provided in many institutions, the long-term care industry has been seriously criticized. Long-term care facilities are all too often isolated from the more extensive backup services of hospitals, from community-based programs, and from major professional schools.

Choosing a Nursing Home

If there is no other solution to the problem and one must go to a nursing home, it's important to have the whole family (children and grandchildren) discuss the move with the patient. The situation may be heavy with all kinds of emotions, most likely guilt on the part of the children and anger in the parent-patient.

All aspects should be brought out in the open, including sadness, worries, and financial problems and agreements. Sometimes outside help—a family physician, a clergyman, or a social service agency—can be brought in. If the patient is going directly from a hospital, its social workers can help. If the patient is convinced that a nursing home is the only solution, the move is easier for everyone.

Once the decision for a nursing home is made, the next important step is choosing one. If investigation is made before the need arises, the selection is not made under pressure.

Three General Types of Nursing Homes

1. *Skilled nursing facilities,* supervised by a medical director, for intensive care.
2. *Intermediate care facilities,* for the person who needs some help with dressing, walking, or eating, but not intensive medical care. The patient is under the care of his or her own physician. At least one registered nurse is on duty during the day.
3. *Nonskilled facilities,* institutions or private residences. The latter are not usually licensed or subject to government inspection. Institutions are subject to state licensing only, which is usually less rigorous than federal standards.

These types are listed in order of expense, but within each type there can be large differences in cost. The most expensive is not necessarily the best, but low-cost facilities can be pretty bad unless they are run by a nonprofit group such as a church, a lodge, or a charity, or are subsidized by the government.

The best solution, for those who belong to such groups or otherwise have access, is to find a nonprofit institution. Waiting lists are very long, however, so you should sign up well in advance.

Nursing home charges are paid by Medicare for persons with coverage, but only for a limited number of days. After that the family pays the charges. Persons under Medicaid (generally those on welfare) can have their nursing home charges paid, but the allowance is very small ($36 a day in 1983). A federally licensed home is required to take a certain number of Medicare and Medicaid patients, but state-licensed homes need not. In general, homes operated for profit that accept Medicaid patients and are not federally licensed have very low standards of care.

The checklist on the following pages is a useful tool for evaluating nursing homes for yourself or on behalf of a relative who may be considering one. Without such a list you can easily overlook some important features that may prove troublesome after the patient has moved in.

Cautions

After the patient has been placed in the nursing home, an occasional check should be made for such symptoms as:

- Overworked, fatigued nurses and aides who are putting in too many hours and are likely to be uncaring or irritable.
- Billing frauds such as unnecessary referrals to other doctors for consultations, false claims for services, or billing for services not rendered or of lower quality than reflected in the bill.
- Embezzling of patient's assets or theft of personal property (or careless security).
- Employing inadequate or unqualified staff in violation of licensing rules.

Nursing Home Checklist

PRELIMINARY QUESTIONS	*Yes*	*No*
1. Do both the home and the administrator have current state licenses on display?	______	______
2. Has the home had frequent violations of state law?*	______	______
3. Is the home certified to participate in government or private programs of financial assistance when needed?	______	______
4. Does the home have extra services that may be needed, such as therapies, special diets, etc.?	______	______
5. Do the residents like the facility? (Ask them when they are free to speak without being overheard.)	______	______
OTHER IMPORTANT QUALIFICATIONS		
1. Is the home convenient for the patient's relatives, friends, and personal physician?	______	______
2. Is it near a hospital?	______	______
3. In case of fire or other emergency:		
a. Are exit doors well marked and easily opened from inside?	______	______
b. Can patients' doors and windows be opened readily?	______	______
c. Are there sprinklers and are fire extinguishers accessible?	______	______
4. Have measures been taken to prevent accidents, such as:		
a. Halls and stairways well lighted?	______	______
b. Handrails in corridors?	______	______
c. Grip bars next to bathtubs, toilets, in showers?	______	______
d. Safety mats or strips in tubs or showers?	______	______
e. Nonskid floors?	______	______
f. Call buttons in rooms and baths?	______	______
g. Few or no stairs, or stairs outlined by a highly visible color?	______	______

*Many states require posting such violations. A call to the state nursing home ombudsman will give you the information.

Nursing Home Checklist (continued)

PRELIMINARY QUESTIONS	*Yes*	*No*
5. Are the rooms comfortable, attractive, safe, and clean?		
a. Is the size adequate for the number of beds?	______	______
b. Is there space for a comfortable chair, personal possessions, and storage?	______	______
c. Does the room have telephone, television, radio, reading light, bedside equipment (water, bedpan) or provision for storing such items?	______	______
d. With multiple beds, are there curtains to protect the patient's privacy?	______	______
e. Are beds, floors, and bathrooms clean and free of trash?	______	______
f. Are all areas free of objectionable odors?	______	______
6. Are the facilities (kitchens, utensils, dining room) clean?	______	______
7. Are there rooms and equipment for individual and group activities?	______	______
8. Are patients encouraged, but not forced, to participate in recreational activities?	______	______
9. Is there a qualified recreation director?	______	______
10. In case of a medical emergency:		
a. Is a doctor readily available? Ambulance, emergency equipment?	______	______
b. Is there a medical director employed at the home? Can he substitute for the patient's attending physician in emergencies? Do patients and relatives have his name and phone?	______	______
11. Is it the policy to notify relatives *before* any relocation of a patient to a hospital or to another room or part of the facility?	______	______
12. Is patient care skilled, adequate, and caring?		
a. Are nurses on duty day and night?	______	______
b. Are aides adequately trained, clean, intelligent?	______	______
c. Does restorative care encourage maximum independence in daily living, in use of devices for walking, hearing, etc.?	______	______
d. Is there retraining, if needed, in bowel and bladder control?	______	______
13. Are the patients' rights respected?		
a. Is a written Patient's Bill of Rights given to each patient or posted?	______	______
b. Are patients encouraged to have visitors, vote, make complaints without fear of retaliation?	______	______
c. Is there no discrimination because of race, creed, color, or national origin?	______	______

Nursing Home Checklist (continued)

PRELIMINARY QUESTIONS	*Yes*	*No*
d. Are patients not used for teaching or research without "informed consent"?	______	______
e. Are patients restrained only on a doctor's order?	______	______
f. Do the patients appear well cared for and not sedated?	______	______
14. Are financial arrangements well defined?		
a. Are written, itemized bills presented every month?	______	______
b. Are payment plans explained?	______	______
c. Are covered items clearly separated from those incurring extra charges?	______	______

A patient in a nursing home is entitled to certain rights.

Nursing Home Patients' Rights

- the right to privacy for visits and for confidential telephone calls
- the right to open his or her own mail
- the right to adequate notice before being transferred
- freedom from verbal, emotional, or physical abuse
- the right not to be inappropriately moved or transferred
- protection from monetary exploitation or outright fraud
- the right to see a printed statement of the Patient's Bill of Rights (see page 182)
- the right to retain and use personal clothing and possessions as space permits (unless medically contraindicated)
- protection from over-drugging
- the right to sanitary conditions in bedroom, bathroom, and kitchen
- the right, if married, to privacy during visits with spouse and the right to share room with spouse if both are in the same facility (unless medically contraindicated)

In some states these rights are guaranteed by law, but in any state they should be insisted on by patients and their relatives.

Be Alert!

What can you do to protect a parent, relative, or friend in a nursing home? Most important, recognize that an interested and involved family member is the best protection a patient has. When you see a problem—maybe the patient is not being treated properly or something has been overlooked—take it up with the nursing staff immediately and/or talk to the person in charge. If that doesn't help, see the administrator and the treating physician. If nothing happens still, contact the nearest Health Service office or call the state's Attorney General.

If you are regularly visiting somebody in a nursing home, become friendly with other patients and note how they are being treated; most of them don't have visitors to protect them.

Some states have an ombudsman for nursing home patients. This person is a government official who investigates citizens' complaints against the government or against violators of laws. If your state (or possibly county) has an ombudsman, he or she has the power to investigate complaints and report problems to the proper legal authorities.

Note: Some of the above material was taken from the publication *Sentinel,* issued by the Crime Prevention Center of the California Department of Justice. Our thanks for this valuable information.

Recommended Reading

Living in a Nursing Home, by Sara Greene Burger and Martha d'Erasmo. New York: Seabury Press, 1976.

Thinking About a Nursing Home? A publication of the American Health Care Association. Write:

American Health Care Association
1200 15th Street NW
Washington, DC 20005

How to Select a Nursing Home, government publication No. HE 22.208:n 93/980, is available from:

Superintendent of Documents
Government Printing Office
Washington, DC 20402

Also, a list of nonprofit nursing homes in your area can be obtained from:

American Association of Homes for the Aging
1050 17th Street NW
Washington, DC 20036

NUTRITION

The principles of good nutrition are about the same at any age; why, then, include nutrition in a book for seniors? For several reasons:

- As we age, we incur increased risk of certain diseases—notably cancer, heart disease, stroke, and diabetes—which can be influenced by diet.
- We need more of certain nutrients, like calcium and zinc, because we metabolize them less well than we used to.
- We have to walk the narrow line between controlling weight (not eating too much) and not eating enough of the right foods.
- Many older people, especially those living alone, have lost interest in food or can't afford a proper diet.
- Evidence increases that what we eat can influence the aging process.

Diseases Related to Nutrition

Some diseases occur more often in older populations, and some appear to be affected by diet, although the actual mechanism is not completely understood. Increasing evidence, however, connects diet with the probability of acquiring certain degenerative diseases.

Heart Disease. The American Heart Association, the U.S. Surgeon General, the National Institutes of Health, and many independent studies agree that diet can affect your chances of heart attack and stroke. Overweight people are more likely to have heart problems, and a definite link has been established between cholesterol levels in the blood and the risk of atherosclerosis' heart disease, and stroke.

High Blood Pressure. This condition can damage your kidneys and heart and increase your risk of heart attack and stroke. Losing excess weight and eliminating salt from the diet may prevent or control the problem.

Cancer. Increasing evidence links certain cancers, particularly those of the colon and the breast, with diets high in fat. A diet low in fiber is linked with colon cancer.

Diabetes. Being overweight increases the risk of diabetes. Moreover, diet can influence the onset and the course of the disease.

Osteoporosis. The loss of bone material and consequent increased fragility of the bones is largely a disease of aging. One out of every four women and one out of eight men over sixty-five have the problem. It can be prevented or alleviated by proper nutrition.

These are the major diseases of older people that have some connection with diet. On the plus side, ample evidence suggests that good nutrition can make you feel better and increase your life span.

Eating Right for Seniors

The vast body of literature telling you what and what not to eat includes some excellent publications and some not so excellent. The basic rule is that there is no magic and no free lunch; to eat right you have to think about it, go to some trouble, and probably change your habits.

Most of the advice about sensible nutrition is similar, although the emphasis may differ from one source to another. The U.S. Departments of Agriculture and of Health and Human Services give these rules for good nutrition:

- Eat a variety of foods.
- Maintain ideal weight.
- Avoid excess fats, saturated fats, and cholesterol.
- Eat foods with adequate starch and fiber.
- Avoid excess salt and sugar.
- If you drink, do so only in moderation.

Obviously, these rules leave lots of room for interpretation; what is a variety, and how much is too much? Interpretations depend on the bias of the interpreter and the amount of good scientific data available. Let's look at some components of nutrition and summarize the evidence.

Variety in the Diet. All authorities agree that you should not concentrate on one food or type of food, because your body needs a number of nutrients (about forty in all), and no class of food contains all of them.

Fats. There is general agreement that Americans get too large a portion (about 40 percent on average) of their total calories in fat. Excess consumption cuts into the variety of foods we eat and also leads to heart disease, probably some cancers, and overweight. Most nutritionists feel that we should get not more than 25 percent of our calories from fat, and some think the limit should be 10 percent.

From the point of view of cholesterol in the blood and arteries, saturated fats (in meat, butter, coconut and palm oil, cheese, whole milk) are harmful; polyunsaturated fats (safflower oil, corn oil, etc.) are beneficial. From the cancer point of view, both kinds are injurious. Additionally, much of the fat we consume comes from fried, broiled, and charcoal-broiled meats and poultry; these types of cooking tend to produce carcinogens (substances known to cause cancer). The best rule is to be very cautious about fats in the diet.

Carbohydrates. Not so long ago, people who wanted to lose weight were told to cut down on all carbohydrates—both the complex (potatoes; whole grain cereals, bread, and pasta; beans) and the simple (sugar, honey, syrups). Now it turns out that complex carbohydrates are not so high in calories and are beneficial because they contain needed nutrients and fiber. Fruit is also healthful for these reasons, but sugar and other natural sweeteners give you only calories. The message is to cut down on cookies, pastries, and doughnuts, and replace them with fruits. And eat your potatoes without sour cream and your bread without butter.

Fiber. Nutritionists now emphasize the importance of fiber; the typical American diet of processed foods doesn't provide the amounts that we were probably designed for when we lived in trees and caves.

For years some people have eaten bran,which is mostly fiber, to alleviate constipation. More recent research suggests that it's better to eat the fiber as it naturally occurs in whole grains, fruits, vegetables, and beans instead of having it separated in the form of bran.

Studies have indicated that a diet high in fiber can prevent or control diverticulosis and diverticulitis, cancer of the colon, hemorrhoids, hiatal hernia, appendicitis, and varicose veins, as well as constipation. Some types of fiber even help with diabetes and atherosclerosis.

Protein. Protein deficiency is still a problem in the poorer parts of the world, but not usually in this country, except for some older people living alone who can't chew meat or can't afford it and don't go to the trouble of finding a substitute. Low-fat dairy products and dried beans and peas are excellent alternatives. It's not by accident that Mexicans eat beans with rice and corn tortillas. (Some excellent cookbooks, with recipes and menus for balanced protein meals, are listed elsewhere in this book.)

The most common sources of protein are meat, fish, and dairy products, from which you also get some of the vitamins you need. Unfortunately, we tend to like fatty meat or to prepare lean protein sources with fat (fried fish or chicken, cream sauces, etc.).

Remember that most of us eat more protein that we need, that many protein foods are high in fat, that protein is high in calories, and that excess protein is stored as body fat and can increase calcium elimination.

Vitamins and Minerals. Older people commonly absorb inadequate amounts of vitamins A, B complex, folic acid, and C;

calcium, iron, and zinc. The solution is not, however, to take megadoses of pills. An excess of A or D can damage the liver severely, and too much C causes kidney or bladder stones or diarrhea in some persons.

Excess amounts of any one mineral pill may upset the balance and function of other minerals in the body. Large doses of some vitamins can contribute to such health problems as anemia and neurological diseases. And recent studies show that overdoses of B^6 may cause ataxia, a crippling (but reversible) loss of the ability to walk.

A registered dietitian or a physician can recommend calcium, iron, or other pills as needed, in the amounts needed. A single multivitamin pill containing minerals may benefit. Even better, cut down on junk foods and processed meals and consult charts or diet books that indicate the amounts of vitamins and minerals in various foods; a nonfaddist diet rich in food-contained vitamins and minerals engenders no problems and usually suffices.

Salt. Americans eat too much salt, most of which comes not from the salt shaker, but from processed foods—canned soups and vegetables, TV dinners, potato chips, snacks, and deli products. Even foods that don't taste salty, like baked goods and cheeses, may contain large amounts. Since salt can contribute to high blood pressure (although it's not the only culprit), avoid it where you can. The body needs salt, but even if you never ate any salted foods, you would get all you need from the foods that naturally contain salt.

Watch nonprescription drugs for sodium content, and avoid bicarbonate of soda. Low-sodium baking powders are available.

To Review

Most of us need to *cut down* on meats, fats, sweets, and salt, and *eat more* vegetables, whole grains, beans, and fruits. Whole fruits are better than fruit juices, the rind or skin containing fiber and nutrients. Processed foods, including TV dinners, are convenient, but usually contain excessive salt, sugar, or additives.

It's more trouble to eat right, but the results are more than worth the trouble.

Recommended Reading

Jane Brody's Nutrition Book: A Lifetime Guide to Good Eating for Better Health and Weight Control by the Personal Health Columnist of The New York Times. New York: Bantam, 1982.

The editor of the Harvard Medical School Health Letter calls this the best home reference on nutrition he has seen.

Salt: The Complete Brand-Name Guide to Sodium Content, by Michael Jacobson et al. New York: Workman, 1983.

Nutrition Action. This monthly publication of the nonprofit Center for Science in the Public Interest often contains long articles on the relation of specific dietary elements to health and disease.

Also available from the Center is a series of posters with easy-to-read information:

"The Anti-Cancer Eating Guide"
"Chemical Cuisine"
"Life Saver Fat and Calorie Guide"
"New American Eating Guide"
"Nutrition Scoreboard"
"Sodium Scoreboard"

For these, and for information on membership, write to:

Center for Science in the Public Interest
1501 16th Street NW
Washington, DC 20036

Good Eating: An Older Consumer's Guide to a Healthful Diet on a Low Budget.
Available from:

Blue Cross and Blue Shield Associations
Consumer Affairs
676 St. Clair
Chicago, IL 60601

Recommended Cookbooks

Craig Claiborne's Gourmet Diet, by Craig Claiborne with Pierre Franey. New York: New York Times Books, 1980.

Claiborne, king of gourmet cooks, threatened with early death from hypertension and obesity if he didn't give up rich foods, managed to work up recipes that both satisfied his fine palate and enabled him to lose weight. His principles and methods can serve as inspirational messages. He is more concerned about salt than fat, but amounts of fat, cholesterol, sodium, and calories per serving are indicated with each recipe. The ones for appetizers, sauces, relishes, and salad dressings alone make the book worth having.

Diet for a Small Planet, by Frances Moore Lappe; and *Great Meatless Meals,* by Lappe with Ellen B. Ewald. New York: Ballantine, 1975 & 1976, paperback.

Lappe believes that one can enjoy an adequate protein diet without meat; the whole world would be better off on a meatless diet, she says, and tells you how to mix whole grains and legumes so as to get all the essential nutrients. Fine not only for vegetarians but also for those whose diet allows only four ounces of meat daily.

Laurel's Kitchen, by Laurel Robertson et al. New York: Bantam, 1981, paperback.

This small but almost encyclopedic book contains many recipes useful to those on fat-free diets; it includes vitamin, mineral, and fat tables for more than 600 foods and recipes. Chiefly for those on organic-food diets, it does include recipes containing eggs, cheese, and oil.

The Pritikin Program for Diet and Exercise, by Nathan Pritikin with Patrick M. McGrady, Jr. New York: Bantam, 1980.

Dubbed the deSade of the diet movement, Pritikin calls for no salt, sugar, or additives, little meat, and almost no fat of any kind. A devotee once jokingly said that only Mr. and Mrs. P. could adhere honestly to that diet. Again, there are fine essays and recipes, and this book can give you something to strive for.

For further titles see *The Subject Guide to Books in Print* in the reference section of your library, under the topics "Cookery for Diabetics, Cookery for the Sick," etc.

For cooking in a small space and for only one or two, try:

Cooking in a Small Kitchen, by Arthur Schwartz. New York: Little Brown, 1979.

Cooking for Two, by Evelyn M. Fett. Hicksville, NY: Exposition Press, 1980.

Cooking for Two, by Sunset Editors. Menlo Park, CA: Lane Books, 1978.

Cooking for One, by Elinor Parker. New York: Thomas Y. Crowell, 1976.

Cooking for One Is Fun, by Henry L. Creel. New York: Times Books, 1976.

See also: ARTERIO- AND ATHEROSCLEROSIS; CHOLESTEROL; cookbooks listed under DIABETES AND HEART DISEASE (good for everyone); DIETING.

NUTRITION PROGRAM FOR THE ELDERLY

If you live alone, perhaps finding it hard to keep up an interest in food, you may be contributing to your own poor health because you aren't getting the proper nutrition. Recognizing this problem among older people, the federal government has set up a Nutrition Program for the Elderly. Hundreds of communities now serve one hot meal a day, at least five days a week, to people sixty years of age or older, at thousands of nutrition sites. The donation for the meal is sometimes set but is very low. If you can't pay the going rate, you may drop what you can afford in the box.

Meals are served in places that are equipped with kitchens and dining facilities—church halls, school lunchrooms, senior centers, and the like.

The meal is important but so is the company. The program offers the opportunity for lonely people to come together. Educational or social programs may precede and follow the meal. In many communities transportation to the dining facilities is provided.

Your Area Agency on Aging, senior center, Info Line, or city hall can tell you whether your community has a Nutrition Program for the Elderly and where group meals are served. Dining or having lunch with others is a sure way to make friends.

O

OLDER WOMEN'S LEAGUE (OWL)

The Older Women's League, which sometimes describes it members as "aging sages," is dedicted solely to the welfare of older women, recognizing that to be old and female doubles the likelihood of ending up alone, impoverished, and even institutionalized. President Trish Sommers, together with Laurie Shields, founded OWL in 1980 to foster consciousness-raising, to effect changes in public policy (national advocacy group), and to change the image of older women.

Sommers, now sixty-nine years old and battling cancer, continues fighting fiercely. Her motto is, "Don't agonize. Organize." It was she who coined the phrase "displaced homemaker" after her own divorce at fifty-seven, and she formed a cancer support group when she found that she needed it.

OWL tells us that the problems of aging are largely women's problems: that three times as many women live in poverty as men; that four million women over forty-five have no health insurance; that more than twelve million senior women have no access to pensions; that sixty percent of women over sixty-five living alone subsist solely on Social Security! The *OWL Observer,* their national newspaper, comes with membership. OWL also publishes informational pamphlets and monographs (not free) on special problems of older women, such as health care, pensions, divorce, and discrimination.

Membership fees are low. Help yourself and all older women by joining this group as well as Gray Panthers.

For further information:

Older Women's League
3800 Harrison St.
Oakland, CA 94611

or

1325 G Street NW
Washington, DC 20005

(See also: DISPLACED HOMEMAKERS; GRAY PANTHERS.)

OSTEOPOROSIS

Are you shorter than you used to be? Are you getting a dowager's hump? Have you fractured a bone lately in a slight accident that shouldn't have caused so much damage? Are you troubled with low back pain? Or with periodontal (gum) disease?

Any one of these symptoms may indicate that you now have osteoporosis, the gradual loss and weakening of bone that comes, with aging, especially to white postmenopausal women, but in time to men also. The postmenopausal type hits twenty-five percent of American women fifty to sixty-five years old; the senile type hits men and women seventy-five and older. It's not usually diagnosed until after a fracture and it's not reversible; but its progress can be halted.

Little is known about the causes of osteoporosis, but possible factors are reduced estrogen levels (in postmenopausal women), high animal protein and coffee consumption, cigarette smoking, lessened ability of the body to absorb calcium, an excess of phosphorus in the diet, and inactivity, especially during prolonged bed rest.

What are the preventive measures and the remedies? At this time medical treatment alone is not expected to replace lost bone, but it can stop the process of bone loss. Doctors often recommend calcium supplements in dosages of 500–1500 mgs. a day, together with daily exercise, especially walking, swimming, or cycling. A diet rich in calcium—milk (if your body tolerates it), yogurt, sardines, shellfish—is also helpful. Vitamin D and fluoride supplements should be considered only under strict medical supervision, because they can have very serious side effects; estrogen therapy, which is sometimes recommended, can cause certain cancers.

According to the *Journal of the American Medical Association*, taking calcium supplements without engaging in physical exercise is like settling for half a loaf:

> Calcium acts to suppress bone resorption, whereas mechanical stress seems to enhance bone formation. Consequently, combining the two measures appears to be the most practical approach....Calcium can, at best, do nothing more than arrest further bone loss....It cannot, by itself, increase bone mass. Only physical exercise can accomplish the latter. (*Journal of the American Medical Association*, Feb. 26, 1982. Vol. 247, No. 8)

Having done what you can to arrest the condition, learn to be very careful about safety, both in and outside the home, as even a minor fall may cause a bone fracture in an older person. And if you're lucky enough to have strong bones still, don't delay, start taking preventive measures tomorrow—or today.

OUT-REACH PROGRAMS

Some senior centers operate Out-Reach programs to inform housebound seniors of services that may help them. Trained volunteers visit the elderly and, after determining their particular needs, link them to the proper community agencies or organizations for legal aid, tax assistance, meals-on-wheels, transportation, financial help, or whatever is indicated.

If this service would help you or someone you know, call your senior center.

P

PAIN RELIEF

George H. suffers from an osteoarthritic hip, but surgery is contraindicated because of a heart condition. Gloria Z. has painful fibro-myalgia, incurable. Paul F. is plagued with blinding headaches.

For such sufferers with chronic pain, pills can help but sometimes are addictive or have other bad side effects. A recent development is the pain clinic, which helped all three of our examples. Pain clinics can be found in most teaching hospitals and some nonteaching ones. The best way to find one is to ask your doctor, since you can be admitted to a pain clinic only on a doctor's recommendation.

The pain clinic uses a whole range of techniques, selecting them on the basis of your condition and what works for you. Some of them are:

- Acupuncture or acupressure
- Biofeedback
- Chiropractic
- Counseling
- Cold or heat application
- Movement and exercise therapy
- Hypnosis and self-hypnosis
- Laughter therapy
- New medications
- Physical therapy
- Relaxation and meditation
- Visualization and guided imagery
- Yoga

Some hospitals are using a new device called the pain pump. It contains the pain medication and is connected to the patient intravenously. It is programmed by a physician, but the patient can press the button for medication when the pain begins instead of waiting for a busy nurse to come and get the request and then make another trip with the medication. It has been shown that patients actually use less medication when they have control of it, and that they are more willing to cooperate in their recovery.

Plans are being made to make the pain pump available at home for chronic pain sufferers and terminal cancer patients. (See also: COUNSELING; YOGA.)

PARAMEDICS

The high mortality rate in the early phase of heart attacks has spurred many programs of emergency paramedic care. These provide prompt life support for victims of life-threatening emergencies. Highly trained technicians staff twenty-four-hour emergency care/rescue vehicles, delivering prehospital care to victims. When appropriate, such care is given at the scene.

The heart attack or stroke victim is stabilized at once and then transported to a medical facility; the accident victim is given first aid and moved speedily to a hospital. The object is immediate therapy for illness or injury that might otherwise be fatal, thus compensating for the usual delays in reaching the hospital and a physician.

Paramedics, in many places part of the fire department but sometimes attached to a hospital or even a private ambulance service, are also known as emergency medical technicians or EMTs. They are trained intensively to meet federal standards. Arriving at the scene, they question the patient if possible, examine him, and immediately institute life-sustaining procedures like CPR. At all times in telephone contact with a physician who directs the course of treatment, they minister to the patient as he is being transported to the hospital.

Call paramedics at once for the following problems:

- severe chest pain
- difficulty in breathing
- paralysis or numbness in part of the body
- diabetic coma
- shock
- sudden impairment of vision or hearing
- sudden mental confusion or amnesia
- loss of consciousness
- fall with possible head or spinal injury
- severe burns
- poisoning
- strongly adverse reaction to medication

Do not call for nonemergencies, such as an illness that has been going on for some time and can wait, or for a simple nosebleed or fracture. The number of paramedics is limited, as is the number of properly outfitted vehicles. If they are called for less-than-life-threatening emergencies, they may not be available to save a life elsewhere.

In many parts of the country the emergency number 911 will reach the paramedics. It may be called without a coin. If 911 isn't in use in your area, find out what the number is, place it in front of this book, and paste it to your telephone.

With luck you'll never need it, but think how you'd hate yourself if you did need it and wasted precious moments finding it. (See also: CARDIOPULMONARY RESUSCITATION or CPR.)

PARENTS, CHILDREN OF AGING

Are you in your sixties or seventies and still postponing that long-planned trip to England or East Africa because of an infirm parent? Do you, unwillingly, still live with that parent, or is your family unhappy because the parent has come to live with you? Do you feel so torn between the needs and demands of your adult children and those of your aging parents that there seems to be nothing left for yourself?

Some of these problems may be insoluble, but many are not. Family Service or some other counseling organization may help you find someone to stay with an aged parent while you get some respite, maybe once or twice a week, maybe for a few weeks. But children of aging parents, particularly seniors, need the comfort and reinforcement of a support group. Such groups exist throughout the country, offering strength and understanding as well as exchange of ideas.

They may not be easy to locate, because names differ. If there is no group in your area, you may have to get together with other people in the same predicament and try to form a group. Already-established groups and the National Self-Help Clearinghouse are glad to advise. Write to:

National Self-Help Clearinghouse
33 West 42nd Street
New York, NY 10036

Children of Aging Parents
2761 Trenton Road
Levittown, PA 19506

Caring Children of Aging Parents
c/o Ethel Burdell
4835 East Anaheim Street #210
Long Beach, CA 90804

Check also in the *Encyclopedia of Associations* at the reference desk or in the reference section of your library.

PATIENTS' RIGHTS

Many states have adopted lists of patients' rights, which are posted in hospitals and in some doctors' offices. Call your librarian, your Area Agency on Aging, or a local hospital to see if your state has one.

Even if it doesn't, these rights are ethically yours. Don't let any doctor practice one-upmanship on you; politely but firmly insist on getting the information you want to know, having errors corrected, and participating intelligently in decisions.

Among the rights listed in California, for example, are these:

- The right of the patient to receive from his physician information about his illness, his course of treatment, and the prospects of his recovery, in terms he can understand.
- The right to participate actively in decisions regarding his medical care. To the extent allowed by law, this includes the right to refuse treatment.
- Knowledge of the name of the physician with primary responsibility for his care, and the names and specialties of other physicians who will see him.
- The right to receive information about any proposed treatment or procedure recommended, in order that he may give intelligent consent or refuse treatment.
- Full privacy about his illness and his treatment and confidential treatment of all records, except by his written consent.
- The right to leave the hospital even against the advice of his physician.
- The right to be told if a physician or hospital plans to use experimental medication, treatment, or care; and the right to refuse to participate in any research projects.
- The right to receive and examine a detailed bill and to question any part of it, regardless of the source of payment.
- These rights also apply to a person who has legal responsibility to make medical care decisions for a patient.

PEACE CORPS

Are you still healthy and eager to be of use to the world? Do you enjoy new adventure and travel, (especially if free)? Try the Peace Corps. If you have any skills in agriculture, mathematics, science, teacher training, manpower training, vocational trades, business and public administration, health, nutrition, home economics, or natural resource development and conservation, the Peace Corps has a place for you. If you have skills that don't quite fit the bill, try to build a bridge in your application between what you can do and what they need.

The Peace Corps actively recruits people, including older people, to serve approximately twenty-seven months as overseas volunteers helping developing nations. Orientation and training last from four to ten weeks and are usually held in the country where you will serve. You will learn a bit of the language of the host country, its history, culture, social and political systems, and you'll get any needed technical training.

Transportation is paid to training sites, to and from the overseas assignment, and for family emergencies, if any. A monthly allowance of $200 (in 1984) for food, travel, rent, and all medical needs, and a vacation are provided. Doesn't sound like much, but it's middle-income level in the country you'll be in. An additional allowance of $175 a month is set aside, payable when you complete your service. Your Peace Corps earnings in no way affect your social security benefits.

A $10,000 insurance policy at minimal cost is optional, but you are covered by the Federal Employees Compensation Act for disabilities incurred either in training or during service.

Ruth M. went to Africa when she was sixty-two and lived "sinfully" well, she said.

Jimmy Carter's mother went to India as a nurse when she was in her seventies. Currently more than 300 Peace Corps workers are over fifty years of age.

You may state a choice of area (S.E. Asia, N.W. Africa, etc.) but you must be flexible in order to be competitive. You'll be put where your skills are most needed. And even if you should sometimes be uncomfortable, you may have the most intriguing experience of your lifetime.

Write to:

Action/Peace Corps
806 Connecticut Ave. NW, Room P-307
Washington, DC 20525
toll free: 800–424–8580, ext. 93
or check your telephone directory for a local office, if you live in a big city.

PENSIONS

Although U.S. pension funds (public and private) exceed a staggering $550 BILLION, more than the combined 1980 Gross

National Product of Great Britain and France, less than half of the U.S. work force in the private sector is covered by a pension plan to supplement social security. Even those who are covered may find, upon retirement, that they have no pension or less than they expected.

Why? Some workers lose out because of breaks in service or insufficient work hours or years to qualify, or because of frequent changes of jobs; others because of shifts and changes in company pension plans.

Until 1974, workers had little or no recourse if their companies went bankrupt, merged with another, or terminated their part of the operation. The Employees Retirement Income Security Act (ERISA) brought standards into employee pension plans and safeguards to employees' pension rights.

Although ERISA eliminated the worst abuse in private pensions, the arena is still riddled with pitfalls. If you are not getting a pension you think you are entitled to, or are getting one but think it is smaller than it should be, investigate! Some pension plans are covered by the Pension Benefit Guaranty Corporation (PBGC), the federal agency that insures pension plans against termination; others are not. (Persons covered by a "defined contribution" plan, such as profit-sharing, are not insured.)

Checking on Discontinued Pension Plans or Unpaid Benefits or Contributions

By law, if your company had a pension plan, you were to be given a Summary Plan Description (SPD) by your retirement plan administrator. Find the SPD. Your SPD must state if your plan was insured by the PBGC. If an employer has terminated your plan, or failed to implement your pension, or has gone out of business, you may still have some protection. If your plan was insured, the PBGC became trustee of the pension plan and information or checks should be coming from there. Contact:

Pension Benefit Guaranty Corporation
2020 K Street NW, Suite 700
Washington, DC 20006
(If your employer is still in business, call there. Sometimes a call will jar funds loose.)

Getting Informed about Pension Rights

For the latest word about ERISA, send for the free booklet, "Often-Asked Questions about the Employment Retirement Security Act" from:

U.S. Department of Labor
Labor-Management Services Administration
Washington, DC 20210

Two groups working for enforcement of existing pension laws and for pension reform also have publications. Write:

Pension Rights Center
1346 Connecticut Avenue NW, Room 1019
Washington, DC 20036

Legislative Department
1909 K Street NW
Washington, DC 20049

(See also: SOCIAL SECURITY; VETERANS' BENEFITS.)

PETS

If you're an animal lover, it will come as no surprise to you that pets are now being prescribed as therapy for the lonely, the ailing, the depressed. It's called PFT, pet-facilitated-therapy. (We always called it getting a cat or a dog.)

PFT for those living alone has been recommended for years. "Dad's alone too much. Let's give him a dog; that'll at least get him out of the house." "Mom needs a dog for protection." Now doctors are also suggesting to some of their patients that they acquire a pet.

A pet well matched to an owner can be very good medicine. Pets get their owners moving. They have to be trained, fed, bathed, brushed, let out and in. Dogs need to be walked and act better if taken to obedience school. Birds have to have their cages cleaned, fish their water changed. And with all that going on, there is less time for owners to think or mourn.

Scientific studies indicate that the benefits of having pets is not limited to the activity that the owner must engage in to take care of them. Stroking an animal may decrease stress and blood pressure, as does observing the undulating motions of fish. And how can anyone's self-esteem be less than satisfactory with all of that adoration poured out by a loving dog? Being an owner involves responsibility and concern for another living creature, and provides someone to talk to. Don't think those animals don't understand. Convinced?

If you want a cat or dog, visit any animal shelter. Some shelters lower the "adoption price" for seniors, or give licenses for the life of the animal, or provide free neutering, or all three.

While you are there, ask about rabies shots—where are they free or low cost? Some communities have clinics once a year in a park or at a public building. If there is one, don't miss it. You'll have the time of your life, with all those dogs straining at the leash and getting acquainted.

Perhaps you already have a pet but because of a move are being told you will have to give it up. Before you resign yourself, investigate. In some cities and states, laws permit older persons to keep their pets, at least in public housing. Who says the government doesn't have a heart? Well, sometimes.

Everybody knows about seeing-eye dogs, but did you know that dogs are also trained to help people with hearing problems—to alert them to such sounds as the phone or the doorbell ringing or a spouse calling for attention? For further information write:

Canine Companions for Independence
P.O. Box 566
Santa Rosa, CA 95402

Hearing Dog Program
Am. Humane Associates
5351 S. Roslyn Street
Englewood, CO 80110

For dogs to perform services for the disabled write:

Handi-Dog
5332 Rosewood Avenue
Tucson, AZ 85711

POWER-OF-ATTORNEY

After Carl S. died, his nephew stood by helplessly as Carl's housekeeper, waving a power-of-attorney, packed up his uncle's possessions and took them away. Earlier, when he had asked about Carl's stock certificates, she had snapped, "He had me sell them."

What Carl's nephew didn't know was that, although the sale of the stock might have been legal, the looting of the house was not—a power-of-attorney becomes void the moment the person who granted it dies.

For those who require help with their affairs, a power-of-attorney in the right hands can be invaluable. However, there is no supervision over persons who have a power-of-attorney, and the person who has it has legal control of the property. Extreme caution must be exercised in granting one.

Carl's needs might have been served adequately by the

power-of-attorney granted by most banks, one that allows access to a bank account with the right to endorse and deposit checks and to write checks, but no more. If Carl really wanted the housekeeper to sell his stock, he could have granted a limited power-of-attorney for that specific act. A power-of-attorney can also be limited to a specific period of time.

A power-of-attorney usually names a spouse or a trusted relative or friend. If you have any doubts, or are being pressured to enter into such an agreement, consult an attorney whom you trust.

Tip: You can buy forms for general or limited power-of-attorney at most stationery stores.

PRENUPTIAL AGREEMENTS

The romance need not be less, but the legal considerations are more for late or second or third marriages. Of course, you're both going to need new wills, but that comes last, after the dust has settled on other decisions and agreements.

Way back in the good old days of your first marriage, situations were less complex. You promised to love, honor, and obey or cherish; you set up joint checking and savings accounts (if you had any money) and you proceeded to build an estate together. You promised to take care of each other in sickness and in health, but you had reason to believe that it would be in health for many years.

Now one or both of you may have a house, a car, a boat, art objects, furniture, crystal, silver, stocks, bonds, pensions, trust funds, annuities, insurance, debts, or even a business or two.

And one or both may have dependents—a parent, two parents, children, other relatives, an ex-spouse with claims upon income.

Before you walk down the aisle and sign the marriage contract, you need to see an attorney to learn all of the ramifications of your proposed change of status.

Does each of you retain title to your own property?

What income or properties become joint? Under what circumstances?

What happens to pensions, annuities, and property when one partner dies?

How can each of you leave your individual property to your own children, if that is what you wish to do?

How can arrangements be made to continue support of dependents?

What responsibility, if any, does one have for the other's debts if such exist?

You need to talk over these and other questions with your prospective spouse and then with an attorney.

Often the interests of both parties and their intended heirs are best served by signing a prenuptial agreement. This is a written contract signed *before marriage.* It usually indicates ownership of properties brought into the marriage and the way the property is to be treated if divorce or death dissolves the marriage.

If the attorney who draws up your prenuptial agreement has a good knowledge of the tax law, he may also point out ways to set up your estate or estates that will save your heirs a bundle.

You may cheerfully mix assets or keep them apart after marriage, but agreeing beforehand about what each individual brings fully into the partnership and what is to be shared or left to others will make for smoother sailing. The agreement *must be signed before marriage.* Even though you and your partner are in perfect accord, state laws may interfere with your desires in case of death. And in the event of a divorce, heaven forbid, you may really be in the soup!

PROBATE

The special court that establishes the validity of wills and administers estates is usually called a probate court. Taking a will through probate can be time-consuming, costly, and complex; but if no will exists, the cost and complexity can be even greater, and the estate will be divided according to state law rather than your wishes.

The most famous book on how to avoid these expenses is Norman F. Dacey's *How to Avoid Probate: Updated!* (Crown, 1980). It's done through gifts, living trusts, and other means, all spelled out. But remember: If you make an error, it can be risky and end up costing more rather than less.

In planning how best to avoid probate court and estate taxes, it's a good idea to consult the best estate attorney you can find. You don't have to have a lawyer if you're submitting a will for probate; you *can* do it yourself. Lawyers exact high fees for probate work, and the larger the estate, the higher the fee—even if the case involves no more work than for a much smaller estate. If the estate is large enough to be subject to state and federal taxes, some executors and heirs suggest that a tax accountant can be a lot more useful than a lawyer, and a great deal cheaper. (See also: WILLS; LIVING TRUSTS.)

PROSTATE PROBLEMS

Prostate problems are the older man's specialty. Benign enlargement affects, to some degree, 10 percent of males aged forty, 50 percent by age fifty, and almost all males by age sixty. Play it safe; *get a digital (done with the fingers) rectal examination once a year.* It's not comfortable, but it can help discriminate between benign prostate enlargement and prostate cancer, which has few or no symptoms before it spreads, and an almost 100 percent cure rate if treated before then.

The symptoms of prostate enlargement are: difficulty in starting to urinate, slowness and hesitancy of the stream, dribbling at the end, and increasingly greater frequency and urgency to urinate, especially at night. Sometimes the condition causes sexual problems, even impotence.

When should you surrender and undergo surgery? When you're fed up with the discomfort or a competent urologist advises it. The consensus is that there's nothing to it for most men, and almost no likelihood of impotence.

The thing to worry about is prostate cancer, the second-most common cause of death from cancer in men, and devastating once it has begun to spread. That's why you should have that digital rectal examination once a year. If the doctor has reason to suspect cancer, he will do a biopsy.

Many such cancers in older men are dormant. Then the surgeon may choose not to operate—just to watch it. If the cancer is not dormant, treatment may be surgery or radiation, both of which may result in impotence. Sometimes it's controlled for a long time by removal of the testicles and administration of a female hormone. Other prostate problems are:

- *Chronic prostatitis:* low-grade infections that aren't serious but cause considerable discomfort and are difficult to treat. Physician may use antibiotics or tranquilizers or both.
- *Acute prostatitis:* burning sensations and pain during urination, chills, and fever, which are signs of urinary infection. See a physician at once.

The prostate is a gland no larger than a walnut, but its disfunction can cause all these difficulties. If watched and cared for in good time, they are neither potency-threatening nor life-threatening.

Remember those regular checkups, even after a benign prostatectomy, which doesn't protect against cancer, since only part of the prostate is removed.

For further information, write to:

The American Cancer Society
777 Third Avenue
New York, NY 10017

(Ask for *Facts on Prostate Cancer.*)

and

The National Cancer Institute
Building 31, Room 10A18
Bethesda, MD 20205

(Ask for the prostate pamphlet in both the *What You Need to Know about Cancer* and the *Progress Against* series.)

Q

QUACKERY

Like bunco artists and purse snatchers, the quack preys particularly on the elderly. He offers a cure for a disability or a disease, frequently indicating that he has a secret formula, a special treatment, or a therapeutic device that has been successful in treating thousands. Often his line is that the American Medical Association (AMA) "medical trust" prevents the treatment from being made available to the public.

Quacks get their victims by advertising, by direct mailing to retired persons or to senior citizens, or by referrals—your name given by someone who has answered the advertisement.

One kind of quackery specializes in ointments, injections, or pills that claim to slow down the aging process, or even to rejuvenate. Remember the old "monkey gland" flap or Royal Jelly? Those injections didn't work, and there is no evidence that anything does.

Another form of quackery is the hearing-aid scheme. Salespeople who have neither the skill nor the training to test hearing try to sell hearing aids to retirees, whether they need them or not. Sometimes they gain entrance to the home by saying they are offering a free hearing device. Once inside, they proceed with "hearing tests" on some kind of machine. The results invariably indicate that the victim has a hearing loss and needs an aid. The free one is still free, but a better one is promoted—one with a sizable price tag.

Sufferers from such diseases as arthritis, cancer, and rheumatism are particularly susceptible to the hope held out by the quack.

Some quackery is harmless—such as copper bracelets or "uranium" mittens for arthritics—but some are hazardous. Untested and unapproved drugs may be dangerous, if not lethal. The Federal Drug Administration has seized many because of the false claims made for them and the risks to the user.

Over-the-counter-drugs get into the act too, advertising "arthritis pain formula" or "arthritis strength" aspirin. This usually means more caffeine or antacid has been added—and a higher price.

Be skeptical of any claims that offer a cure for diseases that are widespread, painful, or greatly feared. If such a cure were available, the newspapers would have banner headlines; nothing could keep the good news from spreading. Some claims should be discussed with a physician or the foundation that is searching for just such a panacea—the National Arthritis Foundation, the National Cancer Society, The Rheumatism Foundation, for example. Ask Information (411) if you can't find them listed in the telephone directory.

And don't bypass a proper diagnosis by a physician because you're relying on an off-beat "cure." Delaying can keep you from getting the proper medical treatment in time to prolong or save your life. If you're not satisfied with the diagnosis of one physician, consult another, or two others. And if the treatment is likewise disappointing, there is no reason why you cannot continue changing physicians—but *don't* fall into the hands of the quacks.

R

RECORD KEEPING

Have you looked at your household files lately? With satisfaction or dismay? For most of us it's the latter, regularly. And if we can't decipher our own files, how could someone else find what's needed in time of emergency?

Retirement or approaching retirement inspires the clean-up, clear-out, get-organized syndrome. A worthy ambition but one that, for best results, should be approached with a plan and caution.

The plan involves setting up categories into which to divide all of that accumulated stuff, and the caution is to make sure you don't discard anything that will be needed later.

Usually six categories will suffice. (If you want to get fancy you can subdivide them later.) Experts recommend the following divisions: family records and documents, financial, health, insurance, property, and taxes.

What to store in each? Your own circumstances will dictate, but general guidelines are in the where-to-put-it, how-long-to-keep it, and where-to-find-it-now list that follows.

And what to keep and what to throw away? Before you discard any of your papers, however limp or dog-eared, consider carefully:

- Is this a record that I or any of my heirs will need to prove a legal right or ownership, verify a financial transaction, recoup a loss in case of fire or theft, or establish a tax deduction? (For example: Don't discard any records that show improvements or major repairs to your house. Should you sell, they are important to show the prospective buyer the condition of the property *and* to establish tax reductions.)
- If I throw this away, will I be able to get the information easily and with little or no cost? Can I throw all but the last bill or statement of this transaction away and still have an adequate record?
- Can I turn over these records—birth certificates, school records, family history—to someone else who will need them or care more about them than I do? Play this one for all it's worth.

Your home file may be a desk drawer, an expandable file, a filing cabinet, or a home safe. Obviously, many of these spaces are not fireproof or burglar proof, which emphasizes the importance of

Record-Keeping Form

	WHERE TO PUT IT (recommended)	*HOW LONG TO KEEP IT*	*WHERE TO FIND IT NOW*
			A—Home file *B—Safe deposit box* *C—*________
Family Records and Documents			
Certificates of marriage, birth, death	Safe deposit box	Indefinitely	________
Adoption, custody, military, naturalization papers	Safe deposit box	Indefinitely	________
Divorce, separation decrees	Safe deposit box	Indefinitely	________
Family tree	Home file	Indefinitely	________
Names and addresses of relatives/friends	Home file	Indefinitely	________
Social Security card	Carry card. Stub in home file	Indefinitely	________
Wills	Original: attorney's office or someone else's safe deposit box. One copy at home; one in safe deposit box	Permanently	________
Financial Records			
Bank documents	Account numbers in safe deposit box; others in home file	While accounts are active	________
Securities	Safe deposit box; record of holdings in home file	Until sold and transaction figured for taxes	________
Credit accounts	Home file	Until superseded by a new record and taxes figured	________
Credit card list	Home file	Until accounts closed	________

Trust agreements	Safe deposit box	Until fulfilled	________
Health Records			
Medical history	Home file	Permanently	________
Prescriptions	Home file	Until new ones given	________
Immunizations and x-ray records	Home file	Permanently	________
Medicare records	Home file	If needed for tax credit, six years	________
Uniform Donor Card	Carry card, copy in home file	Permanently	________
Burial instructions	Home file	Until needed	________
Living Wills	Home file	Until needed	________
Insurance Records	Policies, payments at home; list of policies in safe deposit box	Until expired or claims settled (if out-of-date)	________
Property Records			
Appraisals, inventories	Safe deposit box; copy in home file	Until sold, taxes figured	________
Real estate papers, deeds, mortgages	Safe deposit box	Until sold, taxes determined	________
Titles of vehicles	Safe deposit box	Until sold	________
Tax Records			

Note: Income tax information needs to be kept for six years to cover all of the circumstances of ordinary challenges or transactions with the Internal Revenue Service. A guide to record keeping is available free from your local IRS office, listed in the telephone book under United States Government.

Tax Returns, cancelled checks	Safe deposit box	Six years	________
Receipts, other supporting documents	Home file	Six years	________

keeping irreplaceable papers in your safe deposit box. Even a "fire-resistant" metal box may protect its contents against fire for only an hour, during which they may become charred, so don't be complacent about the safety of valuables you may put into one. Even a home safe should be insulated, and remember also that burglars have been known to walk off with the whole safe.

Once you have set up your file, be sure to update it at least once a year. A great time is in the "doldrums season," right after the winter holidays. That gets you ready for tax calculations too. And be *sure* that a reliable family member or trusted friend knows where your records are.

RENTAL ASSISTANCE

What do you do when you can't pay the rent? If you are old enough to remember the Great Depression, you know that some families doubled up and others got into their rattle-trap cars and set off across the country looking for jobs or a warmer place to winter. The same thing occurred in 1982 and 1983—people living under freeway bridges and in hallways. For some people, however, rental assistance may assure shelter.

Recognizing that older persons on fixed incomes and others are sometimes not able to manage, Congress, in Section 8 of the 1974 Community Development Act, provided for rental subsidies. This program assists lower-income individuals and families to secure decent, safe, and sanitary housing. Eligible for assistance (but subject to change as new laws are adopted) are:

- Individuals sixty-two years of age or older, or families of two persons in which one of the members is sixty-two years of age or older.
- Individuals or families in which one adult member of the household is disabled.
- Individuals or families who have been or are about to be displaced by governmental or private action or by a natural disaster (condo conversions, condemnation of a structure, cyclone destruction, for example).
- Two or more persons living together in a family-type relationship.

Total family income and assets are taken into consideration and must be within the limits set by the federal government. If you are eligible and the owner is willing to participate, assistance may be given for your present residence.

The amount of the assistance depends on your family's annual income, the number of minors, and the extent of medical and unusual problems. Participants pay no more than 30 percent of their adjusted family income.

As you can see, this is not a program strictly for older persons, but it includes older persons who need it.

The local housing authority administers the program. Call it or the United States Department of Housing and Urban Development (HUD) to find out how you can apply.

RETIRED SENIOR VOLUNTEER PROGRAM (RSVP)

RSVP enlists volunteers on a part-time basis and offers almost unlimited opportunities for service through nonprofit private and public community organizations. RSVP volunteers serve in hospitals, schools, correctional facilities, airports, and clinics. They deliver meals to the house-bound, counsel others on tax and social security problems, and assist social service and other agencies in dozens of other ways.

Anyone sixty or older may become an RSVP volunteer. There are no educational, income, or experience requirements. Volunteers serve without compensation but are sometimes reimbursed for such expenses as transportation.

A consultation with the director of the local RSVP office will give you an idea of the volunteer work that is open to you.

To locate the RSVP office call your regional office of ACTION, listed in your telephone directory under United States Government. (See also: ACTION; SCORE; VOLUNTEERING.)

S

SCORE/ACE

The Service Corps of Retired Executives, best known as SCORE, recruits retired businessmen and women with management expertise to help owners of small businesses and community organizations that need management counseling.

SCORE counselors volunteer in their own or nearby communities, helping restaurants, hardware stores, laundries, small manufacturers, and a great variety of other businesses. They may be reimbursed, on request, for out-of-pocket expenses by the Small Business Administration, their sponsor.

Also sponsored by the SBA is the Active Corps of Executives, or ACE, made up of working executive volunteers who give time and talent to help members of the small business community. Both groups have members who serve in all the states and in Puerto Rico.

If you wish either to volunteer or to request advice for a new business or community organization that you are considering or that needs help, call the local SCORE or SBA number or write to:

SCORE/SBA
1441 L Street NW
Washington, DC 20416

SECURITY SYSTEMS: INDIVIDUAL

Would your sense of security be enhanced by knowing that at the touch of a single button you could summon the police or the fire department, or signal to someone that you were in need of medical help? Several such systems are available and beamed toward the retiree market.

In one such system, you push the appropriate button and within seconds you're in direct two-way communication with a trained dispatcher. If for some reason you are no longer at the device, the dispatcher can pick up any sounds within thirty feet of the unit. A special amplifier extends the range even farther. Touching the button for medical help activates a computer before the dispatcher. Your full medical history, including allergies, surgeries, and disabilities, as recorded by you, is displayed. Thus, this vital information is immediately available, should you be unable to speak or lose consciousness.

The same system enables a third party to speak through the summoning equipment to relay possible life-saving information before the paramedics or an ambulance arrives.

A palm-sized medallion worn around the neck or clipped to a belt activates the master unit from as far away as 150 feet if similar buttons on the medallion are pushed.

The units are sold or leased. A monthly subscriber fee is added.

Lifeline is an electronic communication system operated by many hospitals for those with heart problems, diabetes, epilepsy, and the like. The equipment is somewhat different. A small wireless personal "help" button is worn on the wrist, around the neck or attached to your clothing. If you feel an attack coming on you push the button. This activates your home telephone, which dials the emergency center even if the receiver is off the hook or there's a power failure.

Centers exist in forty-eight states and are spreading. The units are low cost and easily installed. The service charges a monthly fee. To locate the nearest hospital or emergency room that has the Lifeline service call 1–800–451–0525 (except in Massachusetts, where the number is 1–617–923–4141).

You can set up a cheaper, though less efficient, system on any telephone with automatic dialing. Program in the emergency numbers, including the friend or relative to be alerted. No need then to search out numbers to dial in case of emergency.

For those who do not have access to any of these systems, remember the space for your emergency numbers inside the front cover of this volume.

SENILITY AND PSEUDOSENILITY

Many older people are diagnosed as suffering from senile dementia when in fact they are lonely, isolated, and depressed. Loss of vision or hearing may also lead to misunderstandings and misdiagnosis. In any illness, according to the National Institutes of Health, a range of symptoms and behaviors may emerge that have no apparent connection to the underlying disorder. Treatable brain syndrome, excess drug use, and alcoholism may all be mistaken for senile dementia.

There is a tendency to underdiagnose organic disorders. Attention should be given to differentiating mood disturbances from reactions associated with physical illness, and to differentiating between depression and senile deterioration. The depressed elderly should be offered psychotherapy more often than they are. (See also: ALZHEIMER'S DISEASE; DEPRESSION; MENTAL HEALTH.)

SENIOR ADULT THEATER

Is there a Katie Hepburn or a Paul Newman in the house? Let your talent no longer be hidden under a bushel; there is a niche for you in SAT, Senior Adult Theater.

Senior drama groups are not new. Since 1959 the Youngstown Players in Arizona have entertained their retirement community. Other groups scattered here and there have honorable histories—San Francisco's Tale Spinners, Chicago's Free Street Too, and others. These groups sprang up spontaneously, started by persons with an avid interest in theater.

In 1973, sensing the possibilities and value of theater for older people, the American Theater Association appointed a committee on theater for retirees. Thus was born Senior Adult Theater (SAT).

The vision, assistance, and guidance of the association has sparked a much broader movement. SATs are reading plays, performing script-in-hand productions, and presenting variety shows and full-blown theater in churches, schools, retirement and senior centers, empty stores, or just in someone's living room or backyard.

In 1981 the association, through the Pennsylvania State University Press, published *Adult Theater,* a practical handbook to help any interested group get started. Along with descriptions of possible theater experiences, the handbook gives hints on raising money and procuring costumes and props, and a list of suitable (often royalty-free) plays with the addresses of the play publishers.

Did I hear someone say, "I'd never be able to learn a part"? Fear not, seniors do. And if you don't want to, there is still a place for you. Clearly, SAT theater production involves a wide range of retirees: carpenters, electricians, painters, artists, metal workers (set and property production); seamstresses, homemakers (construction and care of wardrobe); artists, typists, business professionals (programs, publicity campaigns, fund raising, ticket selling); as well as writers and actors.

Further information is available from:

American Theater Association—Senior Adult
1000 Vermont Avenue NW
Washington, DC 20005

Expansion Arts Program
National Endowment for the Arts
2401 E Street NW
Washington, DC 20506

Life-Long Learning Project
Department of Education
608 13th Street NW
Washington, DC 20005

SENIOR CENTERS

Thousands of senior multipurpose centers are operating in the United States, bringing many senior citizens programs and services under one roof, and making it easier to get help and information. Their services are free and funded under Area Agencies on Aging. Here you may get counseling, financial advice, legal aid, and housing information, and find out about health care and volunteer groups. The centers frequently serve low-cost lunches, provide assistance for the housebound, have classes on safety, and operate transportation programs such as Senior Ride. Veteran counseling is often part of the service. The directors and their assistants have a wealth of information at their finger tips. If they cannot solve your problem, they may refer you to another program.

Most senior centers have a lively social program—games, dances, trips, dinners, and crafts centers where you can pursue a hobby.

A senior citizen center is probably the best place to begin with any question or problem. To find the one nearest to you call your city hall or county administrative offices. (See also: AREA AGENCIES ON AGING.)

SENIOR COMPANION PROGRAM (SCP)

Patterned after the Foster Grandparent Program, SCP provides opportunities for low-income men and women aged sixty and over to serve adults with special needs, especially the elderly, either in their homes or in nursing homes or other institutions. Authorized by the Older Americans Comprehensive Services Amendments of

1973 as a complement to other community programs, it is intended to help fill critical gaps in the provision of services to persons with medical or developmental disabilities.

For further information, call your local Action office or write to:

Action/Senior Companion Program
806 Connecticut Avenue NW
Washington, DC 20525

(See also: ACTION; FOSTER GRANDPARENTS.)

SENIOR OLYMPICS

Have you remained active and vigorous through your fifties, sixties, seventies, or even eighties and nineties? Do you long to pit yourself against others in your age bracket? If your competitive spirit is still strong, or if you are only curious to test yourself against your peers, then Senior Olympics is for you.

The first Senior Olympics, founded by Warren Blaney, took place in 1969 at the Los Angeles Coliseum, with 175 contestants. In 1983 approximately 6,000 participated, and more are expected in 1984; 50 to 60 percent of the participants are age sixty and over; some are in their nineties. The prize winner for age, who also won a medal, was 103!

Contestants are separated into five-year age brackets up to the seventy-five-and-overs. Gold, silver, and bronze medals with ribbons are awarded to the top three in each division of each event, and a Senior Olympics patch is given to all participants.

In 1983 the Olympics featured more than forty different sports—among them archery, basketball, cross country, cycling, equestrian skills, fencing, martial arts, weight lifting, track and field, tennis, racquetball, sailing, swimming, winter sports (at Lake Placid, New York), and wrestling. The most unusual is harmonica, which Mr. Blaney feels is good for the lungs and the Eustachian tubes.

Senior Sports International, the parent organization, is supported by low membership dues. Expenses are met by a low participation fee for each event. Highly recommended by no less a personage than Avery Brundage, Senior Olympics is fun, and a great way to meet men and women with similar interests.

Look for local Senior Olympics in your own community or state. If you can't find any, or there are none and you'd like to start one, send a stamped, self-addressed envelope to Mr. Blaney, who keeps a file of spin-off Olympics in other parts of the country and the world.

No sports event should be undertaken without the OK of a physician, and you must, of course, sign a release certifying that you have no physical defects that would prevent your competing and you understand that you compete at your own risk.

For further information and membership send your stamped, self-addressed envelope to:

Senior Sports International
5726 Wilshire Boulevard
Los Angeles, CA 90036

SEX

"Young people do not have a monopoly on sexuality," says Dr. Mary Calderone of the Sex Information and Education Council of the United States. "It is with you all your life."

Myths about senior sexuality have thrived on media brainwashing that equates sexuality with youth, and on social attitudes that have labeled sex unseemly for older persons. We have been led to believe that sexual desire, response, and capacity decrease with age—to the vanishing point. The realities are quite different. Sex researchers Masters and Johnson revealed that "sexual response may be slowed down by the aging process, but it is certainly not terminated." Not to belittle Masters and Johnson, but Benjamin Franklin, Victor Hugo, and others had already left records attesting to sexual activities that continued into their eighties.

Post-1950 studies reported by Norman M. Lobsenz, in Public Affairs Pamphlet "Sex after Sixty," showed that more than half of all married couples whose ages ranged from the mid-sixties to the mid-nineties "...were sexually active from once a month to three times a week."

Some sexual changes may take place in both men and women as they age. Changes may vary greatly from man to man. An erection may take longer and be less firm and large than it was in earlier years. The sensation that an ejaculation is about to occur may be shorter, and the loss of erection after orgasm more rapid. The length of time between erections will probably be greater. (Or none of this may happen.) These changes and conditioning resulting from the myths about aging may lead men to expect impotence, a dangerous expectation that may be a self-fulfilling prophecy.

Women generally experience little loss of sexual capacity due to age alone. Some changes usually occur in vaginal elasticity, shape, and lubrication. The simplest remedy for the latter condition is use of a water-soluble surgical jelly—*not* petroleum jelly (Vaseline). The safety of estrogen pills and creams is doubtful because of a possible connection with cancer.

The physical changes women experience (including hysterectomy) should make no difference in their capacity to achieve orgasm. (See Kegel exercises in URINARY INCONTINENCE.)

Experts agree that sex with a loving partner helps reduce tensions, depression, and frustrations, and heightens self-worth.

Indeed, sex can be therapeutic and should not be avoided because of illness. Heart disease, especially a heart attack, may cause an older person to give up sex for fear of causing another attack. Yet the risk of death during intercouse is very low. Check with your doctor. Sex usually can and should be resumed an average of twelve to sixteen weeks after a heart attack. An active sex life may, in fact, decrease the risk of a future attack.

A common problem, especially for older women, is finding a sexual partner. A personal solution like masturbation or a vibrator can provide gratification.

Public acceptance of sexuality in later life is slow in coming but gradually increasing. We can hope for the day when it will be generally accepted that older people have the same right to and need for sex as the young.

Recommended Reading

"Sex after Sixty," by Norman M. Lobsenz. Pamphlet #519. Write:

Public Affairs Pamphlets
381 Park Avenue
New York, NY 10016

Sex after Sixty, by Robert N. Butler, M.D., and Myrna I. Lewis. New York: Harper & Row, 1976.

The Starr-Weiner Report on Sex and Sexuality in the Mature Years, by Bernard D. Starr and Marcella Weiner. Briarcliff Manor, NY: Stein and Day, 1981.

Love, Sex, and Aging, by Edward M. Brecher and the Consumer Reports Editors. Boston: Little, Brown, 1984.

Love in the Later Years, by James A. Peterson and Barbara Payne. Chicago: Follett, 1975.

SKIN CARE

Sun damage is the major cause of aging skin—lines and wrinkles, dark patches or "age spots," and thickened, leathery texture. If you've been a suntan addict and your skin is now older looking than it ought to be, the first thing to do is to stop sunning and arrest the damage. If you must or want to be outdoors a great deal, protect your face and neck with a hat and a sunscreen lotion.

Even if your skin is not wrinkled from sun exposure or heredity, you are probably finding that it has become increasingly dry and thin, except perhaps on your feet, where it may have become thick and callused. Women seem to suffer more from dry skin than men.

It's important for older people to use creams and lotions to alleviate the condition. Overheated rooms and harsh soaps or detergents can aggravate the problem, as can daily bathing. That cleanliness is next to godliness becomes less true as you age and your sweat glands become less active.

Slathering cold cream and emollient lotions on your face, throat, back, feet, or any area that feels dry and perhaps itchy will do a world of good. Use a bath oil while bathing or after showering, as directed. Use only mild cold-cream soaps like Dove for washing, and soaps like Ivory for laundering underclothes.

Exposure to the sun's rays can also cause skin cancers, particularly in fair-skinned people. Consult a dermatologist about any pimple or sore that doesn't heal in a reasonable time, or about any growth or mole that grows larger or changes character. If a mole is flat and black or varied in color, however, it could be a melanoma, perhaps the swiftest and deadliest of cancers. Don't wait another day; see a dermatologist at once. Be assured, though, that most types of skin cancer are easily curable if attended to in time.

Recommended Reading

Great Skin at any Age, by James and Thomas Sternberg, M.D.s. New York: Pinnacle Books, 1982.

(See also: AGE SPOTS.)

SOCIAL SECURITY

"We can never insure 100 percent of the population against 100 percent of the hazards and vicissitudes of life," said President

Franklin Roosevelt in 1935 when he signed the Social Security Act, "but we have tried to frame a law which will give some measure of protection to the average citizen and to his family...against poverty-ridden old age." Even with an unstable economy the law has accomplished much of what it was designed to do—to give older people a chance to live independently and with dignity in their old age.

Because of the widespread application of social security, almost all older Americans are acquainted with most of the basic structures affecting them: pensions start at sixty-five, or at sixty-two with reduced benefits; the amount received depends on earnings; a certain number of quarters of work credit are required to get the pension; a spouse can collect on a husband's or wife's coverage.

However, because the law is so comprehensive and has been changed periodically, some new provisions may have escaped notice.

New Provisions under Social Security

These include changes in the law to give divorced spouses coverage, the amount of wages you can earn without losing part of your pension, the age at which restrictions on earnings no longer apply, the change in the law about remarriage.

How has the law been changed about divorced wives? If the marriage lasted ten years or more checks can now go to divorced wives sixty-two or over, or to a surviving divorced wife at sixty, or to a disabled surviving divorced wife fifty or older. Starting in January 1985, a divorced wife who has been divorced at least two years can receive benefits at sixty-two if the former spouse is *eligible* for social security; the former spouse does *not* have to be drawing social security.

What happens to my social security if I work? If you go back to work and are under seventy, your earnings may affect your social security. However, you may earn up to a specified amount (in 1983 $6,600 for people sixty-five or over and $4,920 for people under 65) without loss of benefits. At seventy the ceiling on earnings is lifted completely.

What happens if I am widowed? If you are sixty or older or are younger with unmarried school-age or disabled children, you are eligible for benefits based on your husband's or wife's coverage.

If I remarry will my checks stop? Checks continue if a widow or widower over sixty remarries. Amounts may change.

If the marriage fails will I lose everything? If by everything you mean your social security benefits, no.

How can I find out if I worked long enough to get social security? Ask the Social Security Administration to send you a statement of your social security earnings and the requirements for qualifying. (Don't forget—active military duty counts too. It is counted when a claim for benefits is made. It does not appear on your earnings statement.) And you can still earn more credit if you need it to qualify—even after sixty-five.

What should I do if my check doesn't arrive? If it hasn't arrived by the sixth of the month, get in touch with any social security office. If you suspect that it is lost or stolen, contact your social security office.

Will my check be replaced? Yes, but it will take time. (See DIRECT DEPOSITS.)

The Social Security Administration has numerous booklets and leaflets, as well as a well-trained staff to answer your questions about the benefits of the social security system. Call the office to request information. Two basic booklets available upon request are:

Your Social Security
Your Social Security Rights and Responsibilities

Caution: Be sure to check the date on any information you have, as it changes frequently. In addition, if the information you receive is questionable, try again. Remember also that you can question decisions about changes in checks for you or your dependents. If you feel a decision is in error, ask for the leaflet outlining the steps to take.

STEPFAMILY ASSOCIATION OF AMERICA

Because stepfamilies have even more problems than the ordinary, they often need support and education. One might think, with all the children grown and out of the household, that there wouldn't be a problem. But often grown children (like the young) resent the marriage of an aging parent—partly out of loyalty to the supplanted parent, even though through death; partly because of fear of losing "their" part of the estate; partly because they think it's unseemly for an older person to continue wanting love and romance, and even sex.

Resentments over real or fancied slights can build up and poison the new marriage. Each partner may favor his or her own children. And how heartily will step-grandchildren welcome the newcomer and be welcomed? Will everybody be careful not to make distinctions?

The nonprofit Stepfamily Association acts as a support network and national advocate for stepparents, remarried parents, *and* their children. Membership includes a quarterly bulletin, helpful materials including booklists, discounts on certain books, and membership in local chapters. These may encourage small mutual help groups, stepparenting classes, and seminars and conferences. There are now sixty chapters in thirty states, and the number is growing.

It's enlightening and comforting to discuss problems with others who are similarly distressed, and to read about them too. For further information and membership, write to:

The Stepfamily Association of America, Inc.
28 Allegheny Avenue, Suite 1307
Baltimore, MD 21204

STRESS

Magazines, TV, and radio are filled with talk and advice about stress. There is nothing new about stress, however; it has always been with us. Someone has even collected a set of quotations from Proverbs on the subject. A couple of samples:

> A tranquil mind gives life to the flesh, but passion makes the bones rot. (14:30)
>
> Better is a dry morsel with quiet than a house full of feasting with strife. (17:1)

If we translate "passion" ("envy" in some translations) and "strife" into our modern term *stress,* we find that it's an old problem.

Although it has been recognized for centuries that stress can cause physical symptoms, we are just beginning to understand how mental states can influence the complex web of hormone interactions (and vice versa). There is now strong evidence of

The Social Readjustment Rating Scale*

LIFE EVENT	*MEAN VALUE*
1. Death of spouse	100
2. Divorce	73
3. Marital separation	65
4. Jail term	63
5. Death of close family member	63
6. Personal injury or illness	53
7. Marriage	50
8. Fired at work	47
9. Marital reconciliation	45
10. Retirement	45
11. Change in health of family member	44
12. Pregnancy	40
13. Sex difficulties	39
14. Gain of new family member	39
15. Business readjustment	39
16. Change in financial state	38
17. Death of close friend	37
18. Change to different line of work	36
19. Change in number of arguments with spouse	35
20. Mortgage or loan for major purchase (home, etc.)	31
21. Foreclosure of mortgage or loan	30
22. Change in responsibilities at work	29
23. Son or daughter leaving home	29
24. Trouble with in-laws	29
25. Outstanding personal achievement	28
26. Wife begin or stop work	26
27. Begin or end school	26
28. Change in living conditions	25
29. Revision of personal habits	24
30. Trouble with boss	23
31. Change in work hours or conditions	20
32. Change in residence	20
33. Change in schools	20
34. Change in recreation	19
35. Change in church activities	19
36. Change in social activities	18
37. Mortgage or loan for lesser purchase (car, TV, etc.)	17
38. Change in sleeping habits	16
39. Change in number of family get-togethers	15
40. Change in eating habits	15
41. Vacation	13
42. Christmas	12
43. Minor violations of the law	11

*See Holmes, T. H. and Rahe, R. H.: The Social Readjustment Rating Scale, Journal of *Psychosomatic Research 11*:213-218, 1967, for complete wording of the items. Reprinted from the Journal with permission from Pergamon Press, Ltd. and the author.

connection between stress and such troubles as high blood pressure, colitis, ulcers, and heart disease. Some physicians even assert a link with cancer.

Stress is not necessarily bad. Life with no stress would be boring, and some stress is just normal living. We just shouldn't have too much of it at one time, and we should have ways of dealing with it when it comes.

A popular and much-quoted analysis of stress, "The Social Readjustment Rating Scale" by Thomas H. Holmes, M.D., of the University of Washington, relates it to life events. His work shows that people with a score of over 300 for the past year have an 80 percent chance of getting sick in the near future, and those scoring between 150 and 299 a 50 percent chance. The corresponding probability for those with lower scores is only 30 percent.

Preventive Measures

Looking over this list of life events, you can see that a large number of them are likely to happen to older people. Those "sunset years" are not necessarily a time of less stress—just different kinds of stress.

There is an abundance of additional advice about how to cope with stress. Some people just naturally cope better than others, but nearly everyone can use a little help sometimes. The simplest thing is to take a tranquilizer, but there is increasing evidence that continued use of tranquilizers can lead to addiction and other problems. A pill should be considered only a temporary solution while you work out a long-term strategy for coping.

Basic Coping Strategies

Face It. If your stress is caused by anxiety or fear of what might happen, it can help if you look it right in the eye. Exactly what is it that might happen, and what if it did? What would you do then? Maybe it's not so terrible.

Talk It Over, with a friend or with a professional counselor (see COUNSELING).

Roll with It. That is, don't fight it. Since the change is something you have to accept, figure out how you are going to remake your future under the new circumstances.

Distract Yourself. Throw yourself into some activity that takes all your attention and energy. Organizational work, paid work, gardening, sports—anything that takes you out of yourself.

Nutrition. Be sure you are eating right. Some authorities recommend extra B vitamins, vitamin C, tryptophan, and a generally wholesome diet.

Religion. For centuries, people have been helped through periods of stress by a strong faith. Also, many clergymen act as counselors.

In addition, there are specialized techniques that help cope with stress. A few follow.

Tranquilizing Techniques

Deep Breathing. Relax. With both hands on the abdomen, breathe in slowly through the nose, feeling the abdomen expand as the lungs fill. Then exhale slowly. Repeat several times. This simple exercise will help compose you for sleep and help you wake up in the morning. It's a good thing to do any time you feel angry, frustrated, or upset for any reason—it's better than counting to ten.

Progressive Relaxation. With emptied mind, lie in a quiet room and relax each muscle group in your body, beginning with the feet and working up to the scalp.

Meditation or Relaxation Response. This is a technique for emptying the mind, with muscle relaxation and controlled breathing. See references that follow.

Yoga. This technique combines emptying of the mind and concentration on the inner self with special breathing, relaxation, and exercises that stretch and relax the body (see YOGA).

Biofeedback. Calming yourself is only one of the benefits of biofeedback. A trained therapist and a machine are necessary at the beginning, but you will be trained to use the techniques on your own.

Self-Hypnosis. A hypnotist can tranquilize you, but you can learn to do it to yourself through auto-suggestion.

Visualization or Guided Imagery. Sitting in an easy chair or lying flat with your eyes shut, you can waft yourself or be wafted by the mellifluous voice of a tape or a live leader away to the Elysian Fields, the Fortunate Isles, Avalon, the gardens of the gods—someplace where all is beauty, tranquility, serenity.

All these techniques help tension-tight people to relax. They have numerous elements in common, and there is a normal amount of borrowing and overlap. Try a few and find the one that works best for you.

Recommended Reading

The Relaxation Response, by Herbert Benson, M.D. and Miriam Z. Klipper. New York: Avon, 1976.

The Mind-Body Effect, by Herbert Benson, M.D. New York: Berkley, 1980.

The Stress of Life, by Hans Selye, M.D. New York: McGraw Hill, 1978.

Stress Without Distress, by Hans Selye, M.D. New York: Lippincott, 1974.

Total Breathing, by Philip Smith. New York: McGraw Hill, 1980.

(See also: YOGA.)

STROKE

Strokes, caused by a sudden disruption of the blood supply to the brain, are the third leading cause of death in the United States.

Small strokes called TIAs (transient ischemic attacks) are warnings of possible major strokes to come, and although they leave no residual damage, they should not be ignored.

Symptoms may be any of these: intense, unusual (not migraine) headache; weakness, numbness, or paralysis in arm, leg, or face, usually on one side; sudden difficulty or alteration in speech, hearing, or understanding; difficulty in breathing or swallowing; loss of bladder or bowel control; sudden dizziness, loss of balance, or fainting, which, of course, may be symptomatic of other conditions. Seek medical attention at once if you feel a TIA coming on, and make up your mind to alter your lifestyle radically.

Even though no permanent damage ensues, your doctor may prescribe anticoagulant drugs, a daily dose of aspirin, or stroke-preventing surgery.

Some of the things you can do to prevent another TIA or a stroke are:

- Control your blood pressure.

- Stop smoking.
- Reduce weight if above normal.
- Change your diet (much less meat and dairy fats) to lower your cholesterol and triglyceride levels.
- Exercise aerobically at least three to four times a week, one-half hour each time, as strenuously as your doctor allows.
- Avoid or learn to cope with stress, using techniques described in this book.
- If diabetic, control diet, exercise, and drugs as prescribed.

When a stroke occurs, emergency care is crucial:

- Use CPR (cardiopulmonary resuscitation) if the victim loses consciousness.
- DON'T give fluids.
- Call the paramedics, the doctor, and perhaps the hospital.

Almost immediately after your stroke, appropriate therapy will begin in the hospital. A rehabilitation center may be recommended, and then therapy at home or as an outpatient. It could be speech, physical, occupational, or even recreational therapy. A psychotherapist or a social worker may also be needed.

You *can* survive a major stroke even if it leaves you disabled, if you receive immediate and then regular attention and are determined to recover the use of lost faculties. According to Jane Brody's *Guide to Personal Health,* 30 percent of stroke victims remain unhandicapped, and an additional 55 percent are only partly disabled.

Easter Seal Society Stroke Clubs assist in overcoming post-stroke depression as well as physical difficulties. Many other organizations, both governmental and local nongovernmental, are eager to help. Make use of them; some even provide transportation if needed.

Professionals and organizations will guide and encourage you, but the extent of your recovery will depend largely on your determination to do the prescribed exercises and to live again as normally and richly as possible. Unfortunately, frequent aftermaths of stroke are fatigue, apathy, irritability and other personality changes, any or all of which may make you resistant to renewed activity.

Almost two thousand years ago, Sophocles wrote, "Heaven never helps the men who will not act," and Euripides, in the same vein, said, "He who strives/Will find his gods strive equally for him." It's still true.

Recommended Resources

The Sister Kenny Institute
Chicago Avenue & 27th Street
Minneapolis, MN 55407

Easter Seal Society Stroke Clubs
2023 West Ogden Avenue
Chicago, IL 60612
(Check your local telephone directory first.)

The American Heart Association
7320 Greenville Avenue
Dallas, TX 75231
(Check your local telephone directory first. Ask about their stroke clubs.)

OPUS (Organization of People Undaunted by Stroke)
196-25 Peck Avenue
Fresh Meadows, NY 11365

For additional addresses and information see the U.S. Department of Education's *Directory of National Information Sources on Handicapping Conditions and Related Services,* in your library's reference section. (See also: ATHERO- AND ARTERIO-SCLEROSIS; BLOOD PRESSURE; CHOLESTEROL; EXERCISE; NUTRITION; PARAMEDICS; SECURITY SYSTEMS: INDIVIDUAL; STRESS.)

SUPPLEMENTAL SECURITY INCOME (SSI)

If you are a retiree living on an inadequate pension or without a pension you may be eligible for SSI, Supplemental Security Income. In 1983, although 4 million elderly citizens lived in poverty, another 2.5 million hovered near the poverty line, and another quarter of a million joined the impoverished due to the delay in the cost-of-living increase for social security—only 1.4 million participated in the program.

If you are in need, you may be able to get this assistance. Ask at any social security office. Fill out an application even if you are told you are not eligible. If you are turned down after submitting the application, ask at the social security office for the leaflet that tells you how to appeal a decision. Follow the outlined procedure carefully.

If you are turned down again, seek advice from Legal Aid, the Area Agency on Aging, or some similar group. You may just have made an error on the application.

It's widely known that many eligible people are not getting

the help they need. You may be one of them. (See also: MEDICAID.)

SURGERY—SECOND OPINION

A life-threatening illness with no other possibility of remediation requires immediate surgery; but is most surgery necessary? Deciding whether to have an elective or nonemergency operation is particularly difficult for the elderly, according to the National Institute on Aging. Normal changes that occur with age and disease in later life, particularly heart ailments, often make surgery more risky for them.

The Institute recommends that you begin by consulting your family physician or an internist about your illness and treatment choices because he or she is likely to give equal attention to possible nonsurgical treatment. Consult a surgeon only after you and your doctor have concluded that surgery is the wisest alternative.

When choosing a surgeon, ask if he is board-certified in his field, or if he is an F.A.C.S. (Fellow of the American College of Surgeons), or both. These are indications of high competence. Ask the local medical society, his hospital, or his office.

Some questions the Department of Health and Human Services thinks you should ask are:

- What exactly is wrong with me?
- What is the operation the surgeon plans to do?
- What are the probable benefits of this operation?
- What exactly are the risks, and in what percentage of cases do they occur?
- What will happen to me if I don't have the surgery?
- How long will recovery take, and might there be unfortunate residual effects from the surgery?
- Are there other ways to treat my condition that could be tried first?
- How much will the operation cost?

Then find out whether Medicare and/or your health insurance will cover the costs.

Second Opinion

Sometimes surgery is done on an emergency basis and there is literally no time for a second opinion. But unless the condition is life-threatening, as in many cancers, you may choose to live with your disability rather than correct it. Whenever a doctor suggests nonemergency surgery, it's wise to get a second opinion, an *independent* second opinion. Medicare and most insurance companies are pleased to pay for second opinions, for obvious reasons. You may tell your physician or not—whichever makes you more comfortable—but you will have to tell him if you want to have your medical records (x-rays, etc.) seen by the other doctor.

You can find another competent surgeon through your internist, the local medical school or medical society, or by calling the government's toll-free number: 800–638–6833 except in Maryland, where it's 800–492–6603. If you're on Medicare, you can also ask your local social security office; if you're covered by Medicaid, ask at a local welfare office.

A Cornell study has shown that 18.7 percent of second opinions did not confirm the need for surgery, and other studies show an even higher percentage. In 1976 the United States House Subcommittee on Oversight and Investigations estimated that 2.38 million surgical procedures were unnecessarily performed in 1974 alone, at a cost of some $3.92 billion, and resulting in 11,900 deaths. An eminent Cleveland surgeon maintains that one out of every three operations is unwise.

Remember that it's your body, your life—the only one you'll have, unless reincarnation is a reality. Don't submit with blind, unquestioning faith to a single recommendation. After all, you wouldn't even buy a household appliance without investigation. It's worth your time, trouble, and even expense to make certain that you're choosing the wisest course.

Recommended Reading

Shopping for Health Care, by Harold J. Cornacchia. New York: National American Library; St. Louis, MO: Mosby, 1982.

A Guide to Surgery and Its Alternatives, by the editors of *Prevention Magazine*. Emmaus, PA: Rodale Press, 1980.

T

TAX PREPARATION

You don't have to trundle over to the neighborhood tax preparation service. If you need it, you can get free help in preparing your federal and state income tax returns.

IRS Help

To help unravel the complexities of your federal tax form the IRS has:

- a toll-free number, 1–800–424–1040, to call for answers to perplexing questions.
- a twenty-four-hour number, 1–800–242–4585 to handle requests for forms and publications.
- AND Tele-Tax Information, instant access to 140 recorded explanations of tax stumpers. For the number in your area see: Telephone Assistance in the index to Form 1040 General Instructions. (Push-button telephone users have twenty-four-hour service; rotary dial users must call weekdays during IRS office hours.)

To help you with your tax preparation the IRS has:

- VITA (Volunteer Income Tax Assistance) to prepare returns for low-income or nonEnglish-speaking taxpayers (at IRS offices and other locations).
- TCE (Tax Counseling for the Elderly) to assist those over sixty, especially the disabled, regardless of income.
- OUTREACH, a program to help groups of thirty-five or more. Perfect for senior centers.

To locate the nearest site of VITA, TCE, or OUTREACH instruction call 1–800–424–1040.

Other Assistance

Some colleges and public accounting firms provide income tax preparation for low-income persons. Ask at a senior center.

The American Association of Retired Persons' tax counseling program, *Tax Aide,* is in operation in most communities from

February to April 15. The trained volunteers help with federal and sometimes state returns, cooperating with the IRS. For information call the IRS. AARP has valuable, free tax booklets available to members, write:

Tax Aide
AARP
1909 K Street NW
Washington, DC 20049

Many states have volunteer income tax assistance programs, helping the disabled and the elderly to prepare their state and federal returns. Check at your senior center or call your state tax board.

TAXES

Gold is where you find it, or where you save it.

Tax authorities estimate fully half of older Americans who file tax returns overpay. That's like burning up your fives and tens. A systematic check of tax credits, exemptions and assistance may cut your tax bite substantially, if not spectacularly.

Federal Taxes

Are you taking these credits and exemptions?

	Yes	*No*
Exemption for age—over 65	____	____
Exemption for blindness (Are you "legally" blind?)	____	____
Credit for the elderly	____	____
Residential energy credit	____	____
Exclusion of capital gain on sale of residence	____	____
Qualifying widow or widower	____	____

For explanations and directions for filing each of these, see IRS Publication 554, "Tax Benefits for Older Americans" and the instructions for Form 1040, the long form. If you have been using the short form, pick up the long one at your post office, bank, or library to see if it has advantages for you. It may look pretty complicated, but hang in there. It may save you money.

State and Local Taxes

Are you entitled to any of these tax breaks?

	Yes	No
Renter's Tax Credit	____	____
Senior Citizens Property Tax Assistance	____	____
Senior Citizens Property Tax Postponement	____	____
Senior Citizens Utility Tax Exemption	____	____
Disability Income Exclusion	____	____
Credit for the Elderly	____	____
Exemption of the stipend for:		
Foster Grandparent	____	____
Senior Companion	____	____
Solar Energy Installation Exemption	____	____
Homeowners Exemption	____	____

In most cases you don't get these tax breaks unless you apply for them, so investigate. *(Note:* The exemptions vary from state to state, city to city, and so does the age at which you are eligible. It may be lower than sixty-five. Solar Energy and Homeowners Exemption, for example, have nothing to do with age.)

Nitty-Gritty on the Exemptions

Renter's Tax Credit. In many states where a renter's tax credit is given, many older renters fail to file for it, either being unaware of the break or thinking their income is too high. Ask your tax board or at your senior center.

Senior Citizens Property Tax Assistance. Your state may have property tax assistance. Ask at your senior center or tax board and find out how to apply if you are eligible.

Senior Citizens Property Tax Postponement. In some states seniors may postpone property taxes until property is transferred because of sale or death. The postponed taxes become a lien on the property. If you have no heirs or aren't interested in passing your property on to others, this is a way to "eat up" your estate and leave the world "even," neither owing nor owning.

Senior Citizens Utility Tax Exemption. Depending on your income, you may be exempt from local taxes on gas, electricity, telephone, and water bills. If these are included in your rent, you may be entitled to a refund. (Sometimes these refunds are retroactive.) Inquire at your senior center and/or your utility companies.

Disability Income Exclusion. Certain kinds of income do not have to be reported. If you are on disability, check on this.

Credit for the Elderly. See IRS schedules R and RP to see if you are eligible. Check for similar state credit.

Foster Grandparent and Senior Companion Stipend. If your state exempts the stipend you don't even need to report it. Check your state income tax form or call your tax board.

Solar Energy Installation Credit. Energy-saving devices in your home may give you some tax relief. If you have put them in, apply for any credit you may have earned this way.

Homeowners Exemption. If you are entitled to this exemption, be sure to file. In some places you need apply only once, but in others you must file every year.

Of Special Interest to Homeowners

Beginning in 1984 up to $125,000 of the profit made on the sale of a home is excluded from federal capital gains taxes provided:

- you or your spouse is 65 or older.
- you have owned the property for five years or more and lived in it for three, not necessarily continuously.
- you haven't taken this exemption or a similar one before

(For a detailed explanation, call Tele-Tax, Tape 400. See TAX PREPARATION.)

Danger—Tax Crossing Ahead!

If your income taxes have been withheld from your payroll check, estimated taxes may be a new wrinkle for you. Now you must let Uncle Sam know ahead what your anticipated income for the year is. If your federal income tax indebtedness is more than $200 you must file an estimated tax form. (Some states require it too.) You pay what you expect to owe in quarterly installments, due the fifteenth of April, June, September, and the following January. Watch it; the interest penalty for failing to file is STIFF.

TDD AND OTHER TELEPHONE AIDS

The telephone is so essential for contact with the outside world that those who for any reason can't use it are indeed handicapped. Consequently, many helpful and ingenious aids have been devised. Among these is Telecommunications Device for the Deaf or TDD (formerly known as TTY), a teletypewriter that can be attached to any standard telephone and enable the owner to type messages to any other person or facility that also has the machine.

In some states the device is free to anyone certified as deaf or speech-impaired. It's expensive, however, for anyone who isn't, and a machine is needed at both ends for a teletyped conversation. If you want to communicate with your hard-of-hearing brother by telephone, it may be costly for you. Since an increasing number of hospitals, emergency units, government agencies, catalog order departments, and other businesses have been installing TDDs, it's clearly advantageous for the handicapped person to have one even if friends and family members do not.

Call the local telephone company to find out how to get one. Don't worry about lack of typing skill; it's not essential.

Devices exist to help you with almost any disability:

- Can't hold a receiver? Try a speakerphone (a microphone unit that attaches to your phone) or a flexible arm that clamps to a table top and holds the receiver.
- Dialing is difficult? Get a push-button telephone. If your vision is poor, the telephone company has Braille numbers to superimpose on the buttons; and if you can't get used to these, the operator will be glad to get your number for you.
- Can't hear the phone ring? Install flashing lights, extra-loud bells, or a small electric fan that blows gently on you when the phone rings.

Your telephone company may have many of these devices at low cost; if not, you can get them through a number of commercial firms that supply aids for the disabled. If your doctor certifies that you need aids, the purchase price or rental fee is tax-deductible.

Recommended Reading

The Disabled: Ideas and Inventions for Easier Living, by Suzanne Lunt. New York: Scribner's, 1982.

The Source Book for the Disabled, edited by Glorya Hale. New York: Paddington Press, 1979.

TOLL-FREE NUMBERS

Telephone costs keep rising, but you can often save money on calls that don't cost a cent—the toll-free 800 numbers. Most airlines; motel and hotel chains and some that are not chains; many city, state, and federal government agencies; tour operators; and a surprising number of other businesses have toll-free numbers. Sometimes these are listed in your directory, sometimes not. Before you place a long-distance call, dial 800–555–1212 (long-distance information), which is free also. Often the number is good for all states except the one in which the facility is located. Sometimes there are different 800 numbers for different areas. You'll find the 800 number in your telephone directory, but if you don't, try Information anyway.

TOOTH AND DENTURE CARE

Although new cavities become fewer as you age, gum deterioration can become a serious problem. If you're retired, you can now brush more than once a day. Use a soft brush, because aging tends to make you "long in the tooth"; that is, the gums may recede until the roots of the teeth are exposed. Brush thoroughly, but not too vigorously. Always brush before bed and after eating or drinking sweets of any kind; if possible, brush after meals. If you're not sure of the proper method, ask your dentist or dental hygienist when you get your teeth cleaned (at least once a year). And when you've finished brushing, use dental floss.

If, because of arthritis or some other problem, you have difficulty holding a brush, you can get one of several different types of handle accessories, or make one yourself. Check medical supply catalogs.

The purpose of all this care is to prevent build-up of plaque, which forms on the teeth daily and, if not removed, hardens into calculus, which can be removed only by a dental hygienist or a dentist.

If you don't remove plaque religiously, you risk periodontal disease, (which can also be caused, however, by stress and grinding or clenching of teeth, diabetes, osteoporosis, malocclusion caused by shifting of teeth, or the use of the drug dilantin).

According to the National Institute of Dental Research, current information points to the accumulation of masses of bacteria in the plaque as the primary cause of most periodontal conditions. Dr. Paul H. Keyes formerly of the Institute and now chairman of the board of trustees of the International Dental

Health Foundation, suggests the following regimen to promote the effective daily removal of bacteria and toxic by-products:

- Moisten about two tablespoons of baking soda with a few drops of water and 3 percent hydrogen peroxide, to make a thick mix.
- Work this mix onto and between the teeth and gums with toothbrush and dental floss or Stimudents. Leave the mix on the teeth for one minute. Epsom salt should be used by people on a low sodium diet. Be sure to massage the gums thoroughly.
- Rinse, using a Water Pik, with a salt solution, and then with plain water.
- Brush again, if you wish, with a fluoridated toothpaste.

You can also help keep your teeth and gums in good shape by eating fibrous foods like carrots, which have a cleansing action, and apples, which help prevent plaque formation.

If, despite all your care, your gums begin to bleed easily or are a deeper pink than they were, or your teeth begin to loosen, consult a periodontist quickly. Your dentist or dental society can refer you. If you attend to the problem soon enough, you may be able to arrest the disease, keep it under control for the rest of your life, and retain your teeth.

If you'd like a dentist or a periodontist who has a special interest in the care of older patients, write to:

The American Society for Geriatric Dentistry
1121 West Michigan Street
Indianapolis, IN 46202

For an NIDR fact sheet on periodontal (gum) disease, and for more detailed information about the baking-soda hydrogen-peroxide treatment, write to:

The National Institute of Dental Research
National Institutes of Health
Building 31, Room 2C36
Bethesda, MD 20205

Dr. Paul Keyes
International Dental Health Foundation
11800 Sunrise Valley Drive, Suite 832
Reston, VA 22091

Dentures

Paul Z., tired of dental bills and of visiting the dentist frequently, decided to go to the local university dental school, have all his teeth pulled cheaply, get a set of dentures, and be done with the nuisance of his own teeth.

He came to regret his action, finding that he could no longer enjoy steaks, hard-crusted breads, and sticky foods. Sometimes his dentures slipped during meals, or even when he was talking.

His lower dentures became the big problem. Because of shrunken tissue and bone mass, the dentures had less area on which to rest and less suction. Paul sometimes found that by evening, particularly if he had been doing a lot of talking, his mouth hurt so much that he had to cancel engagements.

Moral: If you've already lost all your teeth, there's nothing you can do about it. But if you still have some, hold onto them as long as you can, and treat them well; partial dentures are easier to live with than a full set.

The change from your own teeth to dentures is never easy. It involves a period of physical and emotional adjustment and considerable practice. When learning to eat with dentures, select soft, nonsticky foods cut in small pieces. Chew slowly, using both sides of the mouth. Be careful about bones and hot or cold foods, to which your mouth will be less sensitive. See your dentist for adjustments till you're satisfied. Afterwards, see him or her annually or whenever you begin to have trouble. Remember that friction can cause oral cancer.

Sensations of discomfort will lessen in time, and gradually you'll learn to eat the firmer foods; 52 million Americans who wear dentures have made it, and with determination you can, too.

Denture Care. Dentures require almost as much daily care as your own teeth did. Brush all surfaces once daily with a special denture brush and dentifrice, NOT the kind you used on your own teeth. Unless your dentist advises otherwise, keep your dentures out of your mouth eight hours a day (or night), placing them in a special denture-cleansing solution or in water—but never hot water. The same care should be taken for partial dentures.

Most partial dentures are matched to the colors and contours of your own teeth and can be undetectable. If you've come to the point where you must wear dentures, remember the plus side: They can be better looking than your own teeth ever were and can allow you a new and brilliant smile. Partial or full, they should look good enough to pass for your own beautiful teeth, even if they don't feel as good.

If you have the money, you should investigate some of the new techniques. Today some periodontists brace loosening teeth at a cost of $15–20,000. Some dentists recommend implants; others say that they can cause severe problems, including infection. A new technique rebuilds the jawbone so that older people can wear dentures more comfortably. This too is costly.

Low-Cost Dentistry

If money is a serious problem, for dental care or dentures, a call to your local dental association or senior citizen center may be beneficial to your purse. These can often give referrals to free clinics, dental schools, and even to dentists who will repair your teeth for less than the usual fees. Or check out the clinic of the nearest university dental school, where students will work on you either free or low-fee.

Check out very carefully those cut-rate dentists and denture makers who advertise low-cost work. You may end up with problems that are a lot more costly than if you'd gone to a reputable dentist or clinic in the first place. Your county dental association can advise you. For further information or referrals write to:

The American Dental Association
211 East Chicago Avenue
Chicago, IL 60601

The National Institute of Dental Research
National Institutes of Health
Bethesda, MD 20205

TRANSPORTATION

As long as you can pilot your own car over the highways and byways or hop on the bus, getting from here to there is chiefly a matter of time and money. But what if getting from point A to point B and back is too costly, or if your arthritis or some other disability makes it hard for you to drive your car or use existing public transportation?

Senior Fares. In most communities the regular transportation system has reduced rates for riders who show their Medicare cards or other evidence of their age or buy senior citizen passes. Ask the bus driver or ticket salesperson.

Senior Ride. Often called Senior Ride, but sometimes operating under other names, it is a free or inexpensive transportation system serving seniors in many localities. Specially marked vans or mini-buses provide door-to-door service from the senior's home to medical or dental offices, shopping centers, banks, and recreation and nutrition sites. Reservations usually must be made twenty-four hours in advance. Call your senior center or Area Agency on Aging for information.

Taxi Discount. Many taxicab companies sell coupon books for prices that cut the cost of rides as much as 50 to 80 percent. If several cab companies operate in your area, it will probably be faster to call Info Line, Area Agency on Aging, or your senior center to find out which one or ones are giving seniors a break. The coupon books make practical gifts for those for whom transportation is a problem.

Transportation for the Handicapped. As the result of a movement to make all public transportation "barrier free" (eliminating high steps, narrow aisles and other inconvenient features that make using public transportation difficult, even impossible, for those in wheelchairs or using crutches or canes), some regular and many special (Senior Ride, etc.) transportation systems operate specially designed cars. These trains or buses are equipped to accommodate the handicapped.

Since 1982, because of lack of support at the federal level, the program has slowed down so that the goal has not been reached. Even in communities where awareness and support of the program is high, the special vehicles are limited. However, if you need this help in getting around, call the office of the transportation company. It just may be that the route you plan to use is equipped to meet your needs. Ask also if the bus or train is marked with the access sign.

Federal Surplus Property Vehicles. Organizations wishing to provide transportation for the elderly can often purchase vehicles cheaply through competitive bidding on government surplus property. Guidelines on bidding are in a pamphlet, "Buying Government Surplus Personal Property" available from:

Office of Personal Property Disposal
Federal Supply Service
General Services Administration
Washington, DC 20405

For information on AMTRAK see: DISCOUNTS.

TRAVEL

Traveling is one of the favorite occupations of retired people, as you can see if you look around any resort area in the off season. Seniors are everywhere: boarding Amtrak, wheeling down the highways in motor homes, and on cruise ships and tours. After all, who else has the time for traveling when it isn't summer vacation or some other holiday?

Senior Tours

If you would prefer a slower pace than the usual tour allows, and want to save money as well, try a senior tour.

Saga, for those over sixty, offers U.S. and international holidays at excellent prices. These cover practically all expenses, so you'll know how much you'll need to spend. There are river and ocean cruises, university dorm holidays, and "stay" holidays in resort areas such as Hawaii, Israel, Spain, and Bermuda. Combination tours can be worked out: coach tours combined with a cruise or a stay holiday in some city, or "add-on" or consecutive holidays.

Because the organization is connected with British Saga, most foreign tours begin and end with one night in London, or longer if you wish. A Saga escort is always present or available to help you. The price of a tour includes cancellation insurance.

A single tour makes you a member of the Saga Club and recipient of a travel periodical that includes a Personals page and Penfriend and Partnership lists.

For information:

Saga International Holidays, Ltd.
31 St. James Avenue
Boston, MA 02116
Tel. 1–800–343–0273

Grand Circle Travel, formerly the travel bureau for AARP, still offers a variety of reasonably priced senior tours as well as apartment vacations in the great cities and resort areas of Europe. Their domestic tours are mostly in the West.

For information:

Grand Circle Travel
555 Madison Avenue
New York, NY 10023
Tel. 1–800–221–2610 or 212–688–5900

AARP Travel Service, now provided by Olson Travelworld, Ltd., offers discounted cruises and fully escorted coach tours in the United States, Europe, and the Orient, and apartment-style holidays with hosts in Europe, Hawaii, Mexico, and Hong Kong. For information:

AARP Travel Service
P.O. Box 92337
Los Angeles, CA 90009
Tel. 1–800–AARP–TVL (1–800–227–7885)

The *American Youth Hostel* (AYH) has "50+ tours," which are much less physically demanding than their trips for youths. Costs are really low and accommodations are simple. Both domestic and foreign trips include transportation from the starting point, medical insurance, and all group expenses, including meals. Tour groups usually consist of only nine people plus a leader. If you can get eight friends to join you, AYH will provide a leader or you can choose your own, who will travel free.

If you would like a cycling rather than a bus trip, some are reserved for adults (but not specifically over fifty). For information:

American Youth Hostel
1332 I Street NW, Suite 800
Washington, DC 20005

Cruises

Whether you go with a group (see previous section) or just as a couple or with friends, a lot can be said for cruises. You don't have to pack and unpack, you always have your cabin to retreat to, you have your own toilet facilities, and you never have to decide where to eat. If you're on a restricted diet, you can usually find something in the extensive menus that will suit (or maybe have it prepared for you).

Cruises provide plenty of entertainment: games, movies, classes, bridge tournaments, dancing, floor shows, and so on. There is always a doctor on board (unless you're on a freighter), and your steward is available at the touch of a button.

Altogether, a cruise is the ultimate in convenience and luxury. Don't expect to see much of the places you visit, however; a few hours in a port city is about all you get. No exploring or visiting galleries, cathedrals, or other attractions.

Any travel agent can provide you information on cruises to anywhere you might want to go. Don't expect bargains.

Freighters

The days when travel by freighter was cheap are gone; most 1984 prices are in the $100-a-day range. Still, it's a peaceful way to travel. A membership organization, *TravLtips*, will help you find a freighter trip to meet your needs. Membership includes eligibility for specially priced trips and cruises and a periodical bulletin, "Roam the World by Freighter." For information:

TravLtips
Box 933
Farmingdale, NY 11737

Ford's Freighter Travel Guide [$7.50 in 1984]
Merrian Clark, publisher
P.O. Box 505
Woodland Hills, CA 91365

Singles Travel

Do you hesitate to travel because you have no one to go with? Try a classified ad in one of the travel, sports, or literary magazines. Exchange letters or phone calls to determine whether you and potential roommates would hit it off together. Singles tour groups are a possibility, but check on the average age of the group before you sign up.

Two special singles groups are oriented toward the outdoor life. *Rainbow Adventures* is for women over thirty who are sports-minded. They do canoeing, trekking, backpacking, riding, and skiing trips. No wilderness experience is needed for most of the adventures; trips are informal and move at a leisurely pace. Prices are not low. For information:

Rainbow Adventures
1308 Sherman Avenue
Evanston, IL 60201
Tel. 1–312–864–4570

Loners on Wheels (LOWS) is for older singles who enjoy camping and own a recreational vehicle. With more than 3000 members in the United States and Canada, they meet in recreational areas to fish, hike, play golf or cards, or just socialize. Sometimes two or three LOWS take to the road together, or those who live in RV parks visit one another. A monthly bulletin lists the upcoming activities of each chapter. For information:

Loners on Wheels (LOWS)
2940 Lane Drive
Concord, CA 94518

Hosteling

If you want to travel on a small budget, check out American Youth Hostels. They don't sound quite right for seniors? In fact, seniors are welcome at hostels all over the world, including 280 in the United States and over 5000 altogether in 60 countries. Seniors can join AYH for $10 a year.

In this country, your hostel may be a college dorm, lighthouse, mountain lodge, or YMCA. In Europe it could be a castle, a Swiss chalet, or an old mill. Most hostels are in scenic, historic, or recreational areas.

The cost is very low, but be prepared for sleeping dormitory style with two to eight in a room. There's an extra charge if you don't bring your own sheets and towels. Hostels provide a common lounge, sometimes a cafeteria, and often a kitchen where you can make your own meals. Maximum stay is three nights, smoking is allowed only in a designated area, and alcohol and drugs are forbidden. Lock-out time is 10 P.M.

The young people will welcome you warmly, but be sure you enjoy youth and exuberance. Avoid school vacation periods, when most hostels are filled. If you carry valuables, check out whether your hostel has lockers.

When you consider hosteling, weigh the disadvantages against the low price, and the convenience as compared with camping. In some areas, like southern Europe, you can have privacy in a *pension* for almost the same price.

If you prefer to be with people your own age, AYH still has bargains for you—the "50+ tours" mentioned earlier, together with the address for both.

Recreational Vehicles (RVs)

The 400,000 membership in the Good Sam Club testifies to the popularity of motor homes and trailers for vacationing or for wintering when the thermometer begins dropping. RV parks span the United States and are edging into Canada and Mexico. Owners of these homes-on-wheels form subgroups that often arrange to meet at Taos or El Paso, for example, and caravan to another destination, sightseeing and socializing en route.

RVs are expensive and present a parking problem when not in use. Before you invest, a trial run in a rental rig may be prudent.

If you're hooked and want to get into RV action, Trailer Life Publications, sponsor of the Good Sam Club, publishes *Trailer, Motor Home, and Rider* (for motorcyclists) as well as an annual

Campground and Service Directory, which rates camps, restrooms, and showers; lists charges, service centers, and dumping stations; and tells you where to find discounts. For information write:

Good Sam Club
P.O. Box 500
Agoura, CA 91301

Home Exchanges

Marilyn K. loves to travel in foreign lands, but her husband Carl detests finding a new hotel every night, packing and unpacking all the time, and deciding where to eat. He doesn't like tours either—too much rushing and being herded here and there.

They have found a solution that suits both of them: house swapping through vacation exchange clubs, which list available homes in all parts of the world. Their directories detail the essentials—number of rooms and baths, appliances, location with respect to transportation and shopping, and so on. Sometimes a car comes with the house, and sometimes household help.

Such home exchanges are available within the United States as well as in foreign countries. Your chances of finding a swapping partner are better, of course, if your house is in New York or Palm Springs or Palm Beach or San Francisco rather than Ottumwa, Iowa, or Fayetteville, Arkansas.

Among the many home exchange services are:

International Home Exchange Service
P.O. Box 3975
San Francisco, CA 94119

Holiday Exchanges
P.O. Box 5294
Ventura, CA 93003

Hideaways International
P.O. Box 1459
Concord, MA 01742

Families Abroad
194 Riverside Drive
New York, NY 10025

Discounted Travel

Stand-Buys specializes in underbooked cruises, charter flights, and tours that the tour operator is glad to fill at a discount in order to cut losses. Retired seniors can most easily take advantage of these opportunities, because one has to be ready to leave on short notice. Offerings sell at 15 to 60 percent discount, and charter flights usually include a hotel room in the destination city.

Membership includes many travel, car-rental, and insurance discounts.

A toll-free hotline announces the latest offerings. At last look, most of these offerings originated in the Midwest and the East. Few flights, even those to Hawaii, left from the West Coast. Check to see whether they have expanded their coverage.

For information:

Stand-Buys, Ltd.
26711 Northwestern Highway, Suite 310
Southfield, MI 48034

Many new organizations offer unspecified travel bargains that may turn out to be useless to you. Check carefully before paying the rather high membership fee.

Tours for the Frail or Disabled

You don't have to be disabled. If you feel too frail or vulnerable to handle a regular tour, try one of these:

Flying Wheels Travel isn't cheap; however, it tailors both tours and individual travel to the varying needs of people with mobility, visual, or hearing disabilities. Barbara and Judd Jacobson (he's a quadriplegic) lead cruises and tours within this country and abroad. If they haven't anything going to the area you want, they'll make all arrangements for you or even attempt to assemble a tour to the area. They also represent Norman Wilkes Tours of Britain (see next section) in the United States. For information:

Flying Wheels Travel
143 West Bridge, Box 382
Owatonna, MN 55060
Tel. 1–800–533–0363 or, in MN, 1–800–722–9351

Norman Wilkes Tours offers a number of personalized special-interest tours of Britain for the disabled and their families and friends. If gardens, dramatic arts, music, cathedrals, or stately homes are your thing, this is the group for you. If you need personal assistance and have no companion, Wilkes will supply a suitable helper for a fee. For information:

Norman Wilkes Tours
2 Lower Sloane Street
London SW 1, England
(or call Flying Wheels Travel, previous section)

Health Tips

- Get health insurance coverage if you're going outside the United States; Medicare won't cover you. Consider trip cancellation insurance.
- Keep an extra pair of glasses and all medications in your hand luggage; your checked baggage may get lost or delayed. Carry prescriptions, too, in case you run out.
- If you have a special problem, wear a Medic-alert tag or keep a warning in your wallet.
- Get a good night's rest before leaving and have a hotel room reserved at your destination.
- Accept your limitations; you may be less spry and energetic than you were. Spend a day in your hotel if you're tired.
- On a long plane or train trip, try to get up and move about frequently. Keep your feet elevated (on your carry-on bag) if possible.
- Avoid alcohol, which aggravates the dehydration caused by low pressure in planes. Drink lots of water.
- Travelers diarrhea is especially bad for the elderly or frail because of the dehydration. Take along some Pepto-Bismol. Lomotil and other prescription medications often have harmful side-effects. If the problem persists, see a doctor.
- You can hire a nurse to accompany you on any trip or tour. For information:

  Medical Personnel Pool of America
  303 Southeast 17th Street, Room 403
  Fort Lauderdale, FL 33316
  (Ask for "The Travel Nurse" brochure.)

- For information on foiling jet lag, read (well in advance): *Overcoming Jet Lag,* by Dr. Charles F. Ehret and Lynn Scaller. New York: Berkley Books, 1983,

  or send an SASE for a leaflet on the subject to:

  Argonne National Laboratory
  9700 South Cass Avenue
  Argonne, IL 60439

- Send a donation to IAMAT for material about world climate, a world immunization chart, a list of approved doctors in foreign lands. Write:

  IAMAT
  736 Center Street
  Lewiston, NY 14902

Getting Special Help

Request special help well in advance if you want it. The FAA defines the disabled passenger as anyone who needs the assistance of another person to exit quickly from an airplane in case of emergency. This includes the blind and deaf, people on crutches or in wheelchairs, *and people who can get around but with limited agility or endurance.* Airlines are glad to make arrangements—eliminating check-in lines and providing wheelchairs, carts, and special meals. For further information, write to:

> **United States Department of Transportation**
> Federal Aviation Administration
> 800 Independence Avenue SW
> Washington, DC 20509
> Ask for Circular AC–120–32, "Air Transportation for Handicapped Persons."

Some people prefer trains to planes, and retired people have the time to travel on them. Amtrak's special services include assistance in boarding and leaving trains; special meals, sleeping accommodations, and bathrooms; and other on-board services.

For a booklet about Amtrak's efforts to make train travel the preferred way to go and booklets on special tours to scenic areas, call 800–USA–RAIL or your nearest Amtrak office.

Recommended Reading

Low-Cost Travel

Europe on $25 a Day and many other books in the Frommer Dollar-a-Day series and the Dollarwise series. Revised annually, and published by Simon & Schuster.

Let's Go and *Let's Go, USA* are Harvard Student Agencies annuals.

All of these are available in most bookstores. You may find that the accommodations listed are too stark for your taste, but give them a try, starting with the higher priced ones. You can always work your way down. These are also excellent guides to inexpensive sightseeing.

The Michelin Red Guides are great books for finding low-cost lodgings and restaurants as well as the finest. And many government tourist bureaus publish lists of low-cost accommodations in their countries; check your telephone book for local addresses.

The Discount Travel Guide for Travelers Over 55 by Caroline and Walter Weintz. New York: E.P. Dutton, 1981. Lists by state and city all sorts of useful information as well as discounts. Most of the information is for the U.S.A., but there is some for other countries.

Where to Stay USA, by Margaret Sherman; edited by Marjorie Cohen. New York: Simon & Schuster, 1980. Unless updated, the prices won't be right, but this is a fine state-by-state guide.

Health and Medical

SAS Exercise in the Chair: An Inflight Exercise Program for the Air Traveler. Ask 800-Information for the SAS number and request this small but excellent pamphlet.

Travel with Health, by Dr. Herbert L. and Margaret W. Dupont. New York: Appleton-Century Crofts, 1980. An excellent preventive guide as well as a handbook on how to deal with problems that may arise when you're away from home.

Access to the World: A Travel Guide for the Handicapped, by Louise Weiss. New York: Facts on File, 1983.

The Wheelchair Traveler, by Douglass R. Annand, editor-publisher. Ball Hill Road, Milfor, NH 03055. 1979 rev. ed. Contains over 6000 listings from fifty states, Canada, Mexico, and Puerto Rico. Lists tourist sites as well as accommodations with easy access for the frail as well as the wheelchair-bound.

General

Fodor, Frommer, and Fielding are the big names in travel guide literature, but the Michelin *Green Guides* to many countries and cities in Europe give superb details about every site worth visiting. The *Blue Guides* published by Ernest Benn, Ltd., London, are also worth studying.

U

URINARY INCONTINENCE

Urinary incontinence isn't necessarily associated with age. Young people also sometimes have lack of urine control or incontinence—leakage while laughing, sneezing, coughing, exercising—anything that puts pressure on the bladder. This is called stress incontinence. Another type is urge incontinence: suddenly and unexpectedly you can't hold it long enough to get to a toilet, the urge coming because you're close to one. Still another is overflow or dribbling incontinence, often caused by enlarged prostate, arteriosclerosis, or diabetes.

Prostate surgery or stress can result in temporary loss of control and some new drugs are also culprits, as are severe depression, pseudodementia, dementia, Parkinson's disease, strokes, and urinary infection.

Whatever the reason, the incidence of incontinence increases with age. Conservative estimates are that by age sixty-five at least one person out of ten has some degree of incontinence, ranging from slight loss of urine to severe and frequent wetting. According to the Step-Up Foundation (for urinary disorders), 15 percent of men and 25 percent of women have problems at age sixty-five, and the percentage rises as age increases.

Incontinent people frequently try to hide their problem from others, even their doctors. However, it can often be cured or controlled, so consult your physician or a urologist. Surgery or medication may eliminate the problem.

Kegel exercises, which strengthen the muscles that help close the bladder outlet, help many women. Developed by Dr. Arnold Kegel, these exercises strengthen the pubococcygeal, or PC, muscle. To identify this muscle, stop the flow when you're urinating. The muscle you are using is the PC muscle. Once you are aware of this muscle, exercise it (not while urinating) as follows:

1. Contract the PC muscle. Hold the squeeze for three seconds, release for three seconds. If you can't manage to contract for three seconds at first, start with two. You can practice at any time—sitting, standing, lying down. Nobody can tell that you're doing it. Increase to ten seconds.
2. Same as above, but squeeze and release as quickly as possible. This is the flutter exercise.
3. Imagine that there is a tampon in the vaginal opening and you're

sucking it up into the vagina. Hold for three seconds.

4. Almost the opposite: bear down as for a bowel movement, but with the vaginal area rather than the anal. Improvement may take six weeks, so don't give up. The exercises may also increase your pleasure during sexual intercourse.

Practice each of these ten times at three times of the day. Other measures to reduce the tensions of incontinence:

- Limit or omit fluid intake in the evening and before going out.
- Empty your bladder every hour, even if you don't feel the need. Gradually lengthen the intervals until you work out a satisfactory schedule.
- Be sure that toilet facilities in the home, including a bedside commode, are easily accessible.

For continued updated information, join the Step-Up Foundation or subscribe to its *Step-Up Informer*, a quarterly publication for urinary-incontinent persons or their friends. Sponsored by Principle Business Enterprises, it has now been separated from them to avoid conflict of interest. (See address following.)

Don't end your social life because of incontinence. Use absorbent pads, waterproof pants with disposable liners, leg bags. These and other accessories are available from Abbey Medical, Sears (ask for *Home Health Care Catalog*), and other firms listed in your classified telephone directory, probably under Hospital Equipment and Sickroom Supplies. Try out several brands to determine which is most absorbent, easy to change and dispose of, convenient to carry, and economical.

If you can't find the following brands locally, write to:

Kimberly Clark
P.O. Box 9123
St. Paul, MN 55190
(for Depend pads)

Humanicare International, Inc.
P.O. Box 838
East Brunswick, NJ 08816
(for Dignity pads)

Principle Business Enterprises, Inc.
Pine Lake Industrial Park
Dunbridge, OH 43414
(for the Tranquility system)

For further information, membership, or publications, write to:

Step-up Foundation
Box 8
Dunbridge, OH 43414

V

VETERANS' BENEFITS

Surprise! If you haven't used your GI Home loan you are still eligible for one. Or, if you didn't use all of your entitlement, you are eligible for the remaining entitlement. (The word *entitlement* means the guaranty benefits available to an eligible veteran—$27,500 in 1983.) The money is in the coffers and the law is on the books. This is not to say you can easily get the loan, but you should investigate.

GI loans may be used to buy a home, a condo, or a mobile home *or* to refinance an existing home loan *or* to repair, alter, or improve a home (including installation of a solar heating and/or cooling system or other weatherization). Check with your lending institution.

If you are a veteran:

- with an honorable or general discharge
- with service-connected disabilities
- disabled by age or disease

or the surviving unmarried spouse or disabled child of a veteran

- who died as a result of service-connected disabilities
- had service-connected disabilities but whose death was not the result of them
- was a member or retired member of the Armed Services

you may be entitled to some or all of the following services:

- a pension
- disability compensation
- medical services
    - hospitalization
    - outpatient and extended care
- dental care
- aids and services to the blind
- prosthetic devices
- mental health care
- nursing home care
- domiciliary care

- alcohol-dependency programs
- drug-dependency programs
- commissary and exchange privileges
- employment assistance
- medical services and supplies
  CHAMPUS (or from civilian sources—CHAMPVA)
- "nonfee" or "free-free" passports (to visit graves of veterans or Tablets of the Missing overseas)
- burial benefits

Veterans' families are entitled to certain death benefits regardless of the time elapsed since the veteran's separation from the service, but application must be made. Funeral directors often help.

- Burial flags. Apply at any VA office or most local post offices.
- Burial in national cemetery. Obtain pamphlet "Interments in National Cemeteries" at any VA office. Also check with the funeral director.
- Headstone or marker. Forward VA form 40-1330 (from any VA Office) to:

  Director, Monument Service (42)
  Department of Memorial Affairs
  Veterans Administration
  Washington, DC 20402

- Allowance for non-Government headstone or marker. Apply at any VA office.
- Residential memorial certificate. Usually sent automatically. If not, see VA office.
- Burial expenses. Amount paid depends on site of burial. Allowance is made for a plot and for burial. Apply to any VA office.

Veterans and veterans' families will make filing a claim or obtaining services easier if they have available:

- the veteran's discharge papers
- his or her "C" file number if a claim has ever been filed
- a statement of his or her burial preference (location and type of burial)

For veterans' benefits information check the white pages of your local telephone directory under United States Government, Veterans Administration, Benefits Information and Assistance, or ask telephone directory assistance. Local veterans' organizations can help too. If the VA disallows any benefit to which you feel you are entitled, ask for advice from the VFW, the American Legion,

Disabled American Veterans, Jewish War Veterans, Vietnam Veterans, or any similar group. They will fight for you if they feel you have a justifiable claim.

A comprehensive guide, "Federal Benefits for Veterans and Dependents," may be ordered from:

Superintendent of Documents
U.S. Government Printing Office
Washington, DC 20402
Price $4.50 (1983)
(Calling VA Information is a better bargain if you have a specific question.)

By now you may need the veterans' benefits that seemed unimportant when you were so overjoyed at leaving the army that you accepted a less-than-honorable-discharge without protest. If you want a review of your military discharge, forms and instructions for filing may be secured by writing:

Department of Defense Discharge Review
P.O. Box 21
St. Louis, MO 63166

Uniformed Services Survivors' Annuities

If you are a widow or widower whose spouse had completed twenty or more years of service in the military and was on active duty at the time of death *before* September 21, 1972, you may be eligible for Survivors' Benefit Plan annuities.

To determine how to apply for benefits contact:

Army: 1–800–428–2290 (Indiana residents, 317–542–3911)
Air Force: 1–800–525–0104 (Colorado residents, 303–307–7051)
Coast Guard: 1–800–638–0205 (Maryland residents, 301–436–7775)
Marine Corps: 816–926–5268
National Oceanic & Atmospheric Administration: 1–800–321–1080 (Ohio residents, 216–522–5955)
Navy: 1–800–321–1080 (Ohio residents, 216–522–5955)
Public Health Service: 202–245–6349

Complaints

Complaints, comments, requests, and suggestions should be directed to the Director of the nearest VA office, VA hospital, VA national cemetery or write:

Veterans' Administration
Washington, DC 20402

VIALS OF LIFE

Created by AARP and administered by some sheriffs' departments, Vials of Life alert rescue teams to the medical history, medications being taken, location of hospital records, names of physicians, and those to notify in an emergency.

The plastic vial containing the information is filled out by the participant and attached to a top shelf in the refrigerator. A Vial of Life sticker on the door of the refrigerator tells paramedics or ambulance attendants that the vital data is inside.

To see if this program operates in your community, call your sheriff's department.

VICTIMS

Many states have programs designed to help victims of crime. The assistance may be financial (to help pay medical bills or restore necessary equipment) or emotional, through individual or group counseling. There are also private assistance agencies in many sections of the country.

If you are the victim of a crime and need help, inquire at your senior center about help or write:

National Organization for Victim Assistance
1757 Park Road NW
Washington, DC 20010

VISTA

Volunteers in Service to America, better known as VISTA, is the domestic equivalent of the Peace Corps. Men and women with particular skills and experience work for a minimum of one year in impoverished rural or urban areas. About 15 percent of these semi-volunteers are over 55. They may live and work with migrant families, on Indian reservations, in institutions for the mentally handicapped, or in a variety of other settings. They may help tackle problems in education, day care, drug abuse, health, legal aid, and city planning.

They receive up to ten days of preservice orientation, plus in-service training as needed. Benefits include a $300 monthly allowance for food, housing, and incidentals; health insurance; and $75-a-month stipend that is paid on completion of service. The VISTA allowance doesn't affect social security or welfare benefits, but it is subject to taxes.

For further information call the local VISTA office or write to:

ACTION/VISTA
806 Connecticut Avenue NW
Washington, DC 20525

(See also: ACTION; PEACE CORPS.)

VOLUNTEERING

Seniors make up an important part of the volunteer force. Some seniors find a place to use their job-related skills; some learn new skills; others carve their own niche.

Although most volunteer assignments are stictly that, involving no pay, some do pay a small stipend. And volunteer jobs have been known to turn into paying ones. The cost of your transportation and any other expenses related to your volunteer work (cost of materials, say), if not reimbursed, are tax deductible.

Some places where you can get involved:

- City or county offices on aging.
- Your local ACTION programs such as Retired Senior Volunteer Program (RSVP), Foster Grandparents, Senior Companion Program (See individual entries for details). Your State Action Office will know the locations of these projects.
- Local chapters of such organizations as the Gray Panthers, SCORE, and dozens of others—fraternal, social, and political.
- Senior centers.
- Community senior food or craft cooperatives.
- Area Agencies on Aging are often a focal point for elderly programs and services that need help.
- Adult day-care centers, convalescent homes, VISTA, the Peace Corps. It takes seniors too.

And watch for "Involvement Opportunities" in your local newspaper.

W

WHEN TO CALL THE DOCTOR

You know the doctor is busy; you also know you don't want to run up any unnecessary medical bills. How do you make the decision to call? Some conditions may be dangerous, a delay even fatal; others are not urgent and can be endured, if not ignored.

The doctor should be called in case of:

severe chest pain
loss of consciousness
a temperature of 102 degrees or higher
breathing difficulties
falls with possible injuries—broken bones, head or spinal injury
poisoning, severe burns or animal bite
continuous vomiting or diarrhea
sudden impairment of vision or hearing
paralysis
bleeding due to a wound (not a minor laceration), or a bloody discharge from any body orifice
signs of internal bleeding: faintness, dizziness, weak but rapid pulse (over 100 beats per minute), shallow, irregular breathing, and clammy skin
reaction to medication

The doctor may have encouraged you to call under other circumstances. Follow his advice. (See also: PARAMEDICS.)

WIDOW AND WIDOWER

When her husband died of a heart attack during the busy Christmas season, Bonnie B. experienced strong feelings of guilt as well as grief. "He was tired, and I accepted invitations; he wanted quiet. Maybe I was responsible for his death."

Bill H., whose wife died after a prolonged bout with cancer, was also riddled with guilt as well as grief. She had become more and more acerbic during her illness, and he hadn't always been patient. He had said things that now tormented him.

After a sixty-year marriage with a man who had become increasingly a recluse and resented her need for people, Nora W.

worried after his peaceful death at age eighty-nine because she wasn't sufficiently grief-stricken, and was actually enjoying her new-found freedom. "I must be an unnatural person," she lamented.

Practical Matters

At first you're numb with shock. People cluster around, supportive and sympathetic. The situation is almost unreal. There will be many things to do that will keep you busy immediately after the funeral. Here are some of them:

- Make six or more copies of the death certificate.
- Apply for changed social security status at the local office, taking with you a copy of the death certificate, the marriage certificate, and the birth certificates for a new claim; if you have already been receiving social security through your spouse, a call to the local office may be enough. In either case, know the social security number or numbers. And if, as the widow of a previous marriage, you formerly drew social security for yourself and minor children, be able to give that social security number also, and the dates.
- If your spouse was a veteran, notify the Veterans Administration and ascertain whether any benefits are due.
- Notify insurance companies of your spouse's death, and provide for each a copy of the death certificate, the obituary notice, and, if the death was caused by accident, the accident report.
- If there is an estate, you must file for probate or get a lawyer to do it for you. (Ask ahead of time what the fee will be.) If the estate is large enough for inheritance taxes, get an accountant.
- Transfer all stocks and bonds, bank accounts, real estate, and credit cards to your own name. It's best to do the credit cards gradually, one at a time.
- If you're no longer covered by health insurance, shop quickly for the best policy you can obtain.

What Not to Do

Don't make any major changes for a year or so. If you need to get away, rent your home; don't sell it. Or sublet your apartment. Strike out in all kinds of new ways if you can, but don't do anything irreversible.

Don't move in with your children unless you have to.

Don't listen to all the well-meaning advice you will receive. Or listen, but then make up your own mind. Only you know what's right for you.

Don't neglect your health. Even if it seems pointless at this time, take care of yourself physically. Walk, exercise. Continue eating properly even though it seems pointless to cook only for yourself. You don't have to cook elaborately to get all the necessary nutrients.

Emotions

Your real pain comes when you begin to grasp all the implications of your loss. Often one feels overcome with a hodgepodge of desolating and strange emotions. In addition to grief and guilt, you may feel anger, loss of self-esteem, loneliness, alienation, longing for the old dependence, helpless awareness of the many ways in which you were dependent, a sense of desertion. Be aware that dreams that the spouse has abandoned or divorced you are are common.

Among the physical symptoms suffered may be: choking, shortness of breath,heart pains, digestive problems, lack of muscular power, debilitating fatigue, insomnia, loss of weight, asthma, hair loss and gum problems (caused by low thyroid), dizziness, ulcers. You may also neglect your health.

It isn't just the loss of the person most important in your life, although that is the greatest loss. It's also the loss of someone to whom you were of first importance that suddenly shreds your ego. It's the change in your social life after the first flurry of calls and letters. It's the terrible guilt about things said that should not have been, and things left unsaid that should have been. You suddenly remember things you could have done for the other and didn't, times when you should have been available and weren't. You can't bear the silence in the house. You hate not being part of a couple when social lives revolve around couples. You're reluctant to entertain without a partner to help you, and so you become increasingly isolated.

Don't heed well-meaning friends who urge you to stop grieving. Working through grief should not be rushed or hurried. Cry all you want, and if you can't find a sympathetic ear among your family and friends, try a therapist. Above all, find a support group in the community; they are active at most senior centers, and frequently in churches, synagogues, and community colleges.

There is no schedule or time limit for either grieving or ceasing to grieve; don't let well-meaning family or friends try to impose one on you. Mourn as long as you need to. How long does one grieve? It will vary, of course, but if at the end of a year you haven't started to work your way out, get help. Don't be like the women in Greece, who donned black from head to foot for the rest of their lives.

Mourn in your own way, not the way that others think you should. Work through your guilt and regrets before you put them away. There will probably be all sorts of unfinished conversations, things you should have asked or said. Write letters to or dialogues with your spouse. Or keep a journal of your feelings, and read it over once a month to see how you and they are changing.

These procedures will help put your guilt and regrets to rest. It should help to remind yourself that *everyone* is left with guilt and regrets, no matter how great the relationship may have seemed. Nobody's marriage, except in cheap romantic novels, was all honey and roses.

Try whatever remedies you can find, other than dependence on alcohol, tranquilizers, or sleeping pills. Occasional use can be very helpful, especially in the beginning, if you're sure you're the type that can taper off.

Exercise—as strenuous as your health allows—can be remarkably beneficial. Try weeding, or cleaning the house at a furious rate, or hiking up a steep hill, or anything that serves as an emotional release. Try the relaxation response, too, or meditation, or yoga.

Make an effort to structure your time, allotting certain hours to certain activities or tasks. Nothing is so demoralizing as unstructured time when you're unhappy.

If you have a job, keep working. If not, try to find part-time or volunteer work to keep both mind and body busy.

Coping in the Long Run

You always relied on your husband to read the road maps, pay the bills, handle money, do the gardening, fix the things that went wrong in the house.

Or you always confined yourself to wage-earning and depended on your wife to cook, clean, shop, take care of the laundry, make social engagements, keep in touch with friends by telephone or mail.

Neither of you realized until too late how dependent you had let yourself become. Now you suddenly have to begin to learn new skills or, failing that, find someone else to do things for you. Remember, however, that new skills can be learned. It will take determination, sometimes new courage, and always, time.

Widowhood is a turning point. You're no longer part of a pair. Couples who you thought were dear friends of both of you no longer include you in their activities. If you and your spouse did everything together, if you were not individuated from him or her, surely you felt frustrated at times about your lack of freedom to get on with what *you* wanted to do, when your spouse didn't. Try to look at this new phase of your life as an opportunity; you now have the freedom to do the things you couldn't do formerly. An opportunity to learn about yourself and to grow again, especially if you hadn't dated, married early, or never worked. You have freedom and time—you don't have to be home at a certain hour to prepare dinner. Freedom to spend money on what *you* want, assuming that you've been left with enough for more than the necessities. Freedom to redecorate your house as you wish or to discard clutter. Freedom to go to school, travel, go on long fishing trips, join the Peace Corps. Freedom to seek out adventure and new relationships.

One good way to cope with the loss of a mate is to find a new one, if possible and desired. This is easier for widowers than for widows, since there are many more available women then men. For either widowers or widows, however, caution is advisable; the success rate for such marriages is not high.

Most people find mates in the same places they find friends, so if you're on the lookout you will have to go out and mix with people who may be compatible. That means hobbies, classes, church, travel, sports, clubs—places where like-minded people get together. When you develop new interests, new relationships usually come along with them, and a new life can begin.

Recommended Reading

On Being Alone, the AARP Guide for Widowed Persons.
For this free booklet write to:

> **AARP Widowed Persons Service**
> Box 199
> Long Beach, CA 90801
> (Ask also if the Service has a group in your area.)

"How to Cope with Crisis."
For this pamphlet write to:

> **Public Affairs Pamphlets**
> 381 Park Avenue South
> New York, NY 10016
> (Ask for their complete list of pamphlets, many of which are useful.)

A Grief Observed, by C. S. Lewis. New York: Bantam, 1976.

Widow, by Lynn Caine. New York: Bantam, 1975.

WILLS

Do you *have* to have a will?

What happens if you don't have one? Then you have left the distribution of your estate up to the state, to be divided among your relatives according to state statutes. Possibly everything will go to the right person or persons, but there is no way for you to give instructions if you haven't done it before you have reached the point of no return.

In most states, if there is no will, children get a substantial part of the estate—often two-thirds or more. And the estate is diminished by costs of administration, not to mention additional delays and a good chance of extra taxes. Yet, despite these disadvantages to the heirs, more than 60 percent of those who die each year die intestate, without a will.

If you make a will you can divide up your estate in any way you like, make bequests, or cut the unworthy out. You may want to give property to your university, the family silver to your favorite granddaughter, your '37 Cadillac to your friend Ed.

Your will can protect your estate for your heirs or from them. If you make a will you can disinherit son Quentin who will just squander what he gets. (Be sure to leave him something though, the proverbial $1 perhaps, to show that you didn't forget him, thus giving him a chance to contest the will.) If you make a will you can name the executor of your estate. You can, with the proper drafting of your will, minimize federal and state taxes.

Having your will drawn up by an attorney well versed in tax and probate law may be the best investment you can make for your heirs.

But, if drawing up your own will—a holographic (in your own handwriting) will or one on a printed form—is legal in your state, such a will is better than no will at all.

Where states will recognize holographic wills, the rules pertaining to such wills are very precise; so if you make one, be careful to comply with the legal requirements.

In California a holographic will must:

- be entirely in your own handwriting, longhand script or printed letter, whichever way you normally write.
- be on completely plain paper having *no* other writing, printing, or typing, not even your letterhead. (The only exception is the lines on lined paper.)
- *not* be witnessed nor notarized.
- be dated, including day, month, and year.
- have the pages numbered, if there are more than one, as, "page 1 of 2 pages," etc.

- have a statement of "testamentary intent," indicating this is your will: "I declare this to be my Last Will and Testament."

This may not be the rule in your state. Witnesses may be required. Printing may be unacceptable. If your holographic will is to be legal, you should know what you're doing. Because of the trouble that can arise due to language used in the body of the will, it is easy to run afoul of the law, so, to be on the safe side, have an attorney review it.

You can make a will on a standardized form from the stationer. In this do-it-yourself number, you fill in the blanks, sign it, and have it witnessed by the required number of persons, usually two. Although this seems simple, the forms won't meet the needs of everyone. The choices given for the disposal of your property are few, and if you want a different arrangement or want to make a number of bequests it won't work. As in the holographic will, you must follow the instructions to the letter.

A seldom-used and very specialized will is an oral will. Its origin is probably the battleground—a dying soldier making his last bequests. It is still reserved for deathbed wishes. The amount of property that may be bequeathed this way is limited, often to $1,000, and the will must be witnessed by two to five witnesses. It is not legal in some states.

Whatever kind of will you make (except the oral one, if you don't recover) is not cast in bronze. It can be modified or changed and you should go over it annually. It should be reviewed by an attorney if:

- you or your heirs marry, remarry, or are divorced or widowed.
- you have new grandchildren.
- you move to, or buy, property in another state. (Laws vary.)
- you change your mind about your beneficiaries or your executors. (Experts suggest appointing more than one executor—two, or even three, so that one can succeed another should the first one become ill, move away, or be unable to assume the duties.)

Wives and single persons are even more remiss than others in not making wills. They too have estates and should draw up wills. Drawing up a simple will is not complicated and not necessarily expensive. Many lawyers charge only modest fees. You may not have to go to a private attorney. Many senior centers have will preparation clinics. Local attorneys sometimes volunteer their services. Grey Law or a similar group may assist you, if fees are a matter of concern.

In whatever form you choose, you owe it to yourself and your heirs to draw up a will. NOW!

X

X-RAYS

Although some physicians still pooh-pooh the idea that x-rays can be injurious, a considerable body of respectable scientific evidence now indicates that excessive radiation (and who knows what's excessive?) can cause cancer and leukemia.

Many of us, throughout our lives, were subjected to unnecessary and excessive radiation. Remember the annual chest x-rays at school? The mobile chest x-ray units? The foot x-ray machines we used to play around with in shoe stores? The x-ray treatments for acne? The routine x-rays some obstetricians took of pregnant women, just to make sure that the baby was in a normal position? The full-mouth x-rays some dentists still insist on annually? The routine mammograms some doctors still order for all women?

In many cases, benefits of diagnostic x-rays outweigh the risks and are, indeed, essential to proper treatment. However, some physicians order x-rays routinely, sometimes in order to protect themselves against the chances of a lawsuit. Be a participant in your own medical care. Ask your doctor or dentist what the x-ray will show, what evidence there is that it will show anything wrong, what is likely to happen if you refuse, and whether any less dangerous tests might give sufficient information.

Keep a record of the dates of all x-rays. Remember that they are legally yours on demand. If you change doctors or hospitals, you have a right to take all x-rays and scans with you; don't subject yourself doubly and unnecessarily to radiation. Find out whether the minimum number of pictures will be taken. In one HMO the technicians routinely take four chest pictures instead of two, on the chance that the first two might not be OK.

But don't refuse an x-ray if the risk of not having it is greater than the risk for radiation.

For an x-ray card to keep in your wallet, and for further information, write to:

FDA
HFX-28 (or X-rays)
Rockville, MD 20857

Y

YOGA

Would you like to have something in common with Gloria Swanson, Yehudi Menuhin, and Jawaharlal Nehru? Try yoga. Once known only as a mystic East Indian philosophy, it has become—at least in part—increasingly familiar to Westerners. Courses in hatha yoga are given in colleges and YMCAs, and many doctors recommend it for stress reduction. Because it's neither competitive nor strenuous, it's particularly suitable for seniors.

Even if you diligently perform your daily aerobic exercise (brisk, rapid walking; swimming; or cycling), you will benefit from yoga because its basic exercises and positions increase flexibility and range of motion, enhance posture, deepen breathing, improve circulation and muscle tone, elasticize the body, and limber the joints and the spine. Hard to believe that one discipline can encompass so much? It really does, and it's great for your psyche besides.

If you disliked exercise in your youth, you'll find yourself becoming more supple than you ever were; if you used to be supple, it should be a delight to regain youthful flexibility and grace.

In addition to the asanas (exercises), yoga, as practiced in the West, frequently includes deep breathing, relaxation, and meditation. Different teachers emphasize different aspects, so try a few before choosing the guru best suited to you.

You can, if you like, substitute an illustrated paperback and attempt yoga on your own. A few months with a teacher is preferable, however, especially if you find one whose soothing voice almost hypnotizes you as she or he croons, "Breathe out all tension and negative feelings... breathe in relaxation and positive thoughts..."

You may also find a yoga course on TV; public TV features Lilias, another station Richard Hittleman.

Some instructors, after an hour of encouraging you to stretch newly discovered muscles and ligaments, end with visualization, a quiet ten minutes learning to recognize tensions, to relax certain parts of your body while you deliberately tense others, and then to relax completely.

The combination of deep breathing, stretching, and emptying your mind of all troubling thoughts...the final Ommm, ommm, shanti...peace be with you...leaves you feeling like a rag doll, calm and relaxed. In India an ideal of yoga is that at fifty-three one should turn worldly cares over to the children and begin to concentrate and work on oneself. Yoga helps you begin.

Recommended Reading

Renew Your Life Through Yoga, by Indra Devi. New York: Warner, 1975.

Yoga for Americans, by Indra Devi. New York: New American Library, 1971.

Yoga for Physical Fitness, by Richard Hittleman. New York: Warner, 1974.

Yoga Twenty-Eight Day Exercise Plan by Richard Hittleman. New York: Bantam, 1973.

Easy Does it: Yoga for People over 60, by Alice Christensen and David Rankin. New York: Harper & Row Pub., 1979.

Z

ZEAL, ZEST, ZING, AND ZIP

All these Zs mean about the same thing, and they (or it) are important for seniors. Gerontologists agree that losing your Zs probably shortens your life. It's not unusual for people as they grow older to slip into passivity and inertia and from there to stagnation and depression, but it's not inevitable. No matter what your age or your condition, there are always things to do and see and challenges to meet. When a friend found Supreme Court Justice Oliver Wendell Holmes studying Greek at the age of ninety, he asked why Holmes was doing it. "Why, to improve my mind, of course," was the reply.

Even if family and friends are gone for one reason or another, there are many other possible interests in life. It's easy to find something to be enthusiastic about, whether it's politics or folk dancing or ethnic cooking or bird-watching or Spanish-American literature—or even learning Greek. And if you are enthusiastic about something you are much more likely to find friends and to be interesting yourself.

So for our final piece of advice: Keep up your Zs!

ADDITIONAL RECOMMENDED READING

We have recommended certain books under topic headings. Here is a list of other books that we think would be of particular interest to senior citizens.

Anatomy of an Illness as Perceived by the Patient, by Norman Cousins. New York: W.W. Norton, 1979.

Aging Is a Family Affair, by Victoria E. Bumagin and Kathryn F. Hirn. New York: Thomas Y. Crowell, 1979.

The Best Years Book, by Hugh Downs and Richard J. Roll. New York: Delacorte Press, 1981.

Dr. Taylor's Self-Help Medical Guide, by Robert B. Taylor, M.D. Arlington House, 1977.

A Good Age, by Alex Comfort. New York: Simon & Schuster, 1978. (mostly supportive and inspirational)

Growing Young, by Ashley Montagu. New York: McGraw-Hill, 1983.

The Harvard Medical School Health Letter Book, edited by G. Timothy Johnson, M.D. and Stephen E. Goldfinger, M.D. New York: Warner Books, 1982.

Health and Healing: Understanding Conventional and Alternative Medicine, by Andrew Weil. Boston: Houghton Mifflin, 1983.

How to Be Your Own Doctor (Sometimes), rev. ed., by Keith W. Sehnert, M.D. with Howard Eisenberg. New York: Grosset & Dunlap, 1981.

It Takes a Long Time to Become Young, by Garson Kanin. New York: Berkley Pub., 1979. (inspirational; stresses the importance of remaining productive)

Jane Brody's The New York Times Guide to Personal Health, by Jane E. Brody. New York: Avon, 1982.

Medical Self-Care: Access to Health Tools, by Tom Ferguson. New York: Summit Books, 1980.

90 Days to Self-Health, by C. Norman Shealy, M.D. New York: Bantam, 1978.

Over 50: The Definitive Guide to Retirement, by Auren Uris. Radnor, PA: Chilton Book Company, 1979.

The Retirement Book, by Joan Adler. New York: Wm. Morrow, 1975.

Sylvia Porter's Money Book for the 80's. New York: Avon, 1980.

The Source Book for the Disabled, edited by Glorya Hale. New York: Holt, Rinehart & Winston, 1982. (excellent not just for the disabled, but for those who find certain tasks growing more difficult)

Take Care of Yourself: A Consumer's Guide to Medical Care, by Donald M. Vickery, M.D. and James F. Fries, M.D. Reading, MA: Addison-Wesley, 1976.

Index